ALSO BY LINDA BIRD FRANCKE

The Ambivalence of Abortion

Linda Bird Francke

Growing Up
Divorced

LINDEN PRESS/SIMON & SCHUSTER
NEW YORK 1983

Published by Linden Press/Simon & Schuster
A Division of Simon & Schuster, Inc.
Simon & Schuster Building
Rockefeller Center
1230 Avenue of the Americas
New York, New York 10020
LINDEN PRESS/SIMON & SCHUSTER and colophon are trademarks of Simon & Schuster, Inc.

Designed by Karolina Harris
Manufactured in the United States of America

1   3   5   7   9   10   8   6   4   2

Library of Congress Cataloging in Publication Data
Francke, Linda Bird.
Growing up divorced.
Includes bibliographical references.
1. Children of divorced parents—United States.
I. Title.
HQ777.5.F72   1983   306.8 9   83-9336
ISBN 0-671-25516-9

FOR H. B. L.

Contents

Acknowledgments

There were many people who helped in the concept, research, and writing of this book, and I welcome this opportunity to thank them publicly. Victoria Balfour, Emily Aspinall, George Margolis, and Peggy Clausen each contributed to the research in her or his separate area of expertise, as did Pam Abramson and Janet Huck. The staff of the Bridgehampton Library was also extremely helpful in tracking down articles and studies in the most remote of publications.

Thanks go also to two eminent divorce researchers, E. Mavis Hetherington at the University of Virginia and Judith S. Wallerstein at the Center for the Family in Transition in Corte Madera, California. They generously shared not only their invaluable research findings but their time as well.

Special thanks go to my agent, Lynn Nesbit, and to my editors at Linden Press, Joni Evans, whose enthusiasm and atten-

Acknowledgments

tion buoyed my confidence throughout the project, and Marjorie Williams, whose organizational skills made sense out of the morass of material.

Closer to home, my gratitude goes to my children, Andrew, Tapp, and Caitlin, whose consideration and self-sufficiency made long work hours possible, and to Albert Francke, who pitched in overtime as a single father to clear more of my time for work. My friends Gail Sheehy, Jane O'Reilly, and Elizabeth Peer also offered continuing interest and advice.

But it was the unfaltering support and encouragement of Harvey Loomis throughout the two years it took to research and write this book that made possible everything that at times seemed impossible. It is to him, then, that this book is gratefully dedicated.

Sagaponack, New York
December 1982

GROWING UP DIVORCED

It started off like any slightly chaotic family lunch. Caitlin, age seven, was lost in reading *Misty of Chincoteague* in her bedroom and had ignored three summonses to lunch. Tapp, five, was trying to coax her all-too-knowing cat out from under the porch so she could give her a bath and also pretended not to hear us call. And for once I was grateful for their contrariness. For this was to be no ordinary lunch. We—my husband and I, our two daughters, and twelve-year-old Andrew, then away at summer camp—were about to become a national statistic. It was time, my husband insisted, to tell the children that we were separating, that he was moving out, that we were never going to live again as an intact family.

And then we were finally at the table. What had prepared the children for this, I wondered numbly, listening to the girls squabble over who got the biggest piece of ham. To my knowl-

edge they had never heard us have an argument, let alone a
knock-down drag-out fight. Their father wasn't a drunk. Nor
was I. He didn't beat me. Or them. Indeed, we really had a very
happy family life, complete with a weekend house by the sea-
shore, beach picnics, and a recent trip to Disney World. What
differences my husband and I had were between us, not involving them. How could we do this to them, I anguished, longing
to have it over with, longing for it never to happen.

And then, of course, it was time. Leaning over the bowl of
cottage cheese, my husband reached for his daughters' hands
on either side of him. "Give me your hands, girls," he said. "I
have something very, very important to tell you." I listened in a
daze to his words, which seemed to go on and on. He and I, he
explained to the girls, had decided to live apart because we
made ourselves unhappy living together. But it was very important, he went on, for the girls to realize he was not leaving
them, that they were not in the least responsible for the
breakup. "I'll still be your father and I'll see you every weekend," he said, explaining that he was going to fix up his family's
beach shack just two miles down the road. "The only difference
in your lives is that sometimes you'll live with me, and sometimes you'll live with your mother."

I watched the tableau at the table with the damnable detach-
ment that is bred into every journalist. Tapp seemed not to be
listening to his words at all, but just kept asking "why, why,
why" in a tone that was more of a squeak than a voice. Caitlin,
being twenty months older, appeared to be listening very hard
to every word and seemed frozen in the moment. Her fork hovered halfway between her plate and her mouth, and the bite of
cottage cheese in her mouth remained unchewed. When he was
finished, saying that he would pack and be out of the house before we returned from the Sunday matinee at the local movie
theater, silence stretched over the table. Finally Caitlin swallowed and slowly put her fork back down. "I knew this hap-

pened to other kids," she said absently into the void. "I just never thought it would happen to me."

Variations on this scene are being played out in living rooms, dining rooms, backyards and kitchens across this country with stunning frequency. In 1963, according to the National Center for Health Statistics, 562,000 children under the age of 18 were involved in marital breakups. By 1980, the numbers had doubled to an annual rate of 1.18 million children. The suddenness of the divorce epidemic has taken everyone by surprise. Though the divorce rate has been rising steadily since World War II, with a brief respite in the fifties, the seventies saw the rate more than double, from a ratio of 47 per 1,000 married persons to 100 per 1,000 in 1980. And over half these couples have children under eighteen. Now, if you add up the total number of children whose parents are divorced, the sum rockets to over 12 million. Presently, nearly one out of every five children under the age of eighteen goes home to only one parent—the great majority because of divorce.[1] And though divorce no longer carries the social stigma it used to, no longer makes outcasts of children, the shock and the personal significance to each family member have not been blunted. The words "I never thought it would happen to me" have become new echoes of childhood.

We settled down fairly quickly after that separation announcement at lunch and the departure of my husband, as planned, before our return from *Star Wars*. For the next few months I worried about the children's reactions to his absence but was continually reassured by their silence about the subject and apparent reluctance to discuss it when I asked them how they felt. I realize now that their silence was a danger signal, but at the time, I was actually grateful that their seeming lack of distress eased what pain and guilt I felt toward them. My son seemed content at boarding school; my daughters continued to do well at their school, and no one started wetting her bed or

13

having more nightmares than seemed appropriate for her age. And as promised, they saw their father every weekend.

Initially, when research came trickling into the public sphere out of psychiatric literature, revealing that perhaps there was more to divorce and its effect on children than most people realized, it piqued only my professional interest. The evidence *was* startling. On the scale of childhood trauma, for example, divorce was second only to parental death. And though each child's circumstances were obviously different, certain reactions from children were almost universal: shock, followed by depression, denial, anger, low self-esteem, shame, and often, among younger children, a feeling that they were somehow responsible for their parents' splitup. Regardless of age, there also appeared to be an obsessive desire to reunite the parents.

I suggested a cover story on the children of divorce to *Newsweek* magazine, where I was then a writer. There had been much to-do in the media about the plight of the single mother followed by the travails of the single father, all of which we had covered in the magazine. Wasn't it time we heard from the children, I suggested, to see how they felt about being part of the divorce epidemic? There were, after all, over one million children a year now going through the dissolution of their families. And though we all know the old saw that children are "resilient" and "flexible," "able to cope" with the most extraordinary adversities and "bounce back" better than ever, perhaps these children of divorce had a different story to tell.

I decided to begin my research with my own children, taking them out to dinner to interview them. At my fingertips were the snippets of information I'd gleaned about the effects of divorce, without ever thinking they would apply to my bright-eyed, seemingly well-adjusted children. It was, after all, three years since that fateful luncheon, and barring normal family crises like a couple of broken arms, a ruptured appendix and a few disagreements that had escalated into such epithets as "I hate you," we seemed as normal as any apple pie that is missing the "Daddy" slice.

The girls were delighted I was going to interview them, and we went to a local restaurant so the setting would be less home-like and more professional. Over our rounds of Shirley Temples, and bowls of chili, I took out my notebook and asked them how they had actually felt during that cataclysmic lunch three years before.

"I was very sad," Tapp said matter-of-factly. "I was going to say, 'No, Dad, don't do it,' but I couldn't get my voice out. I was too much shocked. I couldn't know why. I remembered once he came home late and you got mad at him, but I really thought you got along just fine.

"All the fun things we had done flashed right out of my mind like when he gave me piggy-back rides and when we picked apples and when we drove fast down the roller-coaster road and when we surprised you in the morning and jumped on you. All I could think of was the bad times and all the bad times stayed in my mind, like when he got mad at me and when he had to go to the hospital with his back. The bad thoughts just wouldn't go away.

"My life sort of changed at that moment. Like I used to be always happy and suddenly I was sad."

My pen skittered to a halt on the page. My youngest daughter had been going through all this suffering and I didn't even know? My mind went back to the divorce checklist. Shock. Depression. I looked at this child across the table, the chili spreading down her chin, and wondered if I really knew her after all. I pressed on. "What was it like when you went to school the next day?" I asked her, trying desperately to remember if I had called her teacher to tell her about the separation.

"I pretended it was a regular week and that I'd see Dad just like usual," she continued cheerfully. "I just put it out of my mind. I tried not to think about it. But I wouldn't tell anybody that you and Dad had got a separation. Not for ages and ages. I felt embarrassed.''

Chalk up the next two. Denial. Shame.

In a very small voice now, I asked, "You didn't think you were the cause of our breakup, did you?"

"Oh, yes," she said merrily. "In a way I thought I'd made it happen. I thought maybe I'd acted mean to you and Caitlin and that you couldn't put up with me anymore. I felt I was being punished by God for being really bad, so I tried being really good so God would change His mind. I helped a lot in the house, I asked you if I could get your breakfast, I got up by myself for school without waking you up. I hoped that if I was really good God would change His mind and let Dad come home. I'm used to it now and it's okay. But sometimes when I have an eyelash to wish on, I still wish for Dad to come home.''

I stared at this beautiful child, who was fidgeting now to get to the jukebox. She had opened wounds in me that she had closed in herself. In a detached way, I finished ticking off the checklist. Low self-esteem. Responsibility for the breakup, a desire to reunite the parents. I was struck dumb by my maternal ignorance. How could I have failed to pick up the distress signals that she must have been sending out? I could have comforted her, reassured her, at least *listened* to her. And why hadn't she told me all this before? "Because you never asked," she said with a grin. "Can I have a quarter for the jukebox?"

It was Caitlin's turn now, my bright, puppy-hearted, supersensitive nine-year-old who was two years ahead of herself in school. Like her sister, she had been totally unprepared for the announcement. "I never heard you have any fights. Never," she said firmly, this child who never loses an opportunity to uncover family secrets in bureau drawers, pocketbooks and file cabinets. "It came as a complete surprise. I always thought 'my parents will never get a divorce.' " Had she been reassured by her father's comforting and really very specific speech at the lunch table that though he was leaving me, he was not leaving them? "No," she continued just as firmly. "When I heard Dad say he wasn't going to live here anymore, I thought I was never going to see him again. I was in a daze. I didn't understand what was happening. Finally I heard him say he was coming out every weekend to see us. But I couldn't hear any of the other words."

Shock again. And again, a sense of responsibility for the breakup: "I was mad at myself. I thought you had been fighting about us, over who would get us if you ever got a divorce. I'd seen a show on TV where the parents were screaming at each other over who the kids would live with. I thought just by being alive I had made you and Dad split up."

All of this she, too, had kept to herself. But being older than her sister, Caitlin had worked out at least a reasonable conclusion as to the "whys" of it all that satisfied her. "I just tried to live with it, really," she remembered, attacking her cheese-cake. "I figured out that you weren't getting along because you spent a lot of time on your work and not on Dad, but I knew you didn't hate each other. So it was all right with me." Being an eternal optimist, Caitlin had even turned the separation into a plus. "After I got over being sad, I realized that we'd be better off separated because then I'd look forward to seeing Dad instead of just having him around all the time."

There it was. Not only were we part of a national statistic, we were participants in a totally predictable series of emotional consequences. Sobered by how little I knew about my children, I got the check (Tapp proudly got the receipt for my expense account) and took the children home. Long after the children were asleep, I lay awake, wondering whether other divorced or separated parents knew what their children were thinking, feeling, fantasizing, scheming, suffering. For even though my children and I led very close and interdependent lives, I never had a clue any of this was going on.

*   *   *

The cover story was written in the summer of 1979, then sat around gathering editorial dust for six months. The subject was too heavy, the editors argued, for a "light" summer cover, and besides, everyone's "children of divorce" were at summer camp, out of sight and out of mind. Summer moved into fall and the Pope's visit bumped the cover once again. Winter brought us cover after cover on the oil crises in the Middle East. Around the magazine, the story began to be known as the "grandchildren of divorce."

It was not until the movie lines stretched around the nation's blocks to see *Kramer vs. Kramer* that interest in the cover picked up again. The film was news: here was the ambitious father converted into an instant parent. Here was the modern repressed mother who had to leave both her husband and her son to find an identity of her own. And caught in the middle was a little boy who loved and needed them both. And the timing was perfect: 1979 was the year the divorce rate hit its all-time high of 1.18 million.

A sign of the movie's impact was the intensity of the discussions it provoked. Suddenly everyone was debating the court's decision to award sole custody to the mother, even though she had walked out on her son without even saying good-bye. What struck me through all these heated conversations was how little people really knew or perhaps wanted to know about the effects of divorce on their own children. What they argued about were parental concerns. Women were delighted that men were finally seeing how difficult it was to be a mother, let alone to juggle child care and career. Men were awed by Kramer's obsession to keep his son and started fantasizing about instituting custody suits of their own. But still no one talked about how the little boy felt.

The *Newsweek* cover, slugged "The Children of Divorce," finally ran in February 1980, and reaction to it confirmed the high emotional stakes that divorcing families are gambling for in this decade. Hundreds of letters poured in to the magazine; letters of praise, letters of outrage, letters from children who were miserable, letters from children whose lives had improved since their parents split up. Not one letter was dispassionate, and each had a story to tell.

"The worst day in my life was the day I had to take the witness stand in a court and give the crucial testimony which resulted in my parents obtaining their divorce," wrote a young woman from Canada. "I still bear the scars that I might carry for the rest of my life." Another young woman was equally upset that her parents *hadn't* gotten a divorce. "Some children don't realize how lucky they are to have their parents divorce," the seventeen-year-old wrote to *Newsweek*. "I plead with my parents and encourage their thoughts of divorce. I've given up a dream for a happy household a long time ago."

Other letters belied the comforting fantasy many parents have that they are hiding their hostilities from their children. "I wasn't a stupid kid and me and my brother could hear our mom and dad shouting," wrote an eleven-year-old New Yorker. "Sometimes two people don't mix and I knew it." A thirteen-year-old from Detroit was just as savvy about the reasons for his parents' divorce. "I don't think my parents should get back together because my dad treats my mom like dirt," he wrote. When the "whys" of the divorce had escaped the children, the legacy lingered into adulthood. Like adopted children who want to know their genetic history before having children of their own, these children of divorce wrote of needing to know their psychological heritages before they married. "The divorce was never explained to me as a child," wrote a twenty-one-year-old Ohio woman who was very nervous about her imminent wedding. "I pray that my marriage will work even though my sister just got divorced and I worry about my lack of adequate role models."

I realized that the *Newsweek* cover had just scratched the surface of the real divorce story. For these letters conveyed a depth to the divorce trauma that the magazine only had space to hint at. I determined then to write a book about the children from this divorce epidemic, to find out from them how it felt to have their parents split up, to shuttle back and forth between separate households, to see their single parents go out on dates or have a date sleep over, to see them remarry. I wanted to hear from them how it felt to be part of a court battle over visitation, money, or custody, to be kidnapped or "childsnatched" by one parent from the other, forbidden by one parent even to see the other, or literally abandoned. And I wanted to know how these ruptures in their family lives had influenced their own thoughts about marriage and having families of their own.

I also wanted to know if there was a predictable pattern of behavioral response among children to divorce, and if so, how much difference their specific ages and levels of development played in those responses, if boys and girls reacted differently. I wanted to know if divorce had only an immediate impact on the children, or if there were some effects that didn't show up until later. I wanted to know what parents were doing wrong—or right—in easing their children through divorce—from the children's point of view. For in spite of all the books that have been written about divorce, I had read none that allowed the children to speak. Save for *The Kids' Book of Divorce*, written by kids for kids, there was no forum for children to get their feelings safely across to their parents.

I set out in the fall of 1980 to listen to as many children of divorce as I could. They were remarkably easy to find. I started with the children of my divorced friends, but the familiarity soon began to backfire. The children began to spew out secrets and perceptions about their families that even their parents didn't know. Though I had promised these kids that what they told me would go no further, their parents hovered nervously nearby and couldn't resist asking me what their children had said when the interviews were over. It became increasingly difficult and uncomfortable for me to hole up in a bedroom with child after child, only to stroll downstairs afterward and join the mothers or fathers for dinner as if nothing out of the ordinary had happened. And my relationship with the parents became increasingly strained.

I turned then to interviewing children whose families I didn't know. I found them on the summer beach, on vacation with my own children, at schools, and even on the Long Island Railroad. With the help of a researcher, I broadened my base and sought the cooperation of such groups as Parents without Partners, the Single-Parent Family Project, The Parents' Center, and the Stepfamily Association of America. It didn't matter at all to the children that they didn't know me. In fact it helped them to talk to a stranger about things they wouldn't dare discuss with their parents.

And talk we did, about every facet of divorce from the moment the children learned the news through the anguishing labyrinth of remarriage and stepfamilies. They were just ordinary children, these kids, from a five-year-old in a starched eyelet dress to a cool teenager who resented the time spent out from under his Walkman. But what they had to say about divorce was filled with articulate doses of resentment, resignation, hope, courage, cynicism, and contempt. Two emotions were predominant. Almost all of the approximately 100 kids I talked to expressed sadness. And virtually all of them were angry.

To understand and interpret what these children were telling me, I sought out the help of the top specialists in the divorce field. I traveled to the University of Virginia to meet with the chairman of the Psychology Department, E. Mavis Hetherington, whose twenty-year research of the dynamics of single-parent families proved invaluable. In California, I met with Judith Wallerstein, whose five-year longitudinal study of 131 children, undertaken with Joan Kelly, documents the impact of divorce at different levels of childhood development. Her benchmark research findings helped put much of what I had learned into perspective. Divorce and its aftermath were becoming a much more complicated and far-reaching subject than I had imagined.

I learned quickly that the divorce chain reaches far beyond the confines of the single-parent family. Schools, for example, have been forced to confront the growing numbers and special needs of their pupils of divorce. Among the many schools I visited, some had specific programs for divorced kids, and some purposely offered none. Controversy, I discovered, sharply divides educators in these days of budget cuts as to whether a school's role is simply to educate or to counsel as well.

The courts turned out to be equally divided about handling the growing fury of custody and visitation disputes, having to base their decisions on the murky criteria of "the best interests of the child." But there are some brave innovations. I visited the new Conciliation Courts in cities as dissimilar as Tucson, Arizona, and Los Angeles where many custody and visitation cases are worked out by mental health professionals rather than judges. I spent time at the divorce-spawned mini-industry of mediation and family therapy centers, in California at the Center for Legal Psychiatry in Santa Monica and the Thaliens Community Mental Health Center in Los Angeles, and in New York at the Nathan Ackerman Institute of Family Therapy. I spent rewarding hours discussing therapy for distressed children of divorce with child psychiatrist Gordon Livingston in Columbia, Maryland, and debated the growing controversy over joint custody with divorce lawyers, judges, child psychologists, and even teachers, many of whom keep daily charts on the different home destinations of their students.

Last, I investigated the new and long overdue law reforms concerning children and divorce. In an attempt to crack down on parents who abandon their children financially, federal and state governments now withhold tax rebates to nonpaying parents. Laws concerning the growing number of childsnatchings have been tightened (though not enough) and have even spread worldwide, as more and more childsnatching parents smuggle their children abroad. Even the FBI is now mandated to join the search for parentally kidnapped children—though the bureau balks at doing so.

It took me almost two years to research and put together all that I learned about what must be the greatest social upheaval of this decade. And too much has happened too fast. The courts are floundering. The schools are floundering. Families are floundering. No one knows what to expect of each other in these days of mass divorce as there are no rules, no precedents to follow. Yet the divorce rate continues to add one million new children a year to the confusion.

Only thirty years ago, divorce was still so unusual that my aunt, who had divorced her husband, had to hide in her family's attic when company came because her parents were so ashamed. Now divorce is so common that its very normality may have anesthetized us to our children's pain.

Out of ignorance, many parents actually create or exacerbate the problems of their children during the transition from an intact family to a stable single-parent family. Out of the same ignorance, parents often fail to understand or recognize the distress signals the child is sending out. A four-year-old who suddenly starts wetting her bed again or stops using her fork at dinnertime is not necessarily being ornery, but may be trying to hide from divorce for a while in the safer world of infancy. A six-year-old boy who suddenly starts bullying his friends in first grade is not necessarily turning into a ruffian, but is probably acting out his anger at his father for leaving him, at his mother for allowing it, and at himself for having caused it.

This book is intended to explain why and when such reactions are predictable; to instruct and guide parents through the throes of their children's postdivorce responses. Though every child's situation in divorce is as unique as is that of every family, there are universal reactions that can be reliably predicted on the basis of such things as age, sex, and level of development. For example, studies by Hetherington and Roger and Martha Cox have demonstrated that:

- boys take divorce harder than girls, especially between the ages of three and five and when they are nine and ten
- the worst time for parents to divorce is when their children are between the ages of three and eight
- girls whose fathers leave them at early ages can become sexually precocious as adolescents
- single mothers have much more difficult relationships with their sons than they do with their daughters, and more than do mothers in intact families
- the worst time for parents to remarry is when their children are between nine and fifteen

Each age level, I learned from Judith Wallerstein, has its own pattern of responses which depends on the child's level of development. This may help explain to parents why one of their children reacts so differently from an older or younger sibling. In addition, I learned from Hetherington that there are "sleeper" effects of divorce which crop up in different ways over the years, as the child passes through progressive stages of development. And in my own research, I discovered that the age of the child at the time of the interview contributed heavily to the child's reactions to the divorce—even if it had taken place years before. Each stage of development, it seems, engenders its own emotions and its own need for the separate parents, regardless of the length of time since the divorce.

The general rules that can be relied on by divorcing parents are laid out in the central chapters of this book, which deal sequentially with the ages of the children, from infancy through the teenage years. These concepts are the outgrowth of research originally developed by Judith Wallerstein and Joan Kelly, who were the first to break down children's responses to divorce into age groups and to document their age-specific reactions.

Divorce, like other crises, has its own timetable—one that essentially takes three years to work through. The critical period for all children is the year following the actual physical separation of the parents. Divorcing parents are almost always highly distracted during this initial period, and quite naturally the children react. Rules, household routines, discipline, even play periods are thrown into disarray as the reorganizing family struggles to find its own rhythm.[2] Bewildered and frightened by this sense of domestic instability, the children seek more attention from the preoccupied and often emotionally distanced parent, who can in fact give them less. Many children of divorce essentially go unparented during the first year and seek constant reassurance from other adults as substitute parents.

The second year begins to get better, especially for girls.[3] Things have begun to settle down. The single parent has usually found some sort of job. If the family was forced to move, they have done so. A pattern of visitation (or nonvisitation) has been set. Support (or nonsupport) has been established, and though life may be pretty grim, it is nonetheless more predictable. Boys, however, continue to be more aggressive than their peers in intact families and to have a more difficult relationship with their mothers.[4]

The third year usually sees the end of the divorce cycle if all has gone smoothly enough, but the continuation of stress if it has not. On the good side, both parents have settled down enough now to turn their attention back again to the children. The single-parent family has established new routines and new responsibilities, and though the children (again, especially boys) still exhibit various signs of unhappiness, the future, for the first time, looks brighter. On the bad side, the disruption of divorce can go on and on if the parents continue to fight, if one parent remains severely depressed, or if the custodial parent is so overwhelmed by financial and emotional pressures that she (or he) is unable effectively to take care of the children.

With these cycles in mind, I have limited this book mostly to the first three years following the family breakup. These are the critical years that determine whether the child will integrate the divorce into his or her life, whether "sleeper effects" will show up in years to come, or whether the lack of resolution will result in permanent damage. A child who continues to be caught in the cross-fire between hostile parents, who is abandoned either literally or emotionally by a parent, or who suffers from chronic inattention, never really comes out whole.

We want very much to believe that our children are fine, that divorce has not harmed them, that they will grow up to have happy and even lengthy family lives of their own. But the prognosis is doubtful. E. Mavis Hetherington predicts that three out of four children of divorce will themselves get divorced. And unless we learn more about how our children feel—and how to handle divorce better ourselves—those figures may very well become their heritage.

Some of the children's distress can be alleviated or at least muted by the parent, though some cannot. Children, after all, are dealt the hand in life they must learn to live with. A child cannot keep his parents from fighting; a child cannot keep his parents from getting divorced. But a child can survive and even benefit from a healthy divorce if the parents keep their differences to themselves and both continue a positive involvement with the child. This does not mean to say the child's world will be perfect. Far from it. But at least it will be manageable. And in this day and age, when an increasing number of adults are finding it ever more difficult to manage their own lives, such a legacy is the least we can offer our children.

THE PARENTAL RHYTHMS
OF DIVORCE

Though adults like to think their marriages and their divorces are unique, for the most part they are not—particularly the divorces. The great majority of divorced families have followed a marital timetable as punctual as Mussolini's trains.

According to the 1980 Census Population Report, the average length of first marriages was 6.8 years, up a minuscule five months over 1970. Over half of these divorces—57 percent—included children. Nearly 12 million children at the beginning of the decade lived in a single-parent family created by divorce. The greatest number of children were between six and eight years old at the point of divorce, one of the worst times developmentally for parents to split. (The discrepancy between the ages of the children and the average length of marriage rests on the fact that childless couples divorce sooner than couples with children.)

The highest divorce ratio occurs among blacks—203 divorced per 1,000 married, followed by Hispanics, at 94 per 1,000 and finally whites, at 92 per 1,000. But in terms of total numbers, many more white children are affected by divorce than black or Hispanic children, because there are more whites—and more who marry. Only 23 percent of black single mothers are single because of divorce, compared to 52 percent of white single mothers. Of all age groups, the ratio of divorce is highest among people 30–44.

The financial profile of the single-parent family is bleak, especially if the mother is the custodial parent. In 1982, single-mother families accounted for 15 percent of the population, but 50 percent of all poor families.[1] Divorce can drop a single mother's income by as much as 70 percent, and, as nine out of ten children of divorce live with their mothers, the children suffer accordingly. Shockingly few fathers help support their families. The 1980 census reports that over half of the 3.4 million single mothers who were legally due child support received *none at all*. And the mothers who did received an average of $1,800 a year, or $150 a month. Educational levels directly affected child support probability. Single mothers with college degrees were more likely to receive child support (86 percent) than mothers with high school diplomas (73 percent).[2] For many single mothers, remarriage was the only way to regain some sort of economic stability for their families. A study at the University of Michigan's Institute for Social Research found that over 70 percent of children living below the poverty level with a single parent moved above that level only after the parent had married or remarried.

The sex of the children tends to influence the parents' decision to divorce. Parents who have only sons stay married longer than parents of daughters and sons, who in turn stay married longer than parents of girls only. Five percent more boys than girls live in intact families.[3] Education and income also play a role in divorce probability. Parents with college degrees and higher income levels are less apt to divorce than parents with high school diplomas and lower income levels. In one of the puzzling by-products of numerical profiles, it turns out that women who started college but didn't finish have a higher divorce rate than either women who didn't go to college at all or women who completed their degrees.[4] Higher education seems to create just as much instability. Women with graduate school degrees divorce more frequently than women with college degrees.[5]

Custody battles in court, though often highly publicized, are rare. Over 90 percent of custody arrangements are worked out privately between the parents and their attorneys. And though much has been made of single-father custody,[6] 92 percent of children in single-parent families live with their mothers, either by parental consent or by paternal default. If the father decides to go to court over custody, the statistics change dramatically. Sixty-three percent of custody disputes are now decided in favor of the father.[7] Here again, gender plays a role. Fathers are more likely to win custody if the children are all boys and much less likely if the children are all girls.[8]

The proportion of children living with their divorced fathers has remained constant since 1960, around 88 percent. But because of the increase in divorce, the simple numbers of children in father-custody homes has risen by one-third. In a shift from tradition, more and more very young children now live exclusively with their fathers, especially if the mother has remarried; 9.1 percent of fathers had custody of their preschool-aged children if the mother had remarried and was living with her second husband, compared with only 2.1 percent of fathers of preschoolers whose ex-wives had not remarried.[9]

The children's contact with *both* parents lessens after divorce, regardless of which is the custodial parent. One study found that in the 12 months following separation, the children's time with the parents dropped from 94 hours a week with the mother and 53 hours with the father preseparation to 73 and 20 hours respectively.[10] Noncustodial fathers spend significantly more time with their sons than with their daughters until preadolescence, when girls begin to see their father more frequently than boys. Nine- and ten-year-olds of both sexes have the least contact with their fathers of any age group over three.[11] And the remarriage of the father usually signals a sharp decline in visitation with his own children, especially his daughters.[12]

At any given time, there are many more divorced once-married single women (120 per 1,000) than men (79 per 1,000), because more men remarry than do women.[13] Five out of six men eventually remarry, as compared with three out of four divorced women. Age plays a role here. Women who divorce before the age of thirty are twice as likely to remarry as women who divorce after forty. And they remarry fast—the average time between marriages for women is 3.2 years. Perhaps it is too fast: more second marriages end in divorce (44 percent) than do first marriages (38 percent).

So much for the numbers. Though they paint a precise picture of the predictability of marriage, divorce, and remarriage these days, they do not shade in the consequences of the divorce epidemic. Numbers are simple. Emotions are not. And far from the streamlined Arab custom of saying "I divorce you" three times and being shed of it, marriage in America is still the stuff of invested dreams. The process of uncoupling can be very slow and painful, especially where children are involved.

Divorce is not a self-contained crisis, but the precipitator of a long chain of related crises and changes. And the degree of distress and sometimes damage the children endure is directly related to the way parents handle the divorce process. For very young children especially, the mood and well-being of the parent dictates the atmosphere of the household and colors the child's entire world. The two cannot be isolated. It is important, then, to first understand the dynamics of parental divorce before moving on to the children's experiences. Like the child's game, "Simon Says," progress in the uncoupling process can be measured by giant steps, banana steps, umbrella steps, and inevitably, three steps backward. Every divorce is, in fact, six different divorces.[14]

Psychic Divorce. Just as love and a desire to face the future with each other bring a couple together in marriage, so do hostility and a preference for facing that same future without that partner bring a couple to divorce. In psychic divorce, the partners must renounce each other and admit that the other is not the life partner each had hoped he or she would be. It is not easy to lay such dreams—and ghosts—aside, and the death of that struggle brings with it a period of mourning. Divorce is often lopsided, however, as one partner has made the psychic separation long before the other partner, and well before divorce is even discussed as a possibility.

Legal Divorce. Sometimes this phase is the easiest, especially if the couple has completed the psychic divorce and is not trying to inflict punishment or revenge. Completed in the courts, legal divorce sets up the framework of financial separation for the couple and establishes the custody of the children. Once complete in the eyes of the law, the ramifications of legal divorce are immediate in terms of the redefinition of the couple as single individuals for such purposes as income tax or remarriage.

Community Divorce. The definition of "community" involves much more than the immediate neighborhood one lives in (or often has to move out of, following divorce). Community also includes the friends a married couple has made, the in-laws who come for Christmas and Thanksgiving, even the business

31

colleagues of a working wife and/or husband. All these relationships are in flux during the community divorce and have not only to be redefined, but reestablished. Many divide out of loyalty or along blood lines. A favorite sister-in-law, for example, overnight becomes "the children's aunt." A mother-in-law, though she may be very close to her son's wife, may feel she has to shun her now because of her blood ties. At the same time, divorced people have to form new communities and relearn old techniques of making new friends, many of whom will be divorced themselves. Just as couples seek out couples, divorced people tend to spend more time and share more interests with other divorce veterans.

Property Divorce. This can be one of the toughest phases of divorce because the object here is tangible and not abstract. There is nothing a person can do to make another love her (or him) or to keep that person from loving someone else. But when it comes down to dividing a shared property, from a fishing cabin in Maine to an ashtray bought at a bazaar in Morocco, concrete victories can be won, and thus antagonisms may boil. Suddenly, something that has always been "ours" becomes "yours" or "mine." The disputed property is real, not only in terms of economic worth, but as a sentimental souvenir of happier times. Such division of things is even further complicated by the couple's different attitudes toward "his" and "her" property. He may have loved the fishing cabin in Maine because of the leisure time spent on the water. She may have loved it just as much, but because it was the only place she found time to paint. He may want the ashtray because he bargained the price down to $2.00. She may want it because it is the precise color of red she has always loved and rarely found. Just as some relationships are eroded to the breaking point by such petty actions as leaving the top off the toothpaste, the stages of divorce, which have gone smoothly enough up to now, may explode with mushroom cloud force over the dispersal of the spoils of marriage. After all, even a bad marriage is a part of one's history, and everybody wants the best of the artifacts.

Parental Divorce. Dividing up the children is especially painful, even in the most harmonious of divorces. At the extreme, of course, is a custody fight in which one parent will definitely become the winner, the other the loser. But in all divorces involving children, each parent loses a little. The noncustodial parent, even if he sees his children a great deal, loses the day-to-day contact with them and has little or no say in what decisions the coparent makes concerning schooling, religious training, or even discipline. The custodial parent, on the other hand, loses control of the children while they are visiting the other parent and has no say in what influences or different life-styles are being brought to bear on the children, unless, in the eyes of the court, such differences are thought to be harmful to the children. Even though a single parent may yearn to get out from under the responsibilities of child rearing, it is still very difficult to let the reins go. The situation becomes particularly explosive when another partner for the mother or the father enters the picture and has contact with the children. Many divorced parents never make it entirely through the phase of loosening their control over the children, even though they have successfully managed to give up each other.

Dependency Divorce. The final phase of divorce is perhaps the most difficult for many people to accomplish. There are different kinds of dependence, from economic to emotional, and in this stage of divorce all dependencies have to be lessened, if not severed altogether. Even more than economic dependence (which can be corrected), emotional dependence can be the hardest to shed. Suddenly there is no one to cling to, to be reassured by, to deal with the problems that seem beyond one's emotional, intellectual, or even physical reach. Often, overdependent people remarry immediately, taking their plight on to the next partner without ever learning how to be independent. Or they may try to renew a childish dependence on their own parents, only to reenter the clash of generational wills that never really goes away. But those of the divorced who do shed their dependencies will find in the long run that it is better to want a partner than to need one.

There is just too much at stake in divorce for most couples to kiss each other good-bye gracefully. Divorce, instead, often brings out the worst in everyone. "At the time of the decree, there are likely to be two people who are angry because in the psychic divorce they feel rejected, in the economic divorce they feel cheated, and in the legal divorce they feel misrepresented," says anthropologist Paul Bohannan. "They may be bitter in the co-parental divorce, lonely or badgered or both in the community divorce, and afraid in the divorce from dependency."

It also takes time, a lot of time, to work through these stages of divorce and start a new life with as little scar tissue as possible. Three years, most experts agree, is the minimum time of family adjustment to postdivorce life, a period that often represents half of a child's total lifetime. What follows is an account of the predictable rhythm of the divorce dance, a process most parents—and their children—have to live through to come out whole at the other end.[15]

THE FIRST YEAR

The first year, after a brief honeymoon, gets worse and worse. Whether estranged couples file immediately for a divorce decree, haggle over a legal separation agreement, or just live apart, the twelve to eighteen months following physical separation is a peak period of unavoidable stress. On the "social readjustment scale" compiled by two psychiatrists at the University of Washington Medical School,[16] life events were ranked in terms of the adjustment level they required. The greater the adjustment, the higher the stress. Death of a spouse, not surprisingly, was ranked number 1, with a readjustment rating of 100. Divorce came in second with a rating of 73, followed by marital separation at 65. Fourth, at 63, was a jail sentence!

The Sixty-Day Honeymoon. Immediately following the shock and depression of the physical separation, a feeling of euphoria often envelops one or both of the ex-mates. There is, after all, a ceasefire in the preseparation war, and the postseparation war has not begun. He isn't there to put his feet on the slipcovers, leave pipe ashes everywhere but in the ashtrays, or roll over in bed taking the quilt with him. She isn't there to nag him about the car registration or hog the shower.

For a week, a month, maybe two, the simple absence of tension is a tonic. Reverting to a childish rebellion at authority and routine, the freshly separated are apt to wallow in indulgent disorder, defiantly gorging on ice cream or eating the crumbiest of crackers in bed; staying up until 4:00 A.M., reading a trashy book, or turning off the light at 7:30 P.M. While the children look on in bewilderment, a parent often chooses this time to muse about radically changing the direction of his or her life: off with the old and on to a trendy new hair-do, the beginnings of a beard, or talk of moving to Malibu, to Santa Fe, to Paris! Many parents, charged up with change, become instant superparent and start reading overtime to their children, cooking special treats, and volunteering for the Little League car pool. Others, bent on adolescent hedonism, ignore their children altogether, and revert to a premarriage, preresponsibility state of mind. But the euphoric honeymoon is about to end.

The Two-Month Hostilities. Reality bursts the brief bubble of the postseparation high as the psychological and legal work of the divorce really begins. The novelty of the first flush of singles freedom fades and loneliness begins to set in. This is not the sort of loneliness that comes with an evening's boredom, or the loneliness of having no one to share a sunset with, but loneliness that feeds on the panic that there never, ever will be anyone to share anything with again.

For many newly separated families, there is no avoiding antagonism at this stage. Depression takes the positive form of anger now, and each parent becomes fiercely determined not only to get his or her fair (or unfair) share out of the dead marriage, but to get even as well. Arguments rage about the settlement of property, finances, visitation, and child support. No area seems immune from criticism and sniping by an angry ex-partner, especially the care of the children. Suddenly, a mother and father who have always more or less agreed on the ways of child rearing accuse each other of various ways of mishandling the children. The absent parent, usually the father, tries to reinject himself into a parental role by accusing the mother of such parental crimes as neglecting the children, of being selfish, or thinking only of herself. The mother, on the other hand, finds herself railing at the father with such loaded charges as being inattentive, spoiling the children, letting them stay up too late when they're with him, and returning them home exhausted and half sick. The need to counter the hurt one partner is feeling by hurting the other partner in kind can become almost obsessive. And children are the most valuable battering rams.

The heightening stress on both parents can begin to take its toll. In a study of 425 mothers in the period immediately following separation,[17] the women were found to have such symptoms of distress and tension as insomnia, poorer health, greater loneliness, low work efficiency, memory difficulties, and increased smoking and drinking. It is not uncommon for recently separated mothers to fall into a depression that doesn't seem to lift, which quite naturally frightens the children. It is one thing to share occasional tears of understandable grief with the children. It is quite another for them to witness despair in the one person they perceive as standing between them and their terrors of the greater world.

Men do not appear to fare any better, and in fact initially take separation even harder than their former wives.[18] One study found that recently separated fathers quickly drifted into thinking of themselves as having no identity, complaining of feeling rootless, without a home or structure in their lives. These feelings in turn evoked deeper stirrings of a great loss, especially of their children, of dependency needs the men never knew they had, coupled with the more familiar feelings of guilt, anxiety, and depression. But though these men initially felt worse, they recovered more quickly and more steadily over a two-year period than their ex-wives, who continued to feel some degree of stress and depression.

The struggle to adjust to life without a mate is not self-contained, but spills over into all the areas of an adult's world. Work performance suffers. Tempers and concentration spans shorten. Even health is threatened. Estranged marital partners are both more susceptible to illness and are more accident prone than married people. The driving records of 410 people who were either suing or being sued for divorce in King County, Washington, showed they had 82 percent more car accidents and 195 percent more traffic violations than the average driver in the three-month period following the filing of a divorce petition.[19]

But despite the emotional upheaval at the two-month mark after separation, many ex-couples still feel very much coupled, and some feel even more attached now that the stress of daily confrontation has been removed. In one study, forty-eight white, middle-class, divorced parents were asked to describe their relationships.[20] On the negative side, the list of feelings included "acrimony," "anger," "feelings of desertion," "resentment," and "memories of painful conflict." But the couples' actions were far more ambivalent. Fully 16 percent of these presumed enemies had had sexual intercourse with each other during the two-month period after divorce, and almost 70 percent of the mothers and 60 percent of the fathers admitted that if some sort of crisis arose, the ex-spouse would be the first person they'd call. Some of the fathers even babysat for the mothers when they went out on dates!

The Six- to Twelve-Month Breakdown. As the months roll on, new stresses are added to what have become old familiar ones. In spite of the best of intentions to keep things running smoothly at home for the children's sake, the single-parent home during the first postdivorce year is apt to descend, if not into chaos, at least into a state of domestic disorganization.[21] Daily routines tend to deteriorate: rather than sitting down together for meals, for example, divorced mothers and their children are less apt to eat dinner together. The children's bedtimes become more erratic, and the children are less apt to be read bedtime stories or to be given regular baths. In the morning disorganization begins anew; children of divorce during this period are likely to be late for school.

The emotional states of the recently divorced parents seem to be as shattered as their household routines. Both parents continue to feel increasingly anxious, depressed, angry, rejected, and incompetent. The financial burden of supporting two households hangs heavy on the fathers, who, more than married men, tend to take on heavier workloads—but to do them less effectively. Postdivorce stress caused these men to sleep less, and when they did, to sleep in erratic patterns. At the same time, the mothers were concerned with feeling less attractive physically, losing the status of a married woman, and feeling generally helpless. These feelings were compounded in parents who were older or who had been married the longest.[22]

The Parental Rhythms of Divorce

The single parent's relationship with the children also becomes strained during the first year. The divorcing mother especially seems to lose a lot of her effectiveness. And a vicious cycle can begin, primarily with sons. During this period, single parents communicate less with their children, and when they do, they communicate badly.[23] In two-parent families, mothers traditionally give more than twice as many household commands as do fathers. In single-parent families, the command ratio escalates, and boys start to balk. The conflict is almost inevitable. Single parents simply do not have the energy or the patience to reason endlessly with their children as to why they should brush their teeth or walk the dog. And the coercive cycle between the demands of single mothers and defiant sons begins.

During the first year, preoccupied single parents often show less affection toward their children than do married parents and tend to be inconsistent in maintaining discipline as well.[24] With no backup from the absent parent, the single parent often just gives in—or gives up. Many single parents also seem to lose confidence in helping their children move toward independence, as if unwilling to accept one iota more of risk in their already overstretched lives. Rather than encouraging mature behavior in their children, anxious single mothers tend to be more restrictive and overprotective, which in turn promotes infantile behavior in the very same children these overburdened mothers wish could take more responsibility.

Mothers and fathers also treat the children very differently during the first phases of divorce, which exacerbates the problems even more. Fathers, anxious to spend pleasurable time with their children and not to risk losing their love, often become overly permissive and indulgent, turning more into Santa Claus figures than authoritative ones. To counteract the "every day is Christmas" syndrome that comes with visiting the father, the mother is forced into the role of unloved despot.[25]

The children, bewildered by the polar attitudes of their parents and fairly well disillusioned with both, tend to get even more unruly, a condition that never totally goes away. One classic study states: "Divorced mothers and fathers never gain as much control over their children as their married counterparts."[26]

The Twelve-Month Realities. There have been changes, too many changes, for both parent and child to negotiate gracefully. The reality of divorce has now sunk in and fantasies, at least for the adults, fade. The income level of the mother has dropped as much as 70 percent, and many mothers and their children are embarked on a depressing course of downward mobility. Though the women's movement is justifiably proud of its members newly employed in the executive suite, divorced mothers of small children are not usually part of such career elites and are more apt to struggle along in low-paying, part-time, or temporary jobs. Child-care arrangements tend to be not only erratic, but in many cases, inadequate. Latch-key children are no longer limited to the lowest socioeconomic bracket in this country, but are found increasingly in middle-class neighborhoods where the mother cannot either afford good child care or find it.

In higher socioeconomic brackets, where the effects of divorce do not have such dire financial effects, the result is more subtle, but relatively no less distressing. Suddenly the perks of a more affluent way of life—charge accounts, skiing vacations, piano and ballet lessons—disappear. And the gilt-edged family, which has been protected from the more basic modes of survival, may suffer psychological repercussions from the loss of both financial and social security.

In the middle and upper socioeconomic brackets, the task overload on single mothers can also become a backbreaker at the twelve-month mark. There is less money for household help, for specialty services, for just about everything, but the children of privilege often balk at picking up the domestic slack. It is both the pride and the curse of the middle and upper classes to encourage intellectual (if not physical) independence in their children, and to direct their energies toward self-improvement and self-expression. These ideals don't include such mundane chores as doing the shopping, the laundry, and babysitting for younger siblings. The mother in a higher socio-economic bracket often seems incapable of effectively assigning these chores to the children, while the children, under this strange and demeaning new regime, seem equally incapable of willingly pitching in to help. In lower brackets, where the parental attitude is different, taking on household and child-care responsibilities comes much more naturally.[27] Chores are expected to be accomplished along with self-care, even for children of preschool age. At least in terms of domestic support, therefore, divorced mothers in this bracket have it easier.

The first year after divorce is, in short, the most chaotic. Thus, it is not surprising that it was at the end of the first year that fully 97 percent of the mothers and 81 percent of the fathers in one study[28] admitted that the divorce might have been a mistake and that more effort should have been made to try and resolve their marital differences.

THE SECOND YEAR

Life still isn't any better in the second year. And for many women, the situation is even worse. Regret and ambivalence run deep, as the Promised Land of Singlehood often fails to deliver. Friends who rallied in support at the time of separation tend to fall away, and the mother especially is left in greater isolation than ever. Women who don't work suffer double isolation. Not only do they not have the contact with adult colleagues, they have also lost the friends and colleagues who came along with the business lives of their husbands. Like semi-invalids, many nonworking divorced women describe themselves as feeling shut in or trapped with their children. At the same time, divorced fathers complain of feeling shut out.[29]

To compensate for the loss of a spouse and all the life that revolved around him or her, ex-marrieds at the beginning of the second year often plunge into a frenzy of activity. No project seems too banal for an adult who simply cannot face another evening of being alone. Suddenly, there is a burning need to learn to make jewelry, throw clay pots, take creative writing courses—anything to get out of the house. Men, adrift from family obligations, often go on a social tear and seek companionship, however temporary, in bars, at clubs, and at parties they never would have dreamed of going to while they were still married. Loneliness becomes a malignant enemy, held at bay by a schedule filled to the absurd.

The Twelve- to Eighteen-Month Slump. There is often a time lag in reaction to divorce which has just begun to be recognized. And it makes sense. During the first year, much of the single parent's energy has been consumed by coping with the problems and life changes spawned by divorce. Now the problem becomes learning to live with them. So it is often not for a full year after divorce that indicators of maladjustment show up.[30] In a recent study comparing stress in married and divorced women, the time-lapse results were startling. The stress factors were the same for the "newly marrieds" as for the "newly divorced." The women who had been divorced for over 3.5 years scored the same in self-esteem and depression as the "continually married" group. It was the group in between, living through the twelve to eighteen months following divorce, who were experiencing the most trouble. Women in this time period were experiencing such difficulties as completing tasks they had volunteered to do and enduring mood swings that daily oscillated between "good" and "despair."

The Parental Rhythms of Divorce

There are some women, of course, who experience little or no difficulty ridding themselves of an unhappy marriage, and at the end of the first year proclaim their postdivorce lives to be far more stimulating and happier than their married lives. But paradoxically, the children of these self-fulfilled women often exhibit the most frequent emotional and behavioral problems. The egocentric mother's concentration on her own well-being often means that she overlooks the well-being of her children, who feel lost and ignored.[31] Though it is healthy indeed for a single mother to feel satisfied with her life, the trick is not to find that sense of gratification at the expense of the children.

Second Year Sexuality. The beginning of the second year is apt to be a highly sexual time for both divorced parents, especially the man. But what distinguishes these sexual encounters at the twelve- to eighteen-month mark is the serendipity of them. Casual sex, sex without commitment, sex even with strangers becomes an outlet for those who feel their sexual attractiveness is at a precarious low. In their attempts to recapture a sense of self-worth and sexual attractiveness, otherwise rational and sober adults can find themselves in amazing situations. One man, a partner in a highly respected law firm in Chicago, became so obsessively involved with two Texas women he'd met in a bar that he didn't phone in or show up at his office for two days and missed several important closings. A woman who at home was on the board of deacons of her local church treated herself to a four-day cruise in the Caribbean (which she could ill afford) and wound up not only in the bunk of the ship's navigator, but flauntingly naked in the ship's pool at 3:00 A.M. "I felt crazed, totally out of control," said the woman, who was at the critical eighteen-month mark after divorce. "It just wasn't me. And it was wonderful. Just the memory kept me on a high for months."

Lust runs high, just as high as commitment runs low. It is still too early for the recently divorced to risk wearing a bruised heart on a sleeve. So the body becomes part of the healing process for a wounded self-esteem.

The originator of the divorce action is more apt to enter the sexual arena faster and have more partners than the one who is left. But for men, sexual liaisons are not always successful at first, as even the most eager of Don Juans often suffer some sort of temporary sexual dysfunction following a marital breakup. Guilt and anxiety are not easy emotions to shed. And there is inevitably a sense of failure on the part of both partners, not only as parents, but as spouses, which tends to cloud immediate heterosexual relationships.

During the first few months after divorce, the sex lives of both divorced parents are usually less active than those of married couples. Between the one- and two-year marks, however, divorced men peak in their sexual conquests and surpass married couples in quantity, if not quality. And there is no end of possible partners. Sexual curiosity on the part of both men and women, held in check by an average of six years of marital monogamy, breeds an enthusiastic eagerness to experiment. Having entered marriage in a period when sexuality was more restricted, many divorced people are leaving their marriages now to plunge into an enticing era of sexual laissez-faire. And their median ages at divorce—men in their early thirties and women in their late twenties—give them the confidence and experience to try anything—or anyone. As a salacious result, divorced men in one study reported that as a norm, they made advances on the first or second date. And more often than not, the women accepted.[32]

A new sex life naturally poses a quandary for divorced parents. On the one hand, they must function as family-oriented parents just as much as, if not more than, they did when there were both a mommy and a daddy at home. On the other hand, they must also find adult company and interests for themselves which often have absolutely nothing to do with the children.

Leading such dual lives can be exhausting for the parents and bewildering to the children who don't understand why Mommy or Daddy chooses to go out at night without them. But many divorced parents do not want to risk involving a potential partner in the intimacy of family life for fear of either confusing the children or losing the partner. A relationship between adults has to be fairly well established before it can tolerate the strain or even the possible sabotage of the children.

The Second-Year Lover Loss. While some divorced parents are terrified of finding a permanent lover, others are terrified of not having one. At least for a while. And the second year often sees the termination of a love affair that began at the point of divorce, or even before the marriage was dissolved. In 70 percent of the divorces included in one study, one spouse had been involved with another person during the final phase of the dying marriage. Such triangles often and obviously contribute to the decision to divorce.[33] Indeed, the extramarital affair often gives an unhappily married person the strength and support to end the marriage. Without such support, many divorced people claim, they would have just limped along in the marriage.

But the companion/lover who helps a husband or wife through the breakup rarely wins the prize. Instead, this "transition" person, who has comforted, counseled, and boosted the self-esteem of the divorcing man or woman, is often himself (or herself) abandoned when the stress of the divorce is past. As in the ancient rite of killing the messenger who bears bad news, the extramarital lover can become the target of responsibility for breaking up a family and be blamed for the guilt and disillusionment that often follow. After the emotion of divorce ebbs, moreover, the transition person is looked at more rationally and often found wanting in terms of a permanent future. Fewer than 15 percent of the couples in the study cited above married the person for whom they had left their respective spouses. It is no wonder, then, that divorce veterans shy away from anything more than casual involvement with newly separated or divorced people. "I always ask a woman I've just met how long she's been splitsville," says a New York advertising executive who has been divorced for five years. "If it's under a year, I run like hell."

Even so, for the recently divorced, it is better to take the poetic risk of loving—and losing—than not to get involved at all. Even though the children may suffer through some inattention while their parents are gallivanting about, it is important for divorced adults, who often feel betrayed by the opposite sex, to reestablish some sense of trust. Only by constantly testing the emotional waters do the wary ex-marrieds gain the courage to get their feet wet again and risk commitment. In one study of formerly marrieds, the average man dated fifteen to twenty women in the three years following separation, while the average woman went out with seven to ten different men. And the more, the merrier. For divorced women, the more lovers they have, the more ready they say they are to risk love again and to remarry.[34]

The Third Year. Suddenly, everything seems to improve. New friendships have been made to replace lost ones. Household routines are reestablished, even though they may be very different from the routines before divorce. Parent and child alike gain a new sense of equilibrium both inside and outside the home. The sense of foreignness as a single parent now seems the norm, and the children begin to lose their anxiety. In short, life begins to stabilize. But there are changes.

Some of these changes are for the best. By now, for example, divorced parents have dissected the reasons for their failed marriages so many times that they have come up with a tolerable, if subjective, explanation for the sequence of events.

While some exonerate themselves entirely from blame and level the divorce finger at their ex-spouse, others admit to some human failings on their own part. Regardless of whether the story is "right" or "wrong," fantasized or built on fact, having comfortable answers to "what went wrong with my marriage" is an essential part of closing that chapter and being ready to move on to another. People who are still struggling with the "what if's" and "if only I had's" three years after the fact are not likely candidates for a new and satisfying relationship.

For men, the merry-go-round of self-help projects and mindless social activities slows down to a reasonable rate now, as the terrors of spending Saturday night alone diminish. "It took me three years to be able to sit alone in my apartment and read a book," says a New York editor. "Now I worry that I like being alone too much." Women who had been too much alone the first year after divorce have been steadily increasing social contacts during the second year and, by the three-year mark, are almost at the same level as the reduced social frenzy of their ex-husbands. But they never really catch up. The social life of a divorced woman invariably remains less than that of a married woman—or a divorced man.[35]

Self-esteem and feelings of competence are also welling in the breasts of the new divorce veterans, many of whom by now have established on-going relationships with new partners. The sexual marathon that men, especially, embarked on soon after divorce has been found wanting and has been replaced by a desire for intimacy and meaning. For many women, experimentation has backfired, and prolonged periods of promiscuity have been found to result in feelings of desperation, intense depression, and a bottomed-out self-esteem. Both men and women seem to welcome the return to monogamy with relief, which accounts for the high rate of remarriage at three years after divorce. But still, there is scar tissue. Even after remarriage, newlyweds may score high on the happiness scale, but their ratings for self-esteem and feelings of competence are consistently lower than for parents in intact families.[36]

At three years, the relationship with the children has also smoothed out, especially for the parents of daughters. Single mothers are no longer babying their children and are offering more reasoning and explanation than giving direct orders. Being more relaxed themselves, the mothers are able to be more nurturing of their children, and more consistent. The children respond in kind by being more responsive to the parent and less rebellious. At the same time, the noncustodial father is giving up his permissive attitude toward the children and becoming more demanding, decreasing the reactive gap between the parenting poles each forced the other into.

Yet the single parent, who almost always has had to go to work, is still stretched very thin. There is no room for contingency planning, no backup for an emergency, and the anxiety level remains high. Both parent and child have to readjust their expectations of each other, a process that can produce both pride and resentment.

Strong bonds are apt to develop between the children and the single parent, attachments that are even deeper than those in intact families. More often than not, the single parent is the only adult at the dinner table and is forced to talk to the children. It is inevitable when there are two or more adults at a table that they will talk to each other exclusively until the children start throwing lime Jell-O to gain attention. In a single-parent family, the adult and the children are often each other's regular company, forcing a communion of ages. The bond can be equally strong with the noncustodial parent, most often the father, who, like the mother, does not have the buffer of the other parent between him and the children. In a one-to-one relationship, both the parent and the children come to know each other better and more deeply than if the relationship were diluted or distracted by the presence of another person.

The Parental Rhythms of Divorce

* * *

For better or worse, by the three-year mark most divorced families have set their patterns. If the parents continue to war and are stalled somewhere in the divorce rhythm, the children will continue to carry the double burden of parental hostility and their own development. If the parents are at peace with themselves—and each other—the children have gotten back to the normal tasks of growing up.

It takes time to undo the old family structure and redesign the new. Where there was one family, there are now two. And if and when a parent remarries, the "blended" or "reconstituted" families can turn a single family tree into a forest. In the three or so years it takes for a divorced family to get to "Go" again, parents have had to work through six separate stages of divorce. It is not a time when they can expect themselves to live up to their own images of perfect parents.

But it is important to remember that the parental rhythm of divorce in these first years is different from that of the children. Often the needs of the two generations are completely at odds. The adult has to find new meaning and identity outside the family at the same time that the children have a greater need for security within the family. The adult has to take on a bewildering load of new tasks and responsibilities at the same time that the children anxiously demand an overtime supply of personal attention for themselves. Children simply do not have the experience to understand the adult needs of their parents. And the parents are usually so pressed and preoccupied that they cannot give the children the reassurance they need during this period.

Though it may not be easy to tidy up the fallout from divorce, it is essential to neutralize the anger and resentment that can follow. If the marriage was not a success, at least the divorce can be. Step by step.

THROUGH CHILDREN'S EYES
What Divorce Means

Young children do not understand the word "divorce." Young children do not even understand the word "marriage." Both are adult words evolving from social contracts legitimized by state laws. What children do understand is that they are young, small, and ill-equipped to defend themselves from the demands of the greater world—or even to exist in it—without the protection of adults. And in most cases, those adults are the child's parents.

It is hard to remember as adults just how vulnerable children feel. Adults bear both the security and the weight of human experience and it is difficult, if not impossible, to peel back that experience to join once again the very limited world of the child. Adults often laugh at the plight of the angry child who runs away from home—and doesn't dare cross the street. But few can remember how terrifying it really is for a child who doesn't understand where the cars are coming from, or how to get away from them.

Children are equally helpless in determining the course of their family's lives. Children do not get a chance to choose their parents or to control whatever situation they find themselves in. They are stuck with whatever hand they are dealt, locked into their immediate environments, and dependent on whatever filial relationships present themselves, be they good or bad.

To dispel this sense of vulnerability, children often elevate their parents to exalted levels. A young child doesn't think of his mother or father as an individual with his or her own peculiar quirks or weaknesses, but as a rock-solid institution dropped on earth only to serve and protect him. "To Mary, as to all young children, her parents were no ordinary human beings," wrote child psychiatrist J. Louise Despert of a three-year-old girl. "They could do no wrong; they always knew the answers; they had the magic to dispel every fear, ward off any danger. They were all love, all help and protection, all power. They were God and more than God, because God is someone far away whom you never see, but parents are there and they are real to the touch, the sight, the hearing."[1]

The shock of losing one of those parents to divorce can be devastating to the child, for no matter how hard the child tries to deny it, divorce is a matter of choice. One of the parents chooses to leave the family, and no one—not the remaining parent or the child—can make that parent stay. "The disillusionment that comes with the knowledge that your parents do not love each other anymore and are not going to stay together is probably as profound as the eventual knowledge that someday you are going to die," says Gordon Livingston, director of psychiatry at the Columbia Medical Plan in Columbia, Maryland. "It's not only a tremendous blow to a child's conception of the world as an orderly place, but it shakes his fundamental faith in everything. It's the one thing children expect to persist and when it doesn't, it's scary." The commonness of divorce today has even generated divorce anxiety in children whose families are still intact. "Every time my mother and father argue, I think they're getting a divorce," one nine-year-old girl told me. "I just get so scared."

The isolation of the modern child compounds the shock of divorce and colors its aftermath. A child's world these days has grown dangerously small. The falling birthrate has created a whole generation of only children. The nuclear family does not usually include a nearby network of attentive relatives and in-laws. And divorce makes the family smaller still. This isolation has actually increased the importance of the modern family, rather than decreasing it as the family-is-dead doomsayers claim. So when something goes wrong in a child's tiny little circle, it's apt to go very wrong. "A child learns the rules of human relationships in the immediate household," says Donald Bloch, director of the Nathan Ackerman Institute for Family Therapy in New York. "When the child sees that world splitting up in divorce, he feels his world is shattered and his learned rules no longer make any sense or are true."[2]

Social perceptions of divorce make it harder for these children. Though much of the stigma of divorce has been overcome by the sheer number of single-parent families, vestiges still remain. When families are broken up by the death of a parent, the community often rallies, bringing casseroles, encouragement, and concern for the children. Divorce, on the other hand, tends to isolate the family. There is no wake, no funeral, no support group of relatives and friends. Children of divorce are left to mourn alone. And in smaller communities particularly, their single mothers are often looked upon with suspicion.

To continue the analogy, children who lose parents to death are traditionally excused for any erratic behavior: "The poor little girl, losing her mom (or dad) so young." Even the behavior of children in conflict-ridden homes elicits sympathy: "He has terrible problems at home" is a common excuse offered by a community to explain why a boy slashed tires or threw a rock through a school window. But the same actions from a child of divorce elicit quite a different response. "That boy needs someone to keep him in line," a stern adult might say of an overaggressive boy. Girls do not fare any better. "She's from a broken home," might run the explanation for a girl's misbehavior. "No wonder she's a troublemaker."

The ambience in a household in which there has been a recent divorce is also likely to enforce the child's sense of loss. In a family where a parent has died or even where there is marital violence, the child is often doted on as a love substitute. The single mother or father in these cases is far more likely to say to the child, "I don't know what I'd do without you," whereas the divorced parent, especially during the stress immediately following the splitup, is likely to say—or insinuate—the opposite. "The kids are driving me crazy," is not an uncommon postdivorce reaction. Or "If I don't get out of this house I'm going to go nuts." And the children, either directly or indirectly, get the message of rejection.

Is it worse, then, for the child to have his parents divorce, or to live in a household full of marital acrimony? The elusive answer depends, of course, on the degree of hostility in the still-married household, and the amount of bitterness that might spill over into a divorce. Each is equally destructive at its extreme. But many parents stay together on the pretense—or perhaps in the genuine belief—that they are doing so for the sake of the children, when it is really for their own sakes. Locked in a battle that marriage counselor Isolina Ricci calls "negative intimacy," such parents feed on their hostility until they cannot live without it. Hatred and the desire to punish can be a stronger bond than love and the desire to please. And parents who continue to do battle within a marriage while using the children as matrimonial glue are simply fooling themselves.

And the children show it, especially boys. Not all the rules children learn in their immediate households are positive ones, and when parents abuse each other vocally, physically, or, in a favorite weapon of the upper middle class, silently, the children get the angry message. Study after study has linked parental in-fighting with behavioral problems in children, which sometimes escalate into delinquency. And the longer the discord lasts, the greater the amount of deviant behavior. A classic study in England found that among boys who had already had one brush with the law, those who came from two-parent families with persistent problems were more likely to show up in court again than were boys from either divorced families or nonwarring intact families.[3]

A house filled with tension can take a far greater toll on the children than resolution of the tension through divorce. Twenty-four college students at the State University of New York in Buffalo were asked to evaluate what stage of family disruption centering around their parents' divorces had caused them the most distress. Where the predivorce fighting, often physical, had been intense, the child's stress level was highest. Not unnaturally, the children had been afraid that one of their parents would seriously injure the other, which is hardly the sugarplum stuff of children's dreams. The children had few friends, because they were embarrassed to bring anyone home for fear of witnessing a parental scene. Their family lives were further strained by economic uncertainties. Money is a great weapon, and many of these children's fathers withheld it from their families, ostensibly to punish their wives, but in fact hurting everyone. There was no continuity to their family lives, no one to count on, as one or the other of the parental protagonists kept moving in and out of the house.[4]

The children's reactions to such a turbulent family life were severe, especially if they were under nine years old at the time. Physically, the students reported bouts of vomiting, nervous facial tics, loss of hair, weight loss and gain, and even one ulcer. "I used to think I was in the way when my parents fought," one student recalled. "Sometimes I felt like my insides were tearing." Because of their youth, the children had felt trapped and unable to get away from the conflict. Older children could leave the house to seek refuge with a friend, but these little children could only run upstairs and hide in their bedrooms.

A retreat into fantasy made the situation more bearable for these children, who either made up hero stories about their parents or invented imaginary adults to take the place of those who were letting them down. A few even tried unsuccessfully to intervene in their parents' fights. "Once at the dinner table they were screaming as usual," another student remembered. "I started to write on a piece of paper, "Please stop fighting," but I couldn't remember how to spell "fight." My mother saw me and asked what I was writing. I started to cry and couldn't stop." The fighting continued, and this student, like others who tried to referee their parents' war games, gave it up as futile.

A childhood spent in an atmosphere of such extreme antagonism is an almost unbearable concept. But it happens, and the children cope the best they can. "When I heard my father's car in the drive, I knew it would be a minute before he reached the back door," recalled another student. "In that time I would leave by the front." It is little wonder that these children, who were forced to bear continual witness to their parents' acrimony, found divorce a relief.

Thus it seems obvious that chronic parental fighting is worse for a child than any other family disruption. Children suffer the most in bad marriages—and in bitter divorces. But what about the children in between, the ones whose parents have "drifted apart," whose parents say they no longer have "anything in common," and feel that their marriages are "dead"? Are these children of divorce better off than children whose parents are still together, albeit reluctantly? The evidence would indicate they are not.

It is fairly easy for children to understand why their families are splitting up when they can pin it on some sort of extreme behavior such as alcoholism, drug abuse, or parental violence. The difficulty arises in the often vague and abstract reasons for contemporary divorce. "I have to go find myself," Joanna Kramer explained lamely in the film *Kramer vs. Kramer.* Modern divorce often entails such decisions, by-products of the "Me Decade," which pitted the unfulfilled dreams of one family member against the best interests of the others. "No one knows how unhappy a marriage has to be before it's better that the parents divorce. That's the great unknown," says Andrew Cherlin, assistant professor of social relations at Johns Hopkins University in Baltimore. "No social scientist, no psychiatrist can tell you how unhappy you have to be in order for your kids to be better off if you separate."

Ironically, many of these "life-style" divorces have been preceded by very happy home lives for the children. A middle- and upper-middle-class phenomenon, such divorces come without warning to children accustomed to family tranquillity, caring parents, and an organized household. Though one cannot make the case that it is better for parents to fight openly before divorcing, nonetheless, children who have lived in "ideal" families almost always suffer the most in the upheaval that inevitably follows divorce. Sheltered from any indication of conflict, these children are ill-prepared for the acrimony and confusion between parents who seemed to be happy together just the day before. What happened? The children look everywhere for answers. Limited by their lack of sophistication, they often find answers based more in fantasy than in fact. "My mom likes people with blue eyes and my dad has brown eyes. Maybe that's why it happened," said one seven-year-old boy, struggling to understand.

In cases like these, it is almost always the parents who want the divorce, not the children. And it is the children who have to adjust to visitation schedules, to moving often to less expensive neighborhoods and schools, to watching a new parental partner take over the place of the child's natural parent. Parents may be much happier on the far side of divorce. But it does not necessarily follow that the children will be, too.

Growing up is not easy under any circumstances. Though many adults look back on their childhoods with nostalgia, few would truly opt to live through those years again. And disruption, be it from a hostile home life or from divorce, makes passage to adulthood that much more difficult.

Obviously every situation is different, each family has its own peculiarities and its own way of handling things. But the stress of divorce is universal. And each child has a story to tell, a story that is probably going to be different from that of the parents. Children, especially younger ones, are very reluctant to air negative feelings about their parents for fear of punishment or reprisal. Children often remain silent out of guilt, assuming the blame for what went wrong in the first place. But most important, children keep their mouths shut for fear of losing parental love, the one love a human being can never really do without.

So it's up to us to listen very carefully to these children, and even more important, to try and hear what they don't dare say out loud. Only then can parents begin to understand, at the child's level, how children feel and how some of the pain and confusion can be lifted from their lives. Parents have to look at divorce through their children's eyes, listen to their voices, and remember, if they can, what it was really like to be fourteen or nine or four or even one.

BABIES AND TODDLERS
The Age of Helplessness

No child is too young to experience the fallout from divorce. What affects the parent must also trickle down to the children. Though it is understandable for parents to ease their guilt and sense of parental protectiveness by thinking that children under three are too impossibly young to understand what is going on, quite the opposite is true. During this period of rapid development, children are the most dependent on their parents—and most affected by them.

For babies, the impact of divorce is indirect. What they feel is not their own distress, but that of their custodial parent. A baby's cognitive and emotional growth is directly related to the amount of stimulation and responsiveness he receives from the adults around him. His sense of security is also governed by the quality and consistency of his first attachment. If a parent is tense and distracted, the baby may react by becoming dull and unresponsive at one end of the spectrum, or irritable and hyperactive at the other.[1]

As the baby grows older, he learns to recognize different people, and at six months begins to delight in those differences. Though he is still not sure who these people really are, each adds excitement and instruction to his limited world. The loss of one of these people, presuming it is either his mother or father, cuts his world of outside stimulus in half.

At a year old, a baby has made rapid progress and has begun to "think" for himself. He has mastered rolling over, sitting, and standing, and may even be taking a few steps. He also has the stirring of memory, which brings with it a fear of the unfamiliar. He becomes frightened of strangers (both adult and children), of unfamiliar places, of being separated from the person to whom he has become deeply attached. The impact of divorce at this age now becomes direct. Not only does the child lose one parent whom he knows and trusts, but his other parent usually has to leave him to go to work.

From eighteen months to two years, the toddler imitates the actions of others, mimicking their tones of voices, hugging others as he has been hugged. He can speak now in two- and three-word sentences and feed himself. His independence is hard won, though, for his fears have intensified. Now he's even frightened of going to bed for fear of losing his mother (or father). His imagination knows no limit—and goes far beyond his experience. Unable to differentiate between reality and make-believe, his dreams often become nightmares. Divorce at this age is particularly painful, especially for little boys. Old enough to feel vulnerable and beginning to identify with the father, a little boy is apt to feel not only bereft but unprotected.

Boys of all ages suffer deeper reactions to divorce than girls, partially because 90 percent of the time it is the father who leaves, but also because of both inherent and learned behavior. As early as ten months, for example, boy babies have been observed to be more demanding of a mother's full attention than girl babies, and not to be satisfied until they have it.[2] Further, even before they reach the age of two, little boys have been singled out from little girls in study after study as being more controlling, flouting the rules of the household more often, getting into more mischief than their female toddler peers, and making more demands of the parent. Before they can barely talk, little boys seem set on a collision course with authority, a noncompliance that escalates with age and is intensified by divorce.[3]

Certain ages, though, can be a saving grace for both sexes in divorce. And for these youngest of children, the impact of divorce is muted. Their relationships with their fathers, with the exception of two-year-old boys, are not yet deeply rooted. Though one-year-olds may be delighted to greet a father at night after work, they have not yet learned to miss him. Babies and toddlers are also spared the memory of parental fighting, the legacy of which can haunt older children. "Under the age of three, children have little or no memory of family conflict and what happened in the divorce," says child psychiatrist Gordon Livingston. From the point of view of the children, this, then, is one of the better times to divorce.

But no one gets off scot free. There is a family rupture. The mother is affected, the father is affected, and the children are affected, even, it turns out, before they are born.

THE PREGNANCY DIVORCE

Angela cannot believe what is happening to her. Her husband, Steve, has just announced that he is leaving her. Bam. Just like that. How could Steve do that to her? After all, she is having a baby, *his* baby, *their* baby. They were going to be a *family.* Angela stares down at her swollen stomach, watching her sweater bulge as the baby moves inside her. Whom should she call?

Where will she go? Who is going to take care of her, let alone take care of the baby?

Angela begins to panic. Steve didn't even tell her where he was going, just packed a bag and left. How can she work and take care of the baby at the same time? She doesn't have any money. And she doesn't have the strength. The baby moves again, kicking her painfully in the ribs. Now sobbing, Angela raises her hand and slaps her stomach hard. Stop it, she says. Go away. Just go away.

The immediate prognosis for Angela's marriage to Steve is not good. And neither is the prognosis for the child still developing in Angela's womb. With an irony worthy of *Catch-22,* family problems often erupt before there is even a family, creating shock waves that affect not only present lives, but future lives as well.

Pregnancy can be a flash point in the most solid of marriages, especially when one or both of the partners is emotionally immature. The proof of impending maternity or paternity signals the inescapable end of childhood for both partners, and while most couples adjust to it, some recoil in terror. The reality of becoming a mother or, in Steve's case, a father, is just too grown-up to bear.

But Steve has done more than just walk out on Angela. The developing fetus feels every bit of tension the pregnant woman does. Though the nervous systems of the fetus and the woman are not directly connected, there is a one-way relationship between the two that cannot be severed. When a woman feels such emotions as rage, anxiety, or fear, her nervous system starts pumping extra chemicals into her bloodstream while her adrenal glands quickly send out an assortment of emergency hormones. If she is pregnant, not only does the composition of her own blood change, but so also does the circulatory system of the fetus. The fetus can be so charged up by the mother's stress that it becomes hyperactive in utero, increasing its body movement by as much as 300 percent.[4]

The damage to the baby can be substantial if the pregnant woman's stress continues throughout pregnancy. The baby is apt to be born either prematurely or with a low birth weight. And that's just the beginning. Babies born to unhappy, distressed women are often unhappy and distressed themselves. They tend to be irritable, hyperactive, and squirmy. Their digestive systems do not function smoothly, and they are plagued with excessive bowel movements and gas pains; they have difficulty sleeping, cry excessively, and have an unusual need to be held.[5] Combine these symptoms and needs with those of the new mother whose husband has walked out on her and the miracle of birth comes closer to a nightmare.

THE UNDER-PARENTED BABY

Amy is just waking up. Jerkily, she raises her head and gets herself up on her elbows. She feels wet and a little cold, though at three months she doesn't understand why. She's hungry, too. So hungry that her stomach actually hurts. She starts to cry, signaling to the world at large that she wants help. But nothing happens. She cries harder, more shrilly, as panic now enters her calls. Why doesn't someone come? Maybe no one ever will.

The most important and enduring lesson a child learns in the first year of life is trust, and as early as three months, Amy is learning the reverse: the world is not a very secure and warm place. It is not necessarily her mother or her father that Amy is learning not to count on. Babies under six months old don't know the difference between their parents, a babysitter, or the mailman. But it is very important that someone, anyone, respond quickly to her calls for help and hold her, cuddle her, feed her, soothe her. The old-fashioned theory that babies have to be taught a schedule or else grow up spoiled rotten has mercifully been put to rest. Researchers now agree that the more a baby is tended to, the less often it will cry for attention. Reassured that help is never far away, such babies are more relaxed and less demanding than babies who are neglected or merely ignored.

Babies whose parents are in the process of divorcing are not always ignored, of course. For some parents, a baby provides a welcome distraction from their own problems, and their derailed feelings of love and tenderness for each other reroute themselves to the child. But it is hard, if not impossible, for a mother upset with her own life to continually rise above her own concerns during divorce and selflessly tend to the needs of others. Amy's mother may very well be crying alone in her own bedroom while Amy is crying alone in hers.

It takes a tremendous amount of energy and attention to deal with little babies, and when that energy is shared or at least supported by the father, it all becomes more possible. But if the primary caretaker, usually the mother, is upset and distracted, the quality of the baby's care has to suffer. Technically, the baby may be in fine shape in that it is fed and changed and kept clean. But it is the little extras in a baby's life that begin to determine not only his or her emotional attitude toward life, but the ability to learn as well.

The seemingly idiotic interactions between adults and babies, the cooings, the ticklings, the peek-a-boo games, actually pave the way for a baby's future development. The more a parent talks to a baby, for example, even though he or she cannot understand a word the parent is saying, the sooner the baby will learn to differentiate between speech actually directed to him and general conversation. The more responsive to and relaxed a parent is with a baby, the more responsive the baby will be to all human beings. But if the custodial parent is angry and anxious, the setting is not conducive to such child's play. And though the baby may not actually be damaged, its ability to develop both socially and cognitively may be slowed.

THE OVERPARENTED BABY

Freddy is furious. His mother keeps hugging him, holding him too tightly and too long. He wiggles to get away from her, but she won't let go. He's six months old now and has other things to do. He wants to hold his own bottle. He can sit up with a little help. And this very morning he managed to get up on his knees and actually creep a little, albeit backward. Why won't she let him go?

At six months, an incredibly exciting thing is happening to Freddy. He is beginning the process of emotionally separating himself from his parents, a process that continues through childhood and, for some, even into adulthood. The symptoms of early emancipation are not earth-shattering, of course. A six-month-old baby may try to jerk his bottle away from the mother so he can hold it himself, or wriggle out of her arms when she's feeding him, preferring instead to sit up straight. The real issue is control: until now, a baby like Freddy has been totally dependent on his mother, and under her control. Now the dynamic begins to shift and the baby tries to take charge of his own life.[6]

But Freddy's mother is resisting his bid for independence. She's upset, after all, because of all the bitterness and fighting she's going through with his father. There's even a custody fight brewing, and his mother is panic-stricken that she may lose the one thing she has left to love. So she clings to him, worries over him, babies him just when he is aching to creep off on his own. And in his frustration, he tries to push her out of the way so he can get on with it.

Freddy's response to his mother is healthy, but at his age, his mother's overresponse to him is unhealthy. At six months, a baby has developed just enough to be able to fall back on regression as a respite from the frightening challenges of growing up. If his mother's divorce-generated distress and need to overmother continues to thwart his attempts to pull away from her, he may just give up and return to more infantile behavior.

Divorce now poses a second danger: at six months, a baby "recognizes" his mother, father, and caretakers. He responds to them individually, cooing and smiling happily, realizing for the first time that these people are more than just sources of food and comfort. He begins to form an attachment to the person who cares for him most often, usually the mother. But he is also delighted to see his father, whose deeper voice and more physical way of handling him excite him and broaden his limited experience. The "disappearance" of one of those newly recognized parents from his daily life is his first loss.

In a curious twist of familial fate, the increased participation of the modern father in child care can make divorce more difficult. Traditionally, fathers have expressed little interest in getting involved with young children. One famous study in the early seventies pointed out that fathers spent only thirty-seven seconds a day communicating with their babies, not even time enough for a chorus of "Row, Row, Row Your Boat." The disappearance of such invisible fathers from a baby's life hardly left a ripple. But the growing wave of paternal affection and attention has brought with it not only benefit to the child but the burden of loss as well——on both sides. The fewer the people in the baby's immediate world, the less encouragement and stimulation he will get. And the more distracted the remaining parent, the more diminished still will be the attention a baby this age thrives on.

THE FOURTEEN-MONTH-OLD CLINGER

Johnny is pale and withdrawn. His new babysitter tries to interest him in playing with a plastic truck, but he just sits listlessly on the living-room floor. Johnny is fourteen months old and he is sure his mother has left him for good this time. His father shows up from time to time and takes him for a walk or a drive in the car. But it's his mother Johnny wants. And since the divorce, she leaves him to go to work every day, even though he cries and cries and hangs on to her legs at the front door. When she comes home from work at night, he starts to cry again. He is terrified that once more she will leave him. Sometimes he gets so depressed that he isn't even glad to see her at the end of the day. Instead, he ignores her. He won't even look at her, until it's time for bed. Then he can't get enough of her and clings to her desperately when she tries to put him in the crib. He doesn't even sleep well anymore and often cries in the middle of the night.

Divorce intensifies all sorts of fears in children, fears that appear to be an irrevocable part of normal child development. And to a child between the ages of eight and eighteen months, the repercussions of divorce can be particularly painful. During these sensitive ten months, the child forms a very close emotional attachment—his first—to the most constant person in his life. Inevitably, at the same time, he develops a deep fear of losing that parent. In psychological terms, these phases of child development are called "attachment bonding" and "separation anxiety," and the two go hand in hand.

All children go through these phases in varying degrees. But to a child of divorce like Johnny, they are doubly painful. He is suffering from two separate losses: his father, whose very presence in the house gave Johnny a sense of security; and his mother, who has had to leave him to go to work. Add to this the erratic comings and goings of babysitters at a time when Johnny is also terrified of strangers, and it all adds up to a very unhappy baby.

The single parent doesn't have it easy, either, as the demands of dealing with a baby during this delicate dependency stage would tax Job, let alone Mary Poppins. Just when a baby this age needs love and reassurance the most, the single parent is least able to deliver it. She has to juggle her work life, her social life, and her responsibility as a mother with precious few support systems to help her out. On top of all that, she worries about being able to support a family financially.

An unproductive push-me-pull-you syndrome can develop between the overburdened single parent and the insistent child. The more the baby clings, the more the recipient of such claustrophobic behavior tries to pull away. Feeling defeated and with no other parent to turn to, the baby may then become either hyperactive or withdrawn and unresponsive, making the mother feel even less inclined to put energy into the relationship. The dependency phase may then become more than temporary. Instead of being reassured that the parent will not abandon him, the child will continue to cling to the parent long after the breakaway age of two. And his fear of strangers, rather than diminishing, will persist long after he should be growing out of it.

Many researchers believe that the quality of a baby's first attachment forms the basis for all ensuing relationships. If he has been frustrated by inattention, the ramifications may plague him throughout life. As he grows into childhood, he can become ravenous for attention from any adult in an effort to fill that first, important void. At the other extreme, the child may become a loner, convinced that love is unobtainable—at least for him. Even as an adult, the same themes can play through. Carrying his "separation anxiety" along with him, a man (or woman) may either reject close relationships in a form of self-protection, or hang onto them even when they are no longer productive or fulfilling.

THE FEARFUL TWO-YEAR-OLD

Beth and Sam have come with their mother to see their father's new apartment for the first time since he moved out of their family home. For five-year-old Beth, it is a relief to see his refrigerator, his stove, and his bed. She has been very worried that Daddy would die without food and shelter. But while Beth is reassuring herself by counting the eggs in the refrigerator, two-year-old Sam is getting more and more agitated. To his parents' embarrassment and discomfort, Sam runs fitfully from one to the other, tugging at their hands to draw them close together. Chanting "Mommydaddy, Mommydaddy," Sam starts to cry in frustration and despair when his parents, understandably, are reluctant to touch each other. Sam's escalating distress is so acute that they finally give in and join their hands. To make sure they don't let go, Sam rests his head on their clasped hands and slowly calms down.

Children between the ages of eighteen months and two-and-a-half years are no longer infants. They have learned to feed themselves, to walk, to talk in three-word sentences, even to dress themselves after a fashion. And they are developing the muscle control to consider the potty seat instead of the Pamper. But toddlers are still so very little in the eyes of the parents and so vulnerable to the bumps and bruises of life that parents don't realize how advanced they really are. Sam's parents hadn't even told him about the divorce; their concern had been for his five-year-old sister, who they thought, rightly, would be very concerned about the breakup. They hadn't thought Sam would understand. But they had underestimated him, for a two-year-old cares just as much, although at a different level, especially if he's a boy.

By two, Sam has established a sense of trust in the people around him, the most important, obviously, being his parents. They have, with luck, not let him down. One or the other has come when he has called. They had held him, fed him, played with him, talked to him, encouraged him, comforted him. Sam is not yet too sure about strangers, but he is trying. Slowly and unsteadily, he is pulling away from his dependence on his family to investigate life on his own, and establishing the beginnings of rapport with toddlers his own age.

Then his parents split up. Suddenly, the father who threw

him into the air and always caught him is gone. Suddenly, the mother who read to him before bed doesn't seem to want to now. His sense of trust is threatened. How could these people, who were always so attentive to him, just stop being so? And where, where, is his father?

Sam's behavior changes. He becomes more possessive of favorite objects than the untroubled two-year-old and screams "mine" with a determination that borders on hysteria. He becomes even bossier than other despotic two-year-olds and demands certain foods and objects only to discard them immediately and demand replacements. Sam may also regress not only to a more babylike behavior, but to fears he was beginning to outgrow. The sudden sound of the intercom buzzing or the elevator door slamming in the hall may start to scare Sam half to death again. The big dog down the street that he'd just learned to pat may suddenly revert into a monster. The nights are the worst times. Sam is terrified of going to bed now, not only because he's worried that his mother will leave him too, but because he keeps having nightmares about man-eating monsters. Like other little boys his age whose fathers have left home, Sam feels lost and out of control without the presence of his father. Too young to articulate his distress or to do anything to relieve it, Sam, and other little boys like him, have recurring nightmares filled with terror—and impotence.

It is no wonder, then, that Sam is trying hard to restore order to his uncertain world and bring his mother and father back together. Consistency and routine are essential to the two-year-old who is trying to conquer the confusion of new ideas and the exhilarating but frightening steps toward independence, and his mother and father—together—are very much part of that order.

It is easy for parents to underestimate the depth of reaction in children this young and to overlook their ability to comprehend. But recent research on infancy has turned up some astonishing findings. Babies as young as two weeks old react to their own names, according to one such study.[7] The IQs of babies between the ages of twelve and eighteen months have been raised between five and twenty points with a simple increase of attention from one of the parents, found another.[8] Learning may even begin in the womb.[9] Babies should not be sold short.

How a baby or toddler reacts to divorce depends, of course, on a number of variables no studies can pinpoint. No two babies are alike. Each is born with his or her basic temperament already in place, his own pattern of eating, sleeping, and eliminating.[10] That basic temperament will help determine how the baby, child, or even adult will react to any stressful situation that calls for adaptability. The baby at birth is already a blueprint for what will come later.

HOW PARENTS CAN HELP

Though the temperaments of babies may differ, the need for consistency and affection during these first delicate years is universal. In visitation, a baby under two should not be moved back and forth between the homes of his divorced parents, for example, but should stay put in one place and have the parents visit him. "It's too hard for the young mind to integrate that lack of constancy," says Frank Williams at Thaliens Community Mental Health Center in Los Angeles. "A baby needs not only the familiar parent's face, but the familiar colors on the wall and the familiar shapes of the room and his own crib to make him feel secure." Not until the child is at least two years old does he or she have the maturity to tolerate spending alternate weekends or a summer stint as long as two weeks away from the familiarity of "home." In the interim, the baby will benefit from as much visitation as possible from the noncustodial parent.

A baby should also have as consistent a relationship as possible with one adult (referred to in psychological jargon as the "primary caretaker"), as young babies develop human attachments by bonding to one person. Many people in a baby's life are fine, so long as there is one constant person. But even caring parents are not above using their babies as pawns in their divorce wars. Williams tells the story of a four-month-old baby who is regularly "kidnapped" by each parent from the other. "The mother says she's the best parent and the baby belongs with her," says Williams. "The father says the baby is better off with him because the mother, who had postpartum depression, is crazy and he and his girlfriend can make a better home for the child. But the truth is that this baby, who was born prematurely, needs bonding more than ever, and neither parent is consistent."

A single parent should also make every effort not to over- or under-parent a baby. Babies need stimulation and affection, but they also need calm and rest. The preoccupied parent who responds slowly to the baby's cries of distress or hurries his feedings can make the baby tense and irritable. Conversely, the overdoting parent who clings to the baby for his or her own solace can transmit that adult anxiety to the baby, resulting in the same tension and irritability. Too often in divorce, the parent's distress becomes the baby's distress as well.

Where the parent is too distracted or depressed after divorce to effectively care for a baby, or where divorce forces many changes in a household, the baby may be better off lodged temporarily with a relative or guardian until the single parent is really ready to take on full-time parenting responsibilities. Though the parent may feel guilty about not feeling able to cope, it is far better for the baby to live securely outside the home until he can return to his own, restabilized one.

Babies have a remarkable capacity to endure, however, in spite of early stress. Countless children, after all, grow up whole and strong in spite of their early childhood circum-

stances. And even those babies who suffer from emotional neglect do not have to carry a life sentence. According to child
development specialists, the effects of early childhood neglect
can be reversed if the child's circumstances improve between
the ages of two and six.[11]

And the odds for an improved life for a baby are good. As
the custodial parent of a baby is usually young, the chances of
remarriage and creating a new home for the child to grow up in
are strong. Even if the parent doesn't remarry, a child whose
parents have divorced before he was three has no recollection
of living in a two-parent family, and considers his single-parent
family the norm. But there will be a day of reckoning. If the
noncustodial parent drops out of a young child's life completely, the child will almost always look for him (or her) during
adolescence. During this period of critical identity formation, a
teenager needs to find his missing half.

Though the impact of divorce on babies is the least severe of
any age, with toddlers running second, it should not be mini-
mized. The development rate is extraordinary. In the span of
just twenty-four months, helpless newborns who couldn't even
raise their heads become blustery toddlers. Infants move from
arbitrary dependence on any nurturer to recognizing and developing a strong attachment to one specific custodian. And they
move from a mindless innocence to a highly charged sense of
danger about anyone or anything that is unfamiliar. Above all
else, children these ages need consistency and continuity as
they make their rapid way into an unknown world. Often the
parents are the only people the child truly knows and the only
teachers he has to learn from. At these youngest of ages, the
quality of that care prepares—or ill prepares—the child for
the next and most critical years of his life.

PRESCHOOLERS
The Age of Guilt

The preschool years are critical ones in the development of the child. A working drawing for adolescence, the years between three and five contain many elements that won't appear again until the teens. Many early childhood specialists believe that the successful—or unsuccessful—completion of the developmental tasks facing the preschooler determines his attitudes for the rest of his life.

Psychosocial theorist Erik Erikson, for example, pinpoints these years as the birth of a child's conscience (or superego, to use the psychiatric term) and the beginning of his sense of moral order.[1] Along with his new sense of what is "good" and what is "bad" comes the inevitable burden of guilt. This guilt, coupled with the egocentricity that governs children of this age, often makes them blame themselves for everything that goes wrong, including the breakups of their families.

Starting at three, both boys and girls are also establishing the beginnings of their sex-role identities. A little boy discovers not only that he is a boy, but that he's going to grow up to be a man like his father. Just as a girl at this age starts to mimic her mother, to dress up in her clothes, even to use her tone of voice, boys ape the behavior of their fathers and other males, playing the roles of firemen, policemen, and the father in the favored preschool game of house.

This new sexual identification includes a powerful love for the parent of the opposite sex. During this oedipal period, boys become strongly possessive of their mothers and girls of their fathers. These first flushes of romantic love bring with them all the tensions and jealousies of a more adult love to come. Freud's classic inner conflict develops. The children secretly wish their much-admired but same-sexed mother or father would vanish, but feel guilty for these thoughts and quite frightened that the parent will punish them. In this period of the Great I Am, the child feels he is just as much a threat to that parent as the parent is to him. And because fathers are perceived as more powerful than mothers in a family, the boys are more distressed by the imagined repercussions of this conflict than are girls.

All of these new feelings, combined with an ever increasing sense of imagination unleavened by reality, make divorce particularly painful for children of these ages. Fears common to the children—of the dark, of animals, even of death—escalate with the stress at home. For all their inquisitiveness and curiosity, children at this age can't really integrate their discoveries yet, and divorce leaves them bewildered and confused. In Wallerstein and Kelly's study of the responses of preschool children to the separation of their parents, the typical reactions included regression, heightened aggression, pervasive neediness, low self-esteem, and the overuse of denial. And these feelings did not go away. In their follow-up study one year later, the functioning of nearly half of the preschool children had in fact deteriorated.[2]

THE TOO-GOOD CHILD

Ginny is being very, very good. She sits quietly at the nursery school book table "reading" the same book she read yesterday. And the day before. As she methodically turns the pages, she keeps a watchful eye on the teacher, who is settling a dispute in the block corner. Those naughty children. Anybody can see how good Ginny is, how quiet, how cooperative. If only her mommy and daddy could see her now, they might forgive her for drawing on the wall with her crayon and pouring Daddy's aftershave down the toilet. Then Daddy would come home. And Mommy wouldn't leave her here forever every morning. Ginny smooths her already unwrinkled dress and carefully turns another page. No one will ever know how bad, how *very* bad, she really is.

There is no way to convince Ginny that her parents' separation had nothing to do with her. She *knows* she caused it. It is her terrible secret, and she knows that the only way she can make everything come out all right again is to be relentlessly good. If she can bring herself to put down her treasured book, she'll probably make a present—a fingerpainting, or a butterfly out of pipe cleaners—for her mother and her father to show them just how good she is. She never makes a fuss.

The nursery school teacher and the divorced parent are understandably grateful to have such a quiet child around. "She hasn't been any problem at all," the teacher will say to the mother. Ginny's mother will nod. "I think this whole experience has matured her," she might answer. "She used to get into trouble all the time, drawing on the walls and going through the medicine cabinets."

Only Ginny knows how miserable she is and how much she

craves reassurance. What she really wants to do, of course, is to go bop somebody over the head with a block or just to stand in the middle of the room and scream like the bad person she knows she is. But she doesn't dare. She will wait until her mother has put her to bed at night before she takes her rag doll and smashes its head against the wall, scolding it relentlessly for being so "bad."

The tragedy is that Ginny's act is convincing. Her guilt has left her with a low sense of her self-worth, she has lost whatever self-confidence she had won by partaking in the greater world of nursery school, and she is in fact not learning anything. With luck, someone will notice that this little girl is being too good for her own sake and coax her out of her self-spun cocoon. But if not, Ginny will stay stalled at this level of development long after she should have moved on.

THE CHILD OF DENIAL

Harvey and Sue are playing in the dollhouse corner. While Sue busies herself in the kitchen stacking up tiny dishes in the sink, Harvey reaches into the basket of adult doll figures and takes out every father doll he can find. Carefully, he places a father doll in the living room, in the kitchen, in the bathroom, and in the bedroom. He looks at his arrangement critically, then picks up the father doll in the bedroom and puts it in bed with the mother doll. When Sue starts to remove the father doll from the bed because there are too many fathers in the house, Harvey gets furious and throws her toy dishes all over the room. Not content with that, he savagely kicks the dollhouse, declaring the game over because the dollhouse has just exploded and burned down.

Harvey is stubbornly restoring his family group. A capacity for denial, the mechanism of self-delusion that can forestall truth at any age, begins in the preschool years. Old enough to *sort* of understand what divorce means, but too young to integrate it into his limited scheme of things, Harvey, like other preschoolers, feels deeply threatened and confused. In often pathetic attempts to relieve their distress, preschoolers practice denial in its most literal sense. But though their denial is understandable, the danger is that it often may go on far too long. In one study, some preschoolers were still solemnly putting the father doll in the dollhouse a full year after the parents had separated.[3]

For preschoolers, the denial of divorce often centers around the parental bed.[4] Over and over again, three- or four-year-olds in play will firmly place Mommy and Daddy in their proper supine positions to undo the departure of the parent. The bed remains an important symbol for years, even though the denial mechanisms of the children grow more sophisticated with age. One eight-year-old girl stamped out the words "Mom" and "Dad" on a Dyno labeler and stuck them on the headboard of her parents' king-size bed, even though the father had been gone for two years and another man, of whom the girl was very fond, had been sleeping there for over a year.

The drive to keep the family together is more than just wishful thinking for the preschooler. Even though the child is old enough to realize that his parents are separate people of different sexes, he continues to think of his parents as a single unit, and the loss of one signals the imminent loss of the other. Not understanding the difference between adult-to-adult love and parent-child love, the child also reasons that if his parents can stop loving each other, they can stop loving him. The loss of one parent, then, is a prelude to total abandonment in the mind of the child. His separation anxiety, which at this age should be diminishing, may instead escalate and even include symbolic mothers and fathers such as the nursery school teacher. "I left the room for a minute to make a phone call," one nursery school teacher said. "When I came back in, three children were close to hysteria."

Only with constant reassurance from the custodial parent

(and from *both* parents if possible) that everything is going to be all right, that the child will continue to see the father (or mother), that the child is just as important and loved as he ever was, if not more so, will the child slowly begin to relax and accept reality. But the sad truth is that if the preschooler is still putting the father doll in bed with the mother a year later, everything is not all right. Denial may serve as a temporary buffer against pain, but prolonged denial can prevent the child from integrating the divorce and getting on with his own development.

THE REGRESSIVE CHILD

Sally and Laura are best friends. In their first year of nursery school, they often look at books together, sit together for juice and cookies, even share a mat during rest period. But something funny is happening to Laura. She isn't so nice anymore. When she doesn't get her first choice of a book, she whines and even cries. In outdoor play she won't climb up to the top of the jungle gym with Sally anymore. She hangs around with the teacher a lot, sometimes literally clinging to her skirts. And though all the new kids in nursery school have "accidents" every so often, Laura seems to be forgetting more and more to go into the little bathroom at the side of the classroom and instead wets her pants.

Laura is taking a time-out from growing up. The confusion at home is using all of her energy now, and she doesn't have enough left to move ahead in her own development. Her mother is often short-tempered with her and says she doesn't have time to help her take a bath or even put her to bed. Her father says he's going to see her every weekend, but he doesn't. And when he does, he always brings along a new and different friend. Laura doesn't understand what is happening. All she knows is that she felt a whole lot better when she was younger and people took better care of her. And that's just what she's going to be now, younger.

Regression is the most universal reaction of preschoolers to divorce. It can manifest itself in any number of ways. A child who has learned to use a fork and spoon will suddenly start feeding himself again with his fingers. A child who has mastered toilet training will revert to Pampers—or nothing at all. Courage and fearlessness may be replaced with timidity and caution. Thumb-sucking returns, along with a dependence on an old teddy bear or baby blanket. Even coordination regresses. Instead of moving with a newfound sense of agility, the regressive preschooler can go back to the movements of a two-year-old, using the whole body as a single unit instead of differentiating the actions of the body, the arms, and the legs.[5]

The ability to learn—or even to remember—also suffers. Preschoolers in one classroom wandered aimlessly about asking the same questions time and again about familiar objects: "What's this?" "What's that?" "What goes with what?"[6] In another nursery classroom, the children regressed from playing house with people dolls back to animals. One little boy agreed to play the father role in a dollhouse game, but then pleaded with the little-girl mother for food and to be allowed to sleep in the house, all the while sucking his thumb.[7]

The sadness of these children is profound—and almost impenetrable. Their feelings are so all-encompassing that they can find no surcease in other activities, such as reading or playing. Where the divorce is handled amicably by the parents, the period of regression can be mercifully short. In one study severe regression lasted six to eight weeks before beginning to abate.[8] But where the parents did not successfully complete their separation and the household remained chaotic, some symptoms still lingered a year later in one-third of the preschoolers taking part in another study.[9]

THE ANGRY CHILD

Sam is not winning the popularity award at the birthday party. In the wheelbarrow race, he pushed his partner so fast he fell into the dirt and got a bloody nose. In the three-legged race, he purposely bumped the team next to him so they fell down too. The mother of the five-year-old birthday child wants to strangle him. He has popped half the balloons she spent hours blowing up and thrown the jelly bean favors at the table, hitting one child so hard she cried. So the mother turns her back when the other kids throw jelly beans back at him. One hits him lightly on the face and he screams. The next thing she knows, he's clinging to her legs, crying as if his heart were broken.

An unfocused anger often seems to take possession of pre-school children, an anger that girls and boys express differently. Some girls, like Ginny, are apt to turn their anger inward and become unnaturally quiet and depressed. Others show their anger slightly more, becoming sulky, petulant, whiny, and bossy. At the extreme, girls can harm themselves. One preschool girl kept asking her teacher to tie her shoes tighter and tighter and to pull in her already snug belt, while the child herself pulled up her underpants as high as she could, irritating her skin.[10] Another preschooler picked at her face continually, creating sores and scabs that finally became infected.

Boys, on the other hand, are more likely to direct their anger outward, expressing that same depression in increasingly obnoxious behavior. Often, like Sam, they alternate between being bullies and crybabies, looking for the slightest excuse to run to an adult for comfort. Displacing their anger on their friends, these little boys are the first to knock down block houses others have built, or to throw around their toys and games. But as belligerent as these boys appear, they are confused as to why they are acting this way. One little boy deliberately hurled his juice at the table and when asked why, replied in a puzzled fashion, "I don't know. I'm just not happy anytime anymore."[11]

Sustaining such anger can exhaust these children, an exhaustion that shows in their play. The vivid imaginations of all children this age center on potential violence, and often their games involve explosions, fires, earthquakes—anything that devastates. Children normally work through these threatening fears by becoming Superman, Wonder Woman, a policeman, a doctor who rescues imaginary children (their fantasy surrogates) from impending doom. Under the stress of divorce, however, preschoolers often actually play the victims in these games. Or they give up playing them altogether, as it is too painful to be the victim but their self-esteem is too low for them to think of themselves as Superman.[12]

Though the overaggressiveness or babyish behavior of both boys and girls often alienates their peers and even their teachers in the first year following the breakup of their families, the two sexes are treated very differently. Societal expectation comes down heavily on the boys, making their burden more difficult to bear. Both boys and girls become needy and clinging. Both boys and girls will do anything for adult comfort and attention. But girls achieve their goal far more often than boys. "Crying and distress in boys received less frequent and shorter periods of comforting and more ambivalent comforting than did distress signals by girls," one study states flatly.[13] Where girls had skinned a knee, the adult reaction was directed to the quality of the injury. "Now, that hurt, didn't it?" A boy with the same skinned knee received more negative or denying responses. "There, there! Boys don't cry" or "You're all right now." Whether these different responses are triggered by sex-role stereotyping or the cumulative effect of the more obnoxious behavior of the boys, no one knows. But the differing responses remain.

Preschool boys have a more difficult time socially than girls,

81

too. Contrary to popular belief that little girls are bitchy and unforgiving, the girls of divorce who were originally bossy and unpleasant to their classmates were quickly forgiven by them for their behavior, while the boys were not. Even two years after the divorce, when the behavior of both the boys and girls had improved remarkably, the girls had long since regained their popularity while the boys were still being ostracized by their male peers. As a result, the boys had taken to playing with younger boys—or girls.[14]

The prognosis for Sam, then, is not good in the short run. His anger may abate, but his reputation may linger on. While all the tenets of child psychology stress continuity in the lives of young children, the plight of little boys like Sam seems to deny them. E. Mavis Hetherington, for instance, suggests that changing schools and getting a fresh start with a whole new group of classmates and teachers greatly benefits these boys who cannot live down their postdivorce unpopularity.

THE OEDIPAL CHILD

Jeffrey is scared half to death. He's had another of those nightmares and this time the monster even grabbed hold of his foot. Jeffrey hides his head under the pillow, but the monster is coming out from under the bed. He can hear it. He can feel it. Jeffrey screams, and leaping high over the end of the bed to clear the monster, runs into his mother's bedroom. She hugs him sleepily but he is inconsolable. When she tries to put him back into his bed, he screams even louder. Finally she gives in and takes Jeffrey into bed with her where he slowly calms down and goes to sleep. It is the third time this week that this has happened.

It is not abnormal for a four-year-old to have nightmares and seek the comfort of his mother's bed. What is distressing is the severity and the number of nightmares Jeffrey is having. And the fact that he has finally gained access to his mother's bed.

Jeffrey is in love, and the object of his affection is his mother. Right on schedule he has moved into the oedipal stage of development. The problem is that he feels terrible about it. It was all right when his father still lived here. Then he had someone to compete with for his mother's attention. He wasn't allowed to spend the whole night in their bed, even after a nightmare. And when one or the other of them put him back in his own bed, he always felt somewhat relieved.

But all that has changed since his father left. And he, Jeffrey, is responsible. That is Jeffrey's terrible secret. He had wished his father would just vanish so he could have his mother all to himself. And his father did, just like that. Jeffrey has won, but it is a very uneasy victory. Deep down inside, he knows it is not his place to be in his mother's bed. That place belongs to his father, and Jeffrey expects revenge. His guilt and fear are giving him nightmares, and Jeffrey wishes very much that his father would come home and put an end to this unpleasant turn of events.

The oedipal phase is a very tricky one for both child and parent. The little girl wishes her mother would go away somewhere so she alone could take care of Daddy, the man she is planning to marry. The little boy has the same designs on his mother and the same sinister wishes for his father.

Though many parents consider this phase of romantic involvement with their children as, well, cute, it is not. The oedipal phase is important, acting as a sort of training ground for a child's future involvement with the opposite sex. If the cycle of this first romantic love is interrupted by the departure of the rival parent, the delayed reaction can be deeply damaging. "The oedipal conflict is supposed to be resolved in favor of the parent, not in favor of the child," says child psychiatrist Gordon Livingston. "And yet over and over again now, it's happening the other way."

Children are supposed to fall out of love with their parent of the opposite sex around the age of six and to identify more strongly with their peers of the same sex. It is not that they have lost in their battle to win the heart of the mother or father, but that they realize that the quest is futile and not worth anymore of their time. This oedipal resolution, in Freudian terms, releases the child and allows him or her to move on. But if divorce has intervened, some children can remain stuck in this no-win love affair. Especially girls. Some prolong their oedipal resolution by denying their fathers have even left. "My Daddy sleeps in my bed every night," one little girl claimed emphatically.[15] Other girls keep their oedipal fantasies alive during visitation with their now single fathers. Without the mother around as a tempering presence, the visits can become almost a courtship—even after remarriage. "He might get a divorce [from his new wife], and *then* I would marry him!" said a six-and-a-half-year-old girl.[16]

The departure of the father poses problems of a different sort for boys, who from three to five are in the process of switching their androgynous identification with the mother to the positive male identification with the father. Most little girls still have the mother around after divorce to model themselves upon. But 90 percent of the time, boys do not have the father, and they are more apt to become confused as to just who they are and what behavior is appropriate for them. This confusion may stem from the guilt they feel over defeating their oedipal rival. Further, their increased aggressive behavior, both at home and at school, may stem from the loss of the one person at whom that aggression was safely directed.[17] Little boys may also be frightened by their gender. After all, their fathers were banished from the house. Will they be the next to go?

With little to go on, young boys seem to pick either fantasies of the perceived father to model themselves upon, or fragments of his personality. If the boy thinks of his father as a powerful, macho being, then he too will adopt a strut and a swagger.[18] But if he perceives his father as weak and passive, then he will be more of a whiner and clinger. One reaction among all preschool boys is universal: immediately following divorce, they are mad at all adult females. Whether this anger is based on fear of maternal power or on the boy's perception that his mother caused his father to leave is not known. But that anger continues at a high level for at least two years.[19]

The lack of clear sexual identity became poignantly clear in one study in which preschool boys and girls from both divorced and intact families were asked to draw human figures. Boys in intact families drew a male first. Boys of divorce drew a female. But it was how they depicted the sex differences between the two that emphasized their confusion. Both boys and girls in intact families and girls in divorced families drew explicit pictures of the male and female bodies. The boys of divorce did not.[20]

Some of the effects of divorce on both boys and girls during these critical years will crop up again in early adolescence. Girls whose fathers left home before they were five will often try to make up for that first loss of love by becoming sexually precocious.[21] And boys will often become just as pseudo-mature, acting out macho, hypersexual imitations of what they perceive masculine behavior to be. The girls have never learned how to relate to a man. The boys have never learned how to be one.

HOW PARENTS CAN HELP

If it is at all possible under such highly volatile circumstances, parents are well advised to tell their children about the divorce together, so that the child does not imagine either one to be the culprit. Admit to the children that the parents are sorry that they can no longer live happily together. Children this age are beginning to understand the consequences of their own actions, and if parents admit they are unhappy about the divorce too, the children will feel less isolated in their distress and be less apt to blame one of the parents.

Explain the situation to them in terms the children can understand, avoiding bewildering concepts like "child support" or "visitation rights." "They haven't read the law," points out divorce expert Judith Wallerstein. As yet, they have only a dim grasp of the concept of time, so the phrase "Daddy will see you every weekend" could mean next year or in twenty minutes. It is far more reassuring for a child this age to hear that Daddy (or Mommy) will see him "a lot."

Allay their worries with concrete, step-by-step projections of what is going to happen to them. Say, for example, that "Mommy (or Daddy) is going to take care of you," and that "nice Mrs. Jones next door will take care of you in the afternoons after nursery school because Mommy is going to get a job." Reassure them that one parent will have breakfast and dinner with them, "just like always," and that there will still be bedtime stories. Assure them that when the parent who is leaving is settled, the children will visit and have their own toys there and favorite meals in a new kitchen.

Don't be afraid to admit, however, that things might be a bit mixed up for a while until all these changes fall into place. This at least gives the preschooler some preparation for the confusion that inevitably follows divorce as the family reorganizes.

Above all, parents should do their best to *remain* parents during and after the divorce. A child's reaction to divorce will mirror the way the parents are handling it. If the postdivorce tension escalates between the parents, so also will the tension of the child. And if one parent disappears by choice from a child's life, the child at this age will never really get over it.

Preschoolers

For a preschool boy especially, a constant and continuing involvement with the father can do much to reassure him about his own budding masculinity and also to assuage his self-assumed guilt and fear of revenge for causing the departure of the father in the first place. If that's not possible, a nursery school or day-care center with male teachers, or a male baby-sitter at home can provide a substitute role model.

A single mother can also help sort out a little boy's confusion, for much depends on how she handles the father's absence. Though she may be angry at all men for the moment, especially the father, she should try to keep that anger to herself. Phrases like "all men are alike" or "typical macho" spoken in a tone of derision can make the little boy feel anxious about his newly discovered gender and reluctant to exhibit any of the masculine behavior he has just learned to ape in his father. Indeed, Hetherington found that mother-custody boys at this age temporarily showed more feminine patterns in speech and play than boys in intact families.[22]

Often feeling strung-out and anxious following divorce, a single mother is less apt to encourage or even condone the typically noisy, rough play of little boys this age. Possibly nervous about her responsibility as a single parent, she is also less inclined to encourage her sons *or* daughters in risk-taking activities, such as taking the training wheels off the two-wheeled bicycle or making it to the top of the backyard tree. Instead, she hovers nervously and protectively over the children, sending them the very clear message that what is perceived as masculine behavior is not only dangerous but displeasing to the parent they have to depend on. And the boy's confusion can deepen. "If mothers don't behave in this way, if they are tolerant of rough and tumble play, if they don't demean the father, and if they aren't terribly apprehensive, then you don't get disruptions in sex-typing," says Hetherington.

Unhappy parents cannot put aside their marital antagonisms

just because they have a three- or four- or five-year-old. And though the pain of divorce may be felt more deeply at these ages than at any other, the recovery time is short. The effects for girls are all but washed out in two years. And though some of the problems for boys will persist, they can be considerably reduced. What is essential for the parents to do is to reestablish a sense of continuity and caring in the separate households as soon as possible. Children of these ages are forming the attitudes and emotional makeups that they are going to carry into adulthood. How they perceive the world—and how they feel the world perceives them—is a mirror now for the rest of their lives.

SIX TO EIGHT
The Age of Sadness

Between the ages of six and ten, children enter a developmental stage that Freud called "latency." This stage is broken down into early latency (six to eight) and late latency (nine to twelve). Derived from the Latin word *latens*, meaning "lying hidden," the period of latency is a period of rest from the sexual tensions that have influenced the child during the oedipal phase of development and that will reemerge abruptly during adolescence. Latency is usually a quiet time for children, when all their efforts can be focused without distraction on learning, on moving toward independence from their families, on firming up their identities and self-concepts. Free of emotional and psychological conflicts, these young school-aged children are at their most appealing, not yet rebelling against their parents, and beginning to be able to reason and even to engage in abstract thinking. For most, it is a happy, highly productive time that adults look back on with nostalgia.

Divorce during early latency can be cruel, however, so much so that though children of this age don't face the developmental dangers that preschoolers do, they feel the pain of divorce just as acutely, if not more. Friends have become very important, but parents are still the core of the child's life. And the loss of one of them can be devastating at these ages. The child's parents are strong role models now, and he looks up to them not only in terms of sex-role identification, but as the purveyors of what are becoming his own attitudes and social ideals. He is very proud of his parents, almost deifies them, and bases much of his growing self-concept on their approval or disapproval.

He has also come to appreciate and rely on the security of a family structure as his incursions into the less personal world of school become more daring. He can interpret the disruption of that structure as the collapse of his whole protective environment. Still emotionally immature, he cannot protect himself against these losses. His fears, which are still primitive, escalate. He feels his very survival is threatened, as the loss of one parent implies the loss of the other as well. And his sense of helplessness and lowering self-esteem are confirmed by the fact that he cannot prevent the divorce from happening.

Anger, fear, betrayal, and in the disrupted postdivorce household, a deep sense of deprivation are the characteristic responses of children this age to divorce. But above all, the children feel sad, a persistent and sometimes crippling sadness that even a year after the divorce, they have only been able to mute to resignation.[1]

THE SAD CHILD

Jacob is kicking a soccer ball around his backyard. In the garage he can see the oil stain where his father's car used to be and the hook where his father's golf bag used to hang. There are still a lot of tools on his father's workbench, but Jacob isn't allowed to touch them unless his father is there. And his father hasn't been there for six months. They were going to build a bicycle rack together, but that was before his father left. Now they probably never will. Jacob halfheartedly kicks the ball again. But it isn't fun. Nothing seems to be fun these days.

Like other children his age, Jacob is inconsolable at the breakup of his family. Unlike preschoolers, who can sometimes convince themselves through fantasy play that everything is all right, Jacob, at seven, cannot. His pain is such that the more juvenile mechanism of denial is not sufficient to override it. And he is not yet old enough to use the bereavement mechanism of alternately denying and grieving to incorporate the loss slowly into his life.[2] So consuming is his sadness that he can't even distract himself by losing himself in a good book, or bolster his sense of gratification by kicking a soccer goal. Vulnerable and helpless, he can do nothing to relieve his distress.

Interestingly, the depth of a seven-year-old's sorrow may have little to do with the closeness of the relationship with the departed parent before the splitup. It is as if children this age, who have just begun to recognize the unique benefits of their parents, have lost the promise of a relationship to come, a collaboration they will never know, and the loss they feel is close to the grief of death.[3]

Even if the parent has left the child at an earlier age, the child's grief at the separation often peaks between six and eight. Seven-year-old Danny, for example, had been living happily enough with his father and brother for three years. But now, suddenly, he misses his mother, whom he sees frequently, with a depth that is almost palpable. "I don't laugh a lot now," the towhead told me, sucking on his thumb long after he should have given it up. "I used to laugh more. I don't even play kickball before school anymore. I just want to go inside. I feel so sad. I feel so bad and rotten. I just don't know why."

Though Danny's pain is centered on his mother, most often it is the father who leaves the family, bringing a feeling of unremitting loss to the son left behind. Just out of the oedipal period and still in the process of establishing their sex-role identities, boys can feel particularly devastated by the loss of the father.[4] Conversely, girls who live with their fathers are equally devastated by the loss of the mother. Seven-and-a-half-year-old Antonia, like Danny, was perfectly content living with her father until this age. Now, to prolong the time spent with her mother, Antonia invents her own calendar. "Every Saturday I pretend it's Friday because I don't want to leave the next day." Even school cannot distract these children from their intense grief. "Every time I think of my Mom in school I want to start crying," says Antonia in a small voice. "I don't want to cry in front of my friends so I keep it in my eyes until after school."

Children at these ages cannot even take refuge in feeling angry at the parent, thereby diminishing their distress. At their level of social reasoning they do not understand that they (or anyone else) can both love and be angry at the same person simultaneously. It is one or the other and, most often, they opt for love.[5]

Compounding this sadness is the rejection these latency-aged children feel in the departure of the parent. Though not as burdened with guilt for causing the departure as preschoolers are, these children are apt to take the departure personally, feeling the parent has actively left them.[6] To stave off their feelings of unlovableness, they often make up elaborate stories about the frequency with which they see or have contact with the departed parent. One little boy in California claims that his mother calls every night from Arizona because "she is so lonely for me," when in fact the mother calls only two or three times a year. Another child, an eight-year-old girl, insists her airline pilot father flies her to Los Angeles every weekend to visit him.

A six-year-old boy declares that his father is always waiting to hear from him and he can call him anytime at his office where he is a "big, big boss." The only problem, the boy admits, is that he doesn't know his father's number.

To constantly remind himself of the parent, the child may try to fill his or her role. Little boys may suddenly move to the father's customary place at the table, question a gas station attendant as to whether the air pressure in the tires is right, wear the father's ties to school, or to ask to buy a briefcase instead of a school bag. A little girl whose mother had run off with another man laboriously wrote out a shopping list for her father every morning and insisted on inspecting everyone's hands before they sat down to dinner—including the father's.

This period of intense sadness will pass as the child's experience and maturity level allows him to divert himself from his grief. If Jacob's father and the noncustodial parents of the other children continue to pay close and frequent attention to them, the children will become increasingly reassured that though the family structure may have altered, the children's place in it is assured. But if their parents disappoint them by inattentiveness, the children's sense of rejection may make them less capable of caring for anybody as they grow older.[7]

THE TORN CHILD

Nora is at her father's apartment. So far this weekend they have been to the Central Park Zoo, seen a movie, eaten out at a pizza parlor, and bought a new teddy bear. But still Nora's heart is heavy. "I miss Mommy," she tells her frustrated father. When he returns her home that night, Nora proudly shows her mother the teddy bear and the balloons they bought at the zoo and tells her of the adventures they had over the weekend. But when her mother tucks her into bed, Nora begins to cry. "I want Daddy," she sobs.

Nora is really very lucky. Her father is attentive and caring and sees her almost every weekend. Nora's mother is also loving and sensitive to her daughter and actually spends more time with her now than she did before the splitup. But Nora at seven doesn't know about her luck. All she knows is that she sees one parent or the other, but never the two together.

In one of the conundrums of divorce, the more a child of six, seven, and eight sees the noncustodial parent, the more the child longs to be with him or her. At the same time, the more they see the noncustodial parent, the more they miss the parent left at home. In a push-me-pull-you of emotion, they seem to be unhappy wherever they are.

The phrase "feeling torn in two" has become almost a cliché in talking about the children of divorce. But at this age it is painfully true. "I feel funny going from place to place," says eight-year-old Jerry, who sees his lawyer father one day one weekend, two days the next, and dinner every Thursday night. "I get confused. I don't want to go, then I miss my Mom. At Dad's I don't want to go, then I miss my Dad. I miss my Mom and I miss my Dad." The art work of these children graphically portrays this loyalty tug. One seven-year-old boy drew a picture of himself with a hatchet cleaving his head; another drew a rainbow between two houses with a child sitting in the middle.

A child's sense of time at these ages is still not measured by a calendar or a clock, but by his subjective feelings of need. When he is spending time with one parent, he may feel the eternal loss of the other, leading to feelings of helplessness and deprivation.[8] "It's been so long since I saw Daddy," one six-year-old boy said mournfully, when in fact he had had dinner with him just two nights before.

These children are further burdened by a sense of fragility in their relationships with their parents. They do not understand yet the bond of blood ties and feel that while they are with one parent, the other might stop caring about them altogether. In preschool years, divorce often provokes questions such as

"Will my Daddy find another little boy?"[9] During the latency periods, the child feels less replaceable but more forgettable. One six-year-old girl insisted on wearing her old ratty sweater to go visit her father instead of her new one, so "Daddy will know who I am."

Parents who are hostile to each other make these children's problems far more difficult and even destructive. Not wanting to risk alienating either parent, the child can withdraw from positive relationships with both parents.[10] Or he can appease an angry parent by refusing to see the other, even though he is secretly longing to. But some children show extraordinary courage in maintaining loyalty and contact with both parents.[11] Seven-year-old Freddy has to meet his father at a shopping center because the father refuses to come to the mother's house. Freddy waits in his mother's car until his father's car pulls in. Then he walks by himself to join his father. "They never even say each other's names," says Freddy, whose fingernails are badly bitten. "When I'm with one, I always think the other is dead."

The need for both parents goes so deep at this age that many children will go to any length to keep in contact with the one who has left home. If the parents make it impossible for the child to freely contact the one without angering the other, the child will go underground. One little girl regularly stole dimes from her mother's pocketbook so she could call her father on a pay phone. Another set her alarm clock for 6:00 A.M. so she could call her father before her mother woke up. Still another wrote what she called "secret messages" to her father and dropped them in a mailbox, without an address or a stamp. "I knew the mailman would find him," says the eight-year-old with confidence.

Though joint custody is presently seen as the solution for keeping the child in constant contact with both parents, at this age it has its drawbacks. The sheer logistics of spending, say, three days with one parent and four with another can ask more of a six-, seven- or eight-year-old than he or she is really ready for. Some children get on the school bus each day with a calendar to remind them which house to go home to that afternoon. Teachers have begun to keep charts for their students so they can tell them whether it's the day for dad or the day for mom. All too often, the well-intentioned to-ing and fro-ing becomes incredibly stressful. One seven-year-old girl in San Francisco became so anxious about remembering which house to go home to that she began to vomit every morning before the school bus came. Another child, this one in Boston, became so immobilized by his schedule that one day he didn't dare leave the school at all. "He was so tense and distraught he was almost crying," says his teacher. "He said he didn't know whether he was supposed to go to his mother's or his father's, and if he showed up at the wrong one, they would yell at him."

And as we saw in Nora's case, even weekend visitation at this age can exact an emotional toll. The process of "separating" from one parent and "attaching" to the other, only to turn around in two days and reverse the separation and attachment, often ends in tears and confusion for the child. The results are so predictable that they have been dubbed the "Sunday Night Syndrome." One eight-year-old boy was invariably delivered home late each Sunday night by his father. The mother would have dinner waiting for him and while the little boy picked disconsolately at the dried-out, unappetizing meal, the mother would chastise the father for making the child late and tired. Both parents were angry. The little boy was miserable. And the last thing he wanted to do was eat. Instead, he developed violent headaches or stomachaches and ended the weekend throwing a temper tantrum in his room. "I still dread Sunday nights sometimes," says the boy, who now at thirteen visits his father when he wants to. "They were always so tense. I didn't know where I wanted to be. I was never even quite sure where I was."

Researchers attribute this painful phase to the child's recent resolution of the oedipal conflict and the fear of slowing down his own development by losing one of his parents.[12] Eventually, the child will grow out of this insecurity over his separate parents and his often desperate desire to keep them together. The more frequent the contact with each parent, however painful the separation and reattachment process may be, the more confident the child will become that he is not only loved but remembered. And the closer the proximity of the parents' separate households, the better. In one study, only the children who could ride their bicycles or walk between homes felt they saw each parent almost enough.[13]

THE CHILD OF AVOIDANCE

Robert is sitting ramrod straight on a piano bench at a Long Island school program for divorced kids. Now eight and a half, Robert has been "divorced" for two years and says he sees his father quite enough. Everything about the divorce is fine—just fine—with Robert. "I guess I was sad at first but not now, never," he says, smiling. "I can see my Dad anytime I want. I never do get sad. After the first couple of months you get used to it. I felt I would get over it and I did." He smiles throughout the discussion group, but keeps his arms and legs crossed the entire time.

It may very well be true that Robert *is* just fine. He may even live in a charmed world. He likes being an only child. "I get more toys than anyone else." He likes his father's new wife well enough. "I still think she's just a friend of his." He thinks it's just dandy for his mother to date. "I like her boyfriends." And he has no fantasies about his parents reuniting. "I never dreamed that. If they didn't argue too much, they'd still be together."

But Robert appears much too tense to be as serene as he

claims. And one thing that distinguishes many children of divorce at this age is their capacity for avoidance.[14] They clam up when asked how they feel and either remain silent or say "fine." Instinctively they seem to know just how fragile their defense mechanisms are, and cannot bear to risk being plunged into the uneasiness that lies just below the surface. Kelly and Wallerstein describe an eight-year-old boy who assured them that he was having no trouble with the divorce at all. The truth began to emerge when they asked him to draw a picture of his family. With great elaboration and detail he spent the entire hour drawing his house—and didn't put in one human figure. After a few more sessions, he finally admitted to a "tiny problem" of wanting to see more of his father. And several months later he actually sought out help "because of the awful bad problems I'm having at night," but then couldn't remember what they were.[15]

Repression of feelings is a psychiatric taboo at any age, but during these young years it can set in motion an emotional pattern that will be very difficult to change. In divorce, children sense very early what is safe—or not safe—to say. A mother who feels furious and betrayed by her husband, for example, often wants her children to feel just as furious and betrayed as she does. The child will quickly learn not to say that he misses his father for fear of incurring his mother's wrath. So he keeps his feelings bottled up, and in consequence, grows secretly angry at his mother for forcing him into that position. He doesn't dare express that anger, fearing his mother will turn on him or, worse yet, abandon him. Instead, he sits in lonely silence in the middle, not feeling he can turn to either parent.[16]

Of course, parents, too, practice avoidance, and those who do, by offering no explanation for the divorce, make things even worse for the child. Some parents are so consumed by guilt at having visited this family rupture on the children that they don't talk to them about it at all, leaving the reasons for the upheaval to the child's overripe imagination. Other parents pretend to their children that the divorce hasn't happened and that "Daddy is away on a long business trip," or that "Mommy went to visit her sister for a while," which can drive the child crazy with worry.[17] The strain on the remaining parent is blatantly clear to the child, but what is going on? The continued silence makes the subject taboo, and unasked questions and feelings are bottled up.

The danger, of course, is that the child may get arrested in these unaired emotions. If the parent doesn't admit to his or her own reasonable anxieties or feelings of anger, the child learns not to admit to his, transferring them instead to unreasonable fears, such as a fear of insects or of going to school or even of starvation.[18] One seven-year-old girl gained thirty pounds in the six months after her parents separated. Another compulsive overeater warned a therapist who probed directly, "You'd better not ask me any more about the divorce. I'll get hungry."[19]

Getting children of this age to express how they really feel is not easy, especially for the parent. There is too much at stake for a child—worldly-wise enough to truly recognize his dependency—to risk alienating a parent or losing parental protection. A more neutral person—a teacher, a therapist, or a friend's parent—has a better chance of providing an emotional safety net. But above all else, parents should be honest with their children. If a parent admits to feeling sad, tired, or even angry, the child will then have an opening to express his feeling, too. Divorce involves such a complex array of sometimes conflicting emotions that the more these feelings are aired, the better off both the parent and the child will be.

THE DEPRIVED CHILD

Kate is in the kitchen getting her breakfast. She pulls the chair next to the counter so she can climb up to reach the cereal. Carefully she takes the milk out of the refrigerator with two hands, because her hand isn't big enough to fit around the half-gallon carton. While she stands at the counter spooning cereal into her mouth, she makes herself a peanut butter sandwich for lunch and sticks it into her pocket. She wishes her mother could get up with her for breakfast, but her mother is tired, very tired. "My mom doesn't have to be at her job until nine and she needs to sleep," says the second-grader. Keeping her eye on the "big" and "little" hands on the clock so she won't be late, Kate slips into her mother's bedroom to kiss her good-bye. Kate's mother is having a drink with a friend after work, she tells Kate sleepily, so she won't be home till late tonight. "Just heat up some soup, and I'll try to be home by your bed-time." Kate hurries out the door to catch the school bus. "Good-bye," she yells under her mother's window, and strains to hear if there's a reply.

Kate is certainly old enough to get her own breakfast and make her own lunch. But Kate didn't use to get up all alone. When her father was still home, he often got up with her and they had a good laugh or two before he went off to work and she went off to school. Her mother made her lunch for her the night before and left it in a brown paper bag in the refrigerator. And the three of them had dinner together. But all that has changed now. Her father is gone. And so, much of the time, is her mother. Kate is on her own before school, after school, and sometimes, like tonight, even for dinner.

Kate is just one of many children of divorce who overnight essentially lose both parents. One parent has moved out; the other is likely to be concentrating on a new job or a new life, or, if depressed, retreating into a state of uncommunicativeness and passivity.[20] Left in the postdivorce lurch are the children, who are not only apt to be late for school, but to have erratic meals, bedtimes, and parental attention. They are not being ne-glected in the legal sense of the word. But Kate is not only ex-hausted from taking on all her new responsibilities, she is very,

very lonely as well. Often Kate leaves her mother notes now, like "I lov you, Mommy" and "here is some cinimin tost for yur brekfast."

Psychologists call this condition of reduced parental access "maternal or paternal deprivation." In divorce, at least temporarily, it is almost inevitable, and the children are aware of it. Often the child feels cheated out of what he or she perceives to be the rights of childhood, and the feelings of deprivation and neglect grow to exaggerated proportions. Suddenly the life of every intact family in the neighborhood becomes as perfect as hers is imperfect, and fantasy supersedes reality. She alone has no mother at home to bake cookies in the afternoon, no father to come to soccer practice—*even if the parents rarely did these things before the divorce.* "You were the only mother who didn't come to school," one seven-year-old girl accused her mother, when in fact only three out of ten mothers were there.

But some of their feelings of deprivation are based on fact. Hard-pressed single parents often unload chores and responsibilities on the children that prior to the divorce were shared by the adults. And the children can feel both exhausted and resentful. "I don't even get to be sick," complained one girl. "When Sarah is home with a cold, she has a bell by her bed so she can ring for her mother when she needs something. I have to fold the laundry, empty the dishwasher, and sweep the back porch. It's not fair." Often a stressed single parent will ask more of a child than he or she is up to, inducing a feeling of incompetence in a child who already feels put upon.[21] "I'm only eight," one girl told her mother tearfully after being berated for ruining her wool sweaters in the washing machine. A little boy was equally crushed when he dropped a heavy storm window, smashing the glass. "I just can't do anything right," he said disconsolately, ignoring the fact that the job was too much for him in the first place.

Even a child's social life can diminish. In a cruel twist, just when a child needs friends the most, he often loses them. Because of the lack of adult supervision in many working, single-parent households, parents in intact families frequently forbid their children to play there after school.[22] As all children this age are beginning to define themselves by their friends and their prowess in activities, the loss of home as a social base can be very harsh indeed.

To compensate for their sense of having less, many kids demand more.[23] A new ten-speed bike, an expensive down vest, or a second pair of Nikes suddenly becomes a must. Feelings of deprivation might also account for a tendency to fib. Though tall tales are common for children this age, the children of divorce build even taller ones. One little girl regaled her classmates with stories of a trip she'd taken over vacation which included luxurious stops in Florida and Nassau and time on a yacht, when in fact she had visited her grandparents in Pennsylvania and gone fishing one day in a rowboat on a lake.

During divorce, six-, seven-, and eight-year-olds who were just beginning to be generous with their possessions and to share can suddenly turn relentlessly possessive again.[24] They have already lost enough, they reason, and sense that if they don't clamp down, they will lose even more. Unsure about the future and uneasy in the present, a few even begin to steal. This is not to say that divorce breeds a life of crime. Indeed, the age of seven is a prime age for any child to simply take what he knows does not belong to him. But after divorce the feelings of deprivation can run so deep that the child tries to collect coveted objects with a now-or-never urgency. One seven-year-old girl worked her classmates' houses so thoroughly that when their parents complained, her mother found three computer games, a pearl necklace, an assortment of scarves, two pocket calculators and a big Paddington teddy bear under her bed.

Feelings of deprivation are symptomatic of the anxiety these children feel about the impermanence and the inadequacy of their family support systems. All they see around them is loss—of a parent, of parental attention, of extra money, of a secure future. Not unreasonably, their need for reassurance makes them react by demanding more. Little favors and extras from parents can do a world of good to relieve these anxieties. If not a new sweater, then a finally mended sweater, can prove parental affection. A weekly allowance or a slight increase in an already existing one will make children this age feel more secure. It doesn't take much to relieve the feelings of deprivation. But it does take something.

THE FRIGHTENED CHILD

Johnny is nodding off to sleep again at his desk. This is the third day in a row now that the teacher has noticed how tired Johnny looks. But Johnny won't tell her what's wrong. The teacher is sure it has something to do with his father's leaving home, but Johnny won't talk to her about that. The teacher makes a note to herself to call Johnny's mother at home that evening. Something's really going on with him.

The teacher is right. Something *is* going on with Johnny: Johnny's scared. Without his father around, Johnny feels not only unprotected himself, but responsible in his newfound manhood to take his father's place in protecting his mother and sister. The reason Johnny is so tired is that for the last two nights he has been prowling the house making sure no burglars break in to rob them. He hopes his mother will be proud of him.

Divorce often instills a feeling close to panic in children of six to eight. The departure of one of the parents threatens the security of their whole world and they often feel there is no safe, protected place for them to grow up in.[25] Some children react like Johnny and take on the far too heavy responsibility of protecting their homes and siblings. Others buckle under the panic and become almost paralyzed in their ability to function.

Routines are forgotten, their ability to concentrate at school diminishes. They regularly lose their toys, their school books. They are haunted by dreams of violence and disaster. Little boys, especially, easily break into tears and sobbing.[26]

Separation anxiety, which the child should have grown out of by now, reappears. Where the child used to have two parents to count on, now he only has one. And the fear of losing that parent too, is almost more than he or she can bear. "I always used to get sick or even hurt myself when Mom went out," recalls a teenage girl. "Then I'd stay awake until she got home, even though the babysitter was there." Six-year-old Elsa stays with her grandmother when her mother "goes dating," an arrangement Elsa hates because her grandmother won't let her watch TV "even a little bit." But Elsa's feelings go far beyond missing TV. "I feel terrible," the little girl says. "I cry and cry for Mommy to come back, but I don't want her to hear me."

Parents often unwittingly exacerbate these divorce-centered fears in their children. Though these older children have a firmer grasp on reality than preschoolers, their imaginations still foresee calamity around every corner, and they are old enough to perceive hostile possibilities in the larger world. So when a mother (or father) says despairingly, "What are *we* going to do?" or "What will become of *us*?" the child's worst fears are realized. Translated into the perceptions of the early latency child, such statements clearly mean there will be no Christmas presents, no food, no clothes, maybe not even a bed to sleep in. A child's lurking sense of rejection can also be confirmed by a parent's lament: "Why did he (she) leave *us*?" or "This wouldn't have happened if he (she) hadn't left *us*." It is little wonder, then, that children this age continue to have trouble sleeping and to have more than a normal share of nightmares.

Viewing the exaggerated grief of a parent can also add to a child's fears.[27] And in divorce, it happens time and again. The child is sad. The child cries. The parent comforts the child but his grief is catching. Now the parent starts crying and, once started, can't stop. The child can see that the parent has stopped crying for him and is now crying for herself. The parent seems in worse shape than he is, and he harbors the growing unease that maybe that parent is not going to be able to protect him when he needs it. And the child feels more afraid than ever. "I used to cry every afternoon after school and Mom would cry with me," recalls one girl. "I stopped when I realized Mom was more upset than I was. It made me nervous."

Johnny will stop being so frightened by the breakup of his parents as soon as he learns that his world isn't as threatened as he perceives it to be. Parents can help children like Johnny by not stressing the stereotyped roles of men and women in society and the family. Children these ages are very literal-minded, and for boys to be told they are "the man of the household now" and for girls to hear "you'll just have to be the homemaker now" not only gives them tasks they are far too young to handle, but ill-prepares them for the future in which both sexes will overlap in these outdated values. Johnny and his peers in divorce need to be treated like the six-, seven-, and eight-year-old children that they are, not as miniature versions of their parents. And though it is healthy for parents to share some of their concerns with them, too much can make what is already a distressing situation far worse.

Many of these fears can also be alleviated by frequent visits to the noncustodial parent and the addition of a new male partner for the single mother. Both boys and girls are comforted by the presence of a father figure, and at these presexual ages, remarriage is not as great a risk as it will be when the children are older. A new person around the house is seen less as a threat than as a welcome presence, particularly if the children are included in the new "family" activities. The bigger threat to most children is the diminished attention from the custodial parent, the lessening of the closeness that is apt to mark many parent-child relationships after divorce.

THE FATHER-HUNGRY BOY

Max is hanging around after school again. He waits patiently on the steps for his homeroom teacher to come out. Max likes the way his teacher looks, with his beard and all. And he likes the way he smells, sort of rough. Not the way his mother smells which is sort of softer. Max wants to show him the model plane he's working on. Maybe if he's very lucky, his teacher will come home with him to help him with the plane and even stay for dinner with him and his mother.

Like Max, many boys this age develop what amounts to a father-hunger. Just out of the oedipal stage, these young boys are often nervous and uncomfortable in such close proximity to their mothers without their fathers around.[28] This shakiness, child psychologists believe, contributes heavily to the yearning of these boys for any adult male company. Unsure also about the definition of their newly acquired masculine identities, they look for role models, sometimes with near desperation. "Who are we going to marry next?" one six-year-old boy asked his mother anxiously. "We need to get a daddy around here."

Interestingly, birth order intensifies the extent of these boys' neediness. Eldest or only sons feel the burden of their immature masculinity the most and express more of a need for a father figure than do their siblings of either sex.[29] The traditional pattern of the oldest child is to identify more closely with the parent than with his or her siblings; in keeping with that pattern, these boys feel more than others the weight of living up to some ill-defined expectation.

Boys who feel acutely the lack of a role model are the ones most likely to take sides in the divorce, almost always lining up against the mother. These boys blame the mother for causing the father's departure, regardless of who was to blame. Enraged by that loss, the boys may express their hostility directly at the mother. In a negative way of modeling them-

106

selves after the father, they may ape the darker behavior and attitude of the preseparation parent. One boy, who had seen his father hit his mother on several occasions when dinner was not ready on time, kicked her himself when dinner was not on the table at the prescribed hour. Another little boy compiled a weekly list of complaints to give to his father, then sat back and enjoyed the father's ensuing tirades at the mother.[30]

On a more trivial level, boys feel the lack of a role model in families where the mother is perceived as not being as competent as the departed father. "I miss trying to make things with my Dad," says eight-year-old Mike. "I once tried to make an airplane model with Mom. It came out really weird. By mistake we put the big clips on the back instead of the front. We just laughed." Seven-year-old Gerry has been waiting for someone to fix his bicycle chain for two weeks. "I miss my dad," he admits. "He used to play with me, fix things for me. . . . My mom can't."

Though the longing for their fathers persists, most of these boys, like Max, readily accept substitute fathers. In one study, seven-year-old Jack repeatedly pleaded with his mother to remarry shortly after his parents separated so that he could have "a daddy of my own for myself." Seven-year-old Roy was equally insistent. As he told a researcher, "Well, I'm just used to having a father around the house."[31]

But finding a surrogate father can backfire. Boys who bond to their mothers' boyfriends often grow more attached to them than the mother does herself—and this may involve a new loss. Eight-year-old David still misses a man he calls "Poppa," even though he sees his father often and his mother has remarried. "I like Poppa. I always called him that," says the boy with nostalgia. "Like when I was two I played blocks with him and when I was five he took me to the city to see *Grease*. I saw it the first time it was out. I don't see him anymore and I feel bad about it."

Casual partners for the parent exacerbate the problems of

father-hungry boys even more. Because of their firsthand experience of mothers and fathers sharing a bed, children often attach more significance to parental sleep-overs than the parent does. Not having the sophistication to distinguish between just who and who isn't going to stick around, the boys especially can become attached—again and again. "If the parent is constantly turning over the friends and the child has formed a bond, he'll go through a loss every time," says Hetherington. "In the long run the child may become disengaged and develop a fear of commitment."

Looking for family stability, the children of promiscuous parents often find the opposite. Most children try very hard to please adults to ensure themselves of love and protection. But if they are continually adjusting to the habits and personalities of different parental partners, they can despair of ever finding them. "Sometimes when I see my mommy and daddy with their boyfriends and girlfriends, I think they're all going to get married but then they get divorced," says seven-year-old Daniella. "And then it happens all over again. Each time Daddy brings someone home I think, this girl is going to stay here forever. But it never works out."

While boys may suffer from the turnover of father figures, girls seem more reluctant to accept one in the first place. Though girls are gratified by male attention and seek it out with almost the same verve as boys, they often stop short of welcoming a new partner for the mother into the household. Just out of their own oedipal phase, little girls are apt to remain more loyal to their fathers. Their resistance to a new male is not based on jealousy or competition with the mother at these ages, but on a sort of juvenile monogamy. "I was always expecting Daddy to come at six o'clock and I would run and give him a kiss," recalls a girl whose parents separated when she was seven. "I remember hitting my mom's boyfriend. He explained to me that he wasn't trying to take Daddy's place. But it just felt to me like he was. Instead of Daddy at six o'clock, it was him." Another little girl became downright sinister about her mother's new live-in companion. When she made him an ashtray in ceramics class, her mother complimented her. "Is it for his birthday?" the mother asked. "No," her eight-year-old replied. "It's so he'll die."

It is both the charm and curse of children of this age to wear their hearts so unself-consciously on their sleeves. And parents are well advised to understand how their children of both sexes react to the possibility of new partners in the house. Boys will invest too much. Girls are more apt to resist. But it is the attitude of the parent toward the new partner that is the most important. If the parent is loving toward the new partner, the children are encouraged to be too. If the parent is contemptuous, the children will also be so. And if the parent attaches no significance to the number and quality of the partners, the children will learn to debase the meaning of relationships and sex.

The need for a male in the lives of the boys is understandable. But in many sad cases, the resentment girls carry toward their mothers' partners is a product of self-defense. Divorced fathers tend to remain far more involved with their sons than their daughters, seeing them more frequently and for longer periods of time.[32] The girls are then forced to fantasize about their faithful, loving, "absent" fathers in order to defend themselves against feelings of rejection and unlovableness. And their anger toward a new father figure may just be the displaced anger they don't dare unload on their own rejecting fathers.

HOW PARENTS CAN HELP

Easing the pain of divorce for these children is very difficult. But there are some commonsense rules that can help—if the parents are capable. The cardinal rule, as always, is for parents to present the divorce carefully to the children. Some mental health professionals suggest telling the children about the impending separation a week or two *before it actually happens,* giving the children time to adjust, as well as lessening the shock and salving their feelings of rejection.

The difficulty with this rational suggestion is that the actual timing of the separation is often irrational. Though the marriage has obviously been eroding and the parents have certainly talked about divorce, the flash point of decision is usually spontaneous and arbitrary. A sentence spoken in the wrong tone of voice, a skipped dinner date, one load of laundry too much can trigger activity out of passivity, and shazam—one parent is gone.

For 80 percent of the children there is no warning at all. "A child is better prepared by his parents for a tonsillectomy or an appendectomy than he is for divorce," says Hugh McIsaac, director of the Conciliation Court in Los Angeles. "He wakes up one morning and one very significant person in his life has moved out. You can't imagine how destructive that is to a child."

The reasons for the divorce should be spelled out in terms the child can understand, so he is less apt to blame one parent more than the other—or to take the blame on himself. But at least one child psychiatrist draws a much harder line. Just telling the children "we don't love each other anymore" is a cop-out, according to Richard Gardiner, the author of several books about children and divorce. "Tell them, for instance, 'your father drinks too much' or 'I've met someone else I care about more' or 'I don't respect your father as much as I used to and although he's well meaning, he's weak,' " suggests Gardiner. But parental deficiencies must be countered by strengths as well. "Real people have flaws as well as admirable qualities," says the respected psychiatrist. "The parent who won't tell is depriving the child of useful information."[33]

For all that parents can do to make the divorce passage easier, however, the children will still go through a period of intense pain. Kelly and Wallerstein's study of children of these ages found that *not one* of them was happy with the divorce, even where there had been histories of chronic and even violent conflict. More than anything else, these children want their parents back together. And their persistent reconciliation fantasies, often centering around weddings, are poignant. "They'll run into each other at somebody's wedding," an eight-year-old boy told me. "They'd both be invited. And they fall in love and have a double wedding." A seven-and-a-half-year-old girl in Cleveland has the same fantasy, even two years after her parents' divorce. "I daydream that I am at their second wedding," she says, her cheeks flushed. "They are kissing. They are happy. And so am I."

NINE TO TWELVE
The Age of Anger

For children in late latency (nine to twelve) divorce bears with it both good news and bad. The good news centers around their gains in both physical and emotional maturity. Coordinated enough now to ride a bike safely around the neighborhood, actually hit the baseball, and master the intricate dance steps that escape their parents, children this age are able to expand their worlds and to exact a true sense of gratification from extrafamilial activities. Continuing to distance themselves from their family dependencies, these children are not only developing individual friendships with their same-sex peers, but plunging with great enthusiasm into being team players. Their developing sense of self-worth in sports, in school work, and in social life has built a buffer against the diminished self-esteem that often follows divorce.

Late latency-aged children are still at peace with their parents, a peace that becomes more strained as they approach adolescence. But even these older children of eleven and twelve have not yet begun their teenage rebellion and still seek out and accept their parents' interpretations of morality and sociability. In fact, parents are often even more exalted by children at these ages than at seven or eight: a strong feeling of family solidarity has developed, and the children not only boast of their parents' accomplishments, but quickly punch out anyone who dares to criticize or insult a family member. At the same time, a sense of sympathy and understanding has also begun to stir, and, more grounded in reality than younger children, these children are able to see the divorce as their parents' problem, not their own.

The bad news follows naturally from much of the good news. As team players, children have a very strict sense of fairness, of what is right and what is wrong. In these Girl Scout and Boy Scout years, children live by a rigid code of ethics that stresses black-and-white definitions of loyalty and behavior. When the very parent who taught the child these rules does not abide by them, the child becomes angry—*very* angry. And it is this deep and unrelenting anger that most characterizes the reaction to divorce of late latency-aged children.[1] Unlike younger children, who fight against feelings of anger toward a parent, these children seem to seek it out. Often the child chooses between the "good" parent and the "bad" parent, reserving so much hostility for the latter that visitation with the noncustodial parent sinks to an all-time low, especially for boys.[2]

Sexuality begins to complicate the problems of divorce at this age, especially for girls. At ten—two years ahead of boys—girls start their maturation process. Overnight, it seems, their breasts begin to bud and their bodies to soften into curves. Their growth spurts begin hurtling them upward by three or three-and-a-half inches a year, while their weight gain escalates from seven or eight pounds a year to ten or even twenty pounds. Their interest in the opposite sex and in sex itself intensifies, becoming highly volatile at the end of their preteen years, when most girls begin to menstruate. A second, milder oedipal phase takes hold for girls (boys will follow later), which divorce exacerbates.

All in all, children this age, both boys and girls, are filled with energy and action. They do not take the divorce sitting down. They channel their sense of righteous anger into every aspect of their lives, but they cannot effectively stem their feelings of shame, resentment, rejection, loneliness, and eventually exhaustion.[3] Though divorce may be easier on them than younger children, these children don't know it. And usually they don't hesitate to let their parents know exactly how they feel.

THE ANGRY CHILD

Abbie is disgusted. A very bright, rather intense eleven-year-old, she is articulating her anger against her father, his live-in girlfriend, her classmates, indeed everyone in her formerly tidy world, which has turned topsy-turvy. "I never knew he was having an affair with Lois," she says, her brown eyes flashing. "He used to bring us to visit her at her ice cream shop. We used to love her so much. She was like a friend, you know, she'd play frisbee with us. He didn't need to do that to us. And he even took Mom to one of her parties. That's pretty ignorant. And it was probably mean. I don't know what his problem was. He was probably just having a middle-aged crisis. I cannot believe he could be that mean.

"We had to spend Christmas Eve at Dad's house and she was there and I just hated her so much that I started crying. I hated my father. They gave us all these presents like he was trying to make it up or something, but I just hated it. I ran upstairs to the bedroom to get out of there and Lois came after me. 'I know you hate me,' she said, and I said, 'Yeah, you got it. You're totally right there.' "

Abbie's anger typifies the outrage of many children her age who feel deceived and betrayed by a parent. Abbie has looked up to her father, almost revered him, and the dissolution of that image is extremely hard for her to take. Her father has violated almost every rule in her new and rigid scheme of things. He has broken the promise of marriage. He has made her mother, who is probably the best mother in the world, unhappy. He has lied both to her and to her mother, who would never, *never* tell a lie. And he expects Abbie not only to forgive him, but to go on feeling about him the way she always has. Can you imagine?

With astonishing bravery, children this age will use anger as a defense against their feelings of shock and depression and not hesitate to let both parents know about it. They often align themselves with one parent whom they elevate to nobility to the virtual exclusion of the other, and nothing the "bad" parent does will defuse that contempt. Especially if he or she tries to "buy" the child's affection, as did Abbie's father that fateful Christmas. "I said, 'Dad, are you trying to outdo Mom with all these presents? Because I think it's really terrible of you,' and he said, 'No, it's just that I love you so much.' So I said, 'Look, I don't need all this.' He gave me an album, a pair of gold earrings with Chinese writing on them saying 'May your life be long,' and a gold initial ring. Gold? Mom gave me a Fair Isle sweater. I mean what's my mother supposed to do? Go out and buy me another gold initial ring?"

Most children go through a period of general anger—and get over it. "I got mad at first at my mom for kicking my dad out and my dad for leaving," says nine-year-old Mike, whose parents have been split for a year. "I usually went up to my room and threw things around. I don't do that anymore." But though this anger may be a successful way to sidetrack sadness, in some cases it can perpetuate the sense of family disruption long after the child should have consolidated it. Ten-year-old Raoul, for example, who has been living with his father and stepmother for six years, is still angry at his father for leaving his mother. "I beat up my pillow. I scream. I miss my mother. I cry," says the boy. "I called my father a rat and I was gounded for two days. But he was being a rat."

The anger of these children may spill over into the classroom, where their behavior can become disruptive. Boys often throw temper tantrums and overreact to ordinary discipline and setbacks with violent outbursts; girls are apt to be more devious. One ten-year-old girl, whose father left the house with no explanation at all, terrorized her classmates for months afterward by pinching them, tripping them, and stealing their possessions. It wasn't until the mother, the father, and the little girl all sat down together with a therapist and aired the reasons for the divorce that she began to accept it.

Other children can become immobilized by their anger. "I daydreamed at the beginning of the divorce," says a nine-year-old boy. "I flunked all my tests. I was thinking that I wished this never happened. Why can't it happen to someone else?" But not all children can sustain this anger, and many finally give in to the depression. "It was really tough," says a sixth grader in Washington. "At school, I felt like I was an onlooker and I became like an outcast. I went into a depression. I just felt withdrawn and wouldn't say a lot and I think it scared my friends."

Visits with the noncustodial parent can also fall off during this period of anger, especially for boys. The angry child takes his resentment out on the part-time parent. Rebuffed, the parent either makes less effort to see the child or becomes erratic in his visitation schedule. This makes the child even angrier. And so it goes, until visitation tapers off to its lowest frequency at any age over two.[4]

At home, the coercive cycle between boys and their single mothers can escalate.[5] Not only is the boy apt to blame the mother for banishing the father from the household, but in the increasing separation of the sexes he perceives her as being less powerful and authoritative than his father. He balks at her commands. He bridles at her negative sanctions—"Don't do that again" or "Stop making so much noise"—wanting instead a reasonable explanation of why he should do what she wants. The more defiant he becomes, the more demanding she becomes, especially in the first year after divorce when discipline is apt to be erratic and dictatorial. And so the cycle perpetuates itself, taking its toll on both the boys and their single mothers. Across the board, divorced mothers of boys report feeling more stress, depression, and incompetence than do mothers of girls.

THE VENGEFUL CHILD

Steeped in revenge, some children become intent on punishing the parent they hold responsible for the divorce. Even after two years, twelve-year-old Sophie still hasn't forgiven her mother for leaving her idolized father for another man. Her story is chilling in its frankness. "I try to get even," says the beautiful preteen, whose hair is done in elaborate braids. "I play my parents off against the other. Mom makes me go to bed at nine-thirty. I tell her Dad lets me stay up till eleven. I want to make my mother feel bad. I resent her. No matter what she says, I say the opposite. I want her to feel guilty. I want revenge. I say 'everything was so much fun when we lived with Dad,' things like that. I want to make her cry, but I never can. I probably would feel guilty if I did. But she doesn't cry very much anyway. I don't think I've ever seen her cry."

Sophie is so used to her anger that her voice is completely matter-of-fact. "We moved right in with her boyfriend," she says, chewing on a blade of grass. "After we settled in I started to hate him, too. I blamed him for the separation. I say bad things about him to Mommy. I confront her with it. I mean I talk to him and everything. I just resent him. If he hugs me, I hug him back just enough so he won't hate me." Sophie smiles and pulls another blade of grass out of the lawn.

Much of the need for revenge that festers in children this

age is kept very much alive by a parent who feels the same need to get even. Sophie's father, for example, refuses to give any alimony or child support to the mother and instead pays the child's expenses directly, making the mother seem less deserving to Sophie. He also refuses to drive his daughter to the mother's new house and instead leaves her on the corner. And he has forbidden her ever to mention the name of her mother's lover in front of him, thereby increasing Sophie's concept of her mother—and her companion—as deserving of punishment.

Whereas younger children are often protected from their parents' feelings of anger and from the more lurid facts surrounding the breakup, these children aren't. They look more grown-up physically than they are emotionally, and their sense of "good guys" versus the "bad guys" at this age makes them prime candidates for actively taking sides, even if they were very close to the now outcast parent before the divorce.[6] One mother hid with her ten-year-old son in the bushes outside the father's house until he left for work. Together they jimmied a window; then the boy slipped inside. His mission? To sneak the father's checkbook out to his mother so she could see just how much money he had. "We'll get him," the little boy said with glee.

THE CHILD IN THE MIDDLE

It is no wonder that the form for legal separation often includes a clause that stipulates: "The parties shall exert every reasonable effort to maintain free access between themselves and the children and to foster a feeling of affection between themselves and the children. Neither party shall do anything to hamper the natural development of the children's love for the other. Husband and wife shall not allow the children to witness their disputes." Too often the words aren't worth the legal paper they're written on. "Both parents speak about the other like pieces of dirt," says nine-year-old Dana. "I try to believe both stories. I'll mix the two together. I don't care what the real story is."

Warring parents often use their children as go-betweens, an easier way for them to communicate than having to confront each other. But the child, as the messenger of bad news, often bears the brunt of their anger—which adds to his own. "Mom tells me to tell Dad that the reason my pants look ratty is that he owes her money," says a ten-year-old boy. "Then Dad yells at me and says that she's spending all his money on her new boyfriend and to tell her that. Then she yells at me. Why can't they just yell at each other and leave me out of it?" An eleven-year-old girl is just as fed up with her parents. "In a way I hate them both," she says quietly. "What they've put on me. What they talk to me about."

If parents don't successfully complete their divorce, their children can be caught in the highly destructive middle for years. The Coopers, for example, broke up five years ago. The father has remarried and has a three-year-old son, but the original couple's three daughters are still locked in their parents' ongoing hatred. "Mom doesn't want me to like Dad," says twelve-year-old Nancy angrily. "She tells me awful things he did. He tells me more awful things about her. I try not to listen." Her eleven-year-old sister Ella feels just as trapped. "I've sort of become a divorce expert at school, and I tell my friends who are going through it to try and stay out of the middle," says the sixth grader. "But it's hard. And parents think they are the only ones hurting, without thinking of you."

At the extreme, children who continue to bear the anger of their parents can become suicidal. Much has been written about the increasing suicide rate among teenagers, but the age appears to be coming down. "I'm seeing many, many more troubled families and a lot more troubled children than we saw ten years ago," says Wallerstein, who has been studying divorced families since 1970. "There is no question the stress is more. We're seeing a number of suicidal children as young as nine, eleven. I'm very worried about them."

Her concern is shared by Frank Williams, a psychiatrist at the Thaliens Community Mental Health Center in Los Angeles. "Some of the stories are heart-wrenching," says Williams. He tells the story of a ten-year-old boy who lives with his father on alternate weekends. The mother wanted to treat the boy to a five-day trip to San Diego and called the father to rearrange the schedule. "Sure," the father replied, "if he can make up the weekend later and takes his schoolwork with him." "You can't make conditions," the mother bristled. The father stubbornly repeated: "I give you permission with that condition. Period." The mother then called the boy to the phone. "Eddie, come listen to why your father won't let you go to San Diego," she said. Crying, Eddie took the phone. "Why, Daddy? Why?" he sobbed into the phone. "Because your mother is screwing it up so you can't go," the father told him. Williams shrugs his shoulders in frustrated resignation. "The boy is a high suicide risk," he says. "A lot of young suicides can be traced to these kinds of things."

THE UNDERSTANDING CHILD

Tommy is standing in the stationery store, trying to decide what to spend his allowance on. He's hungry, so he buys himself some Reese's Pieces. He remembers that his mother likes Reese's Pieces too, and as he's going to see her this weekend, he also buys a packet for her. He feels a little guilty about his father, so he buys him a package of pipe cleaners. Now content, Tommy goes home. It's not so bad, really, this divorce. His father pays a lot more attention to him now that they live alone. And he sees his mother every week, sometimes more.

There's no fighting in the apartment now, and Tommy sleeps better at night. Sometimes, of course, he wishes his mother and father still lived together. But they are all really better off apart, what with all that fighting and everything.

Children of this age have a firmer grasp on the reasons their parents have split up. They have begun to understand the foibles of human relationships and to see that the divorce was the result of problems between the parents, not between parent and child.[7] Though there are still vestiges of guilt, especially at the younger end of this age group, for the most part these children do not consider themselves responsible for the breakup. "I always heard them fighting," says eleven-year-old Noah. "Mom used to throw plates at Dad in the kitchen. I never thought it was my fault." The truly wise in this age group can even come to a sort of peace of their own with their parents' divorce. "I used to feel I was supposed to be someone with two parents—a normal family, a dog, a cat, a father," says eleven-year-old Gwen. "I was mad at both of them, I guess, because I thought if they *really* loved me, they would have stuck together and made me happy. Now I realize they had to make their happiness by themselves."

For the first time, children of this age can actually feel relieved by their parents' divorce, especially if their home lives have been disrupted by cronic tension or even violence. And again, it is boys who have borne more of the brunt of their parents' discontent. Out of insensitivity to their sons' feelings, or possibly out of a desire to enlist their sympathy, parents fight more openly in front of boys than girls and for longer periods of time.[8] It is little wonder that children of this age can find divorce a surcease of sorts.

The degree of unhappiness it takes to cause a divorce, of course, is highly subjective, both for the parents and the children. But though parents may think they are hiding their disputes from the children, most often they are not. Children this age are very sensitive—and savvy. "They were fighting quite a lot, though I didn't know what they were fighting about, because they'd usually do it at night and I would be sleeping and they would wake me up," says ten-year-old Angela. "They said they were argumenting [*sic*] over disagreements or something but I never really knew. It made me very nervous." True to her spunky age, Angela had no compunction about getting into the middle of her parents' fights. "I'd try to break it up," she says. "I'd say 'Why are you fighting? Why are you yelling? Why are you screaming?'" She tried to patch up the trouble by putting herself center stage. "I'd cry sometimes because it would upset me very much," says Angela, who developed severe headaches. "I thought it might help if I cried and they would stop fighting and do something about me. I never thought I was the reason for them to fight so much. But I did think I could fix it."

But she couldn't, and six months ago her parents separated. Though she still has trouble getting to sleep, her headaches have become less frequent and less severe. And Angela realizes that divorce is better than a stormy marriage. "I just don't think they got along together anymore," she says rather solemnly. "My mother was very demanding. A lot of people are getting divorced now like mine. I think they get bored of a person, just like you can get bored of a friend, and so they just go away from each other." Angela stares out the window. "A lot of kids think it was their fault that the parents split," she says thoughtfully, "But it's not really. I don't think it would make any difference if I got in trouble or ran away or something to try and get them back together. They have to love each other, and if a kid was threatening to run away, that would just give them a nervous breakdown but it wouldn't make them love each other."

Other children this age can also see the benefit of divorce for their parents, if not for themselves. "My mother is much more independent now, like, she has a job," says ten-year-old Fred. "Before she'd just hang around and do the laundry and wait for my father to come home. It's like she's more together." The improved mental outlook of their parents cheers other children who were anxious about parental health before the divorce. "My dad is drinking a lot less now, which is good," says an eleven-year-old girl matter-of-factly. "He always said my mother was driving him to drink. And I guess she was."

But reconciliation fantasies persist no matter how understanding these children are. Though they are old enough to understand the "whys" of divorce and even its benefits, there is always the hope that someday. . . . Eleven-year-old Gwen still hasn't given up, even though her parents separated when she was five. And her fantasies have changed through her different levels of development. "When I was five I thought if I was really supergood, they'd get back together," the girl recalls with a smile. "I tried to do the dishes but I couldn't reach the sink." By eight, her efforts had grown bigger than the immediate household. "I thought then if I ran away, they'd both be looking for me and they'd bump into one another," says the bright-eyed girl. "My mother would ask him to come for dinner and he'd say 'sure' and everything would be okay again." Unsuccessful but undaunted, she practiced psychological warfare at the age of ten. "I was jealous of my friends with two parents," she says. "So I thought if I acted just like them, the exact carbon copy of them, then I would have two parents together again. I told my mother things like 'Sasha has shoes with straps—I want them too,' I wanted the same outfits that she had. I thought if I became her, my parents would get back together. It didn't work." What does Gwen have up her reconciliation sleeve this year? "I'll tell you if it works," she grins.

THE "POOR CHILD"

Robert is carefully filling out the Publishers Clearing House Sweepstakes entry form. This is the fourth one he has filled out in three months, and he knows just where to paste the bonus coupon and the address label. He looks longingly at the picture of the vacation house they may or may not win, along with the Cadillac Seville, then leaves the form for his mother to mail right away so they will qualify for the Early Bird Bonus. This time Robert does something different though. He also sends a self-addressed, stamped envelope so that he will receive the list of winners. He's no dope. He wants to make sure his mother isn't cheated out of the money he can't think how to get for her any other way.

Money becomes a multi-use weapon in divorce. Many divorced fathers withhold it to punish their ex-wives, pay erratically or don't pay at all. Other fathers (and mothers) shower their children with presents to assuage their own guilt or to try to buy the child's loyalty. The abuses of money following divorce are legion, and inevitably, it is the mother and the children who come out on the short end of the financial stick. For children of this age, who are just beginning to understand the power and the value of money, the dollar war between their parents breeds equal parts of anxiety and anger.

All children like to make money. The misspelled "lemonad" stands that pepper suburban and city streets in the summer may seem merely cute to grown-ups, but to the children, adding up the nickels it is a full-scale business. The difference between children in intact families and the children of divorce is that the former usually keep their profits for themselves. The latter often hand over their earnings to their strapped single parents.

The children are worried—very worried—by all the talk they hear about money. "My father hasn't been paying my child support," says twelve-year-old George. "It's been bothering me. My mother has to write to the court almost every month. She gets three hundred dollars a month and she has to keep asking her boss for more money. She's a nurse's aide at a hospital and she works every other night from three to eleven. And my dad owes about three thousand dollars. He says 'I'm going to pay it' but buys a Mazda instead."

Nine to Twelve

It can be argued that children in our society have been too protected, too pampered, too removed from the realities of day-to-day existence. But overnight the children of divorce seem catapulted into a life of economic uncertainty and forced to face situations they don't have the sophistication to understand. "My mom's two months behind in mortgage payments," says eleven-year-old Andy, whose mother is a dental hygienist. "She can never pay all her bills. Say she gets eight bills a month. She can only pay six. She's always two bills behind." His voice drops to a whisper. "We just asked Dad for $16 more a month. We said it was for food but it's really for cable TV. Don't tell him." Like many children his age, Andy is frustrated that he can't help his mother out by working. "In the old days kids could work, but not now," he says. "Now you have to have a work permit."

Withholding money from an ex-spouse is an age-old game in divorce, but it can violate the fairness principles of children and embitter them against the defaulting parent for life. Paul's father, for example, a successful art illustrator in New York, cut off support payments to his ex-wife two years ago and has been in court with her ever since. Every time Paul needs money, he has to call his father and beg him for it. And twelve-year-old Paul is furious. "He lies. This guy lies like a dog," says Paul, whose anger is almost palpable. "He says he's going bankrupt. Ha! He bought a new house in Connecticut, two houses in Vermont, and three cars, a Jeep, a Saab, and a BMW. One is for his girlfriend. I'm furious at him. How does he think he can get away with it?" Paul rolls up a magazine and swats the arm of his chair with it. "He says he's renting the house in Connecticut. Bullshit. When I went there I looked in the garage and saw the cars. He said one was his girlfriend's car. Double bullshit. In Vermont he lives near Sugarbush. That's one of the most expensive areas in Vermont. I know. I read the real estate sections."

Paul's voice is filled with scorn as he starts a litany of contempt. "He's a creep. He's an ass. He likes lying. He can't face reality. He's a kid. His cars are toys. His house is a toy," he says. "My mom has been working for twenty years and she's getting tired. I want her to do what she really wants to do, like open a gourmet shop or something. Boy, I hope she wins that court case. I hope she kills him."

At least Paul's mother is going after the nonpaying father. All too often women cave in during divorce negotiations, agreeing to far less support than they're entitled to. And legal expenses to sue later are often prohibitive. Of course the children lose, too, and often more than money. They can feel abandoned and unprotected by the parent who won't go to financial bat for them, or pressured if their mothers expect them to carry out their own economic battles alone. Getting money for school trips, summer camp, even Christmas presents often becomes the child's responsibility rather than the single parent's. "I needed a hundred and twenty dollars for our class ski trip and I asked Mom and she said she didn't have it and to ask Dad," says twelve-year-old Andy. "But I needed it that day or I'd lose my place. I asked her to call him but she wouldn't. She said she was tired of begging." Unable to reach his father in time, Andy had to ask his teacher to advance him the money, which his father subsequently repaid. Andy, quite naturally, was angry and embarrassed. "Dad's got three times the money Mom has," he says. "Why didn't she get more out of him? Why doesn't he just give her more? Why does it all have to be up to me?"

Even if the child isn't placed directly in the middle of the money conflict, the battle between parents can backfire onto him. One ten-year-old boy waited days for the report card that never came from school because his father hadn't paid the tuition. An eleven-year-old girl was humiliated in the waiting room of the orthodontist when she reported for her regular appointment. "They said right out loud so everyone could hear that my

appointment had been cancelled because my father was so behind on payments," she says bitterly. "It was the first I knew
about it." A ten-year-old girl went to the riding stable only to
find her pony had been leased to someone else because neither
parent, both of whom could well afford it, would consent to pay
the bill for its board. Some children become highly skilled in financial maneuvers before they've even mastered long division.
"His checks were bouncing a lot," says a ten-year-old girl of
her father. "He can bounce them personally by switching his
bank account around."

In a chilling but practical approach to financial stability, divorce veterans taking part in a program at the Lexington High
School in Lexington, Massachusetts, advise children as young
as eleven to read their parents' separation agreement for their
own self-protection. "You should read [it] so you can make
sure that you'll have a place to live and money to support you,"
advises a seventeen-year-old member of the school's divorce
group. "There should be something that says what will happen
when you turn eighteen so you don't get kicked out then. That
there will be money if you want to go to college . . . so that all
of a sudden you're not left in the cold. Read it and tell your parents you want something in there about college in writing."[9]

Meanwhile, many of these kids do their best to pitch in. "I
do jobs," says eleven-year-old Bryan. "I got a paper route—
fifty-four papers on Sundays, thirty-seven weekly. I get between twenty and thirty dollars a week. Three dollars is my allowance. I give the rest to Mom." Children of single fathers are
not immune from money problems either. "I'm the money-
maker around here these days," says ten-and-a-half-year-old
Steve, whose father is a free-lance writer. "Nobody at those
magazines sends Dad the money on time. So I deliver papers.
Yesterday I collected a hundred and twenty-seven dollars and
got to keep seventy as my share. I lend it to Dad. And when he
gets paid, he pays me back."

Younger children try their luck at contests. "Our Dad doesn't give us much money, so I enter all these contests and sweepstakes but I never win," says eight-and-a-half-year-old Roy. "I try to earn money because Mom's worried." Nine-year-old Tara had tried the cereal-box route. "There was a thing on the back of Fruity Pebbles," says the little girl. "You could win four trips to Hollywood or four hundred different kinds of bicycles. I thought I could take my mom to Hollywood for a vacation or sell the bicycles for her." Twelve-year-old Alan is more realistic. He's looking for a man for his mother to marry. "She's going to have to marry somebody," says the boy. "There's nobody else to help her, to bring in money, too."

Even where there is money, indeed lots of money, embittered parents can still make a child feel very poor. And very insecure. In one of the most devious strategies of postdivorce hostilities, some parents lie to their children about the amount of support they receive in order to win the child's sympathy and alienate him from the other parent. Twelve-year-old Polly, for example, lives in the Beacon Hill section of Boston with her mother, brother, and housekeeper. She goes to a private school and summers on the North Shore with her father, an attorney. But even though her father pays more than $15,000 a year in alimony and child support, Polly doesn't know it and is getting increasingly anxious. "When Mom's upset she talks to me about money," says Polly in a strained voice. "She thinks Dad should give her more. She says things like we won't be able to buy food or get shoes. I believe her. I get real worried and upset and then I can't get to sleep and I'm real tired in the morning."

At this age when clothes and conformity are life's breath to a child, Polly has been so traumatized by her mother's threats that she doesn't see that she has all the things her friends have. Not having the economic facts with which to face down her mother, she takes her anxieties out on her friends. "Most of my friends are really spoiled," she says with disgust. "They show off all their neat clothes and make me really mad. They do it on purpose. I know they do."

THE UNPARENTED CHILD

Lucy is hurrying home from school. She's late picking up her four-year-old brother from nursery school, and she knows he'll be bratty all afternoon if he has to wait too long for her. The teachers have already spoken to her about it, saying it makes Teddy feel even more insecure if all the other children are picked up before he is. She hurries also because she doesn't want her mother to be mad when she gets home from work. Everybody seems so mad lately. Her brother whines and throws things and won't eat. And Lucy's mother loses her temper over almost anything. If it weren't for her, Lucy thinks to herself, not for the first time, the whole family would come apart. With that thought, the ten-year-old breaks into a run, her fifth-grade homework banging on her back.

At ten, Lucy is effectively running a good part of the family life. She doesn't really stop to think whether it is a good thing or a bad thing. It's just the way life has gone since her father left and her mother went back to work. In fact, quite a lot of the time it makes her proud, especially when her mother says, "I don't know what I'd do without you." Sure, there are times when Lucy would rather go to gymnastics or just hang out with her friends. But she can't. She has a job, a responsibility. And there's no one else to do it.

There are many, many Lucys among the children of divorce. At this age, when in an intact family Lucy would probably have a babysitter for herself, she has instead become not only her own babysitter, but her brother's as well. There's no way around it, really. Her mother doesn't make enough money to have someone come in. And Lucy is certainly capable of keeping her brother alive in the afternoons. The fear that she and her mother share is that Teddy will get a cold or something and won't be able to go to nursery school. They talk about it sometimes at night, and they've just decided that Lucy will have to stay home from school when it happens, because her mother can't afford to take any time off from her job—which pays by the hour.

Children of divorce grow up very fast, often too fast. A large part of the problem is economic, of course. There are very few families, intact or not, who haven't felt the pinch of inflation and haven't had to cut back somewhere. Because of the number of mothers in the work force, even most intact families have had to reorganize. But for divorced children of these ages, the shuffle in responsibilities is often overwhelming. Andrew was ten years old when his mother and father separated and his life changed overnight. His mother started spending a lot of time away from home, leaving Andrew to take almost complete care of his five-year-old brother. "She was going out with a lot of guys and she wasn't home much," explains Andrew. "I had to take care of the baby. I had to walk him to school, walk him home, feed him lunch and dinner, even put him to bed. He wouldn't listen to me. And I wasn't allowed to yell at him. I really hated him. And her."

The forced solitude of divorced children also contributes to hurrying them into a maturity many of them wish they didn't have. Teenagers seem more capable of being alone, and even seek out solitude as a surcease from the emotional and social frenzy that often dominates their lives. Much younger children are less apt to be left alone for long periods of time. But late-latency children are caught betwixt and between. They are old enough to take care of themselves, but not old enough to enjoy it. And they can feel very much alone.

"My life suddenly seemed empty," says eleven-year-old Alison, whose father left the family a year ago. "I was best friends with my father. I feel the emptiness in our house. Our dog still waits at the door for him. He used to lie down and leap at my father when he came in at six." Like many divorced kids, Alison also "lost" her mother. "My mother has gone back to work and back to school," says the girl, sitting cross-legged in a chair. "She isn't home three nights out of the week. Sometimes I feel I've learned too quickly to be independent. Sometimes I feel so lonely in my house. I feel the emptiness of going to bed when my parents aren't home."

Eleven-year-old Christine also feels a hole in her life. "Now I come home and the house is quiet," says the blonde, whose mother has gone back to college. "When my mom comes home, she's tired or reads or does homework. On weekends, she'll clean and do shopping. We don't have much spare time together. Mom used to have a part-time job so she got home early. I could spend time with either my father or mother. Now I'm always the first one home. Sometimes at night when my mom has classes, the house feels all creepy. Someone could be hiding behind the chair."

Christine's forced leap into maturity has coincided, as it does in many single-parent families, with her mother's new sense of freedom. "I feel like I'm her older sister," Christine says of her mother. "She feels that she's free—that she'll fly like a bird. She acts like 'I'm in college—I can do whatever I want.' " Christine sighs and draws a deep breath. "I feel more like I'm alone than in a family. Now I feel alone even when people are around."

Often, lonely children this age fantasize about living with the other parent, as if simply changing houses would solve their problems. This concentration on the magic of externally controlled happiness often postpones their ability to face problems and solve them. Just as teenagers can turn to drugs and alcohol to "tune out," children this age can "escape" through the imagined qualities of the other parent who would love them, be home, and buy them whatever they want. But it rarely turns out that way. One eleven-year-old who switched households came back home after three months. "I had to take out the garbage, walk the dog, keep my room neat, and babysit the baby," he said with disgust. "It was worse with Dad than Mom."

Other children, especially girls, can turn to "substitute" families to replace the loneliness in their own. "Yesterday at Erica's house I felt like staying there and not coming home," says ten-year-old Ellen. "I feel like Erica and me are sisters. We're very close to each other. Lisa [Erica's mother] is like my mother. I didn't want to leave." Twelve-year-old Sally is more philosophical in her choice of surrogate family. "My best friend Amalie has a house like a picture house and a picture family," muses the girl. "She has a mother who stays home and cooks wonderful French food. When I'm there I have a peek into a little dollhouse. I can't imagine what it would be like to live like that. I'd be a different person."

Separation anxiety can also return to plague these children who now only have one parent to rely on. Old enough to understand the precariousness of life, they often worry excessively about the parent's safety.[10] "I have these feelings when my mother leaves for work or goes out on a date that she'll be in an accident," says ten-year-old Amy worriedly. Luckily, these children are old enough to distract themselves from their fears. "While she's out, I clean the house so it's all shining clean when she gets home," says Amy. "I started cleaning the house because I was so worried about getting a phone call: 'Your mother is dead.'" Other children worry about the parent's health and even take responsibility for it as a sort of insurance policy against being orphaned. More than one child confessed to hiding or throwing away the parent's cigarettes. One boy brazenly poured a bottle of vodka down the sink right in front of his mother. Still another spent his allowance on vitamin pills for his mother. "Someone's got to make sure she's all right," the nine-year-old said. "I guess it's me."

Nine to Twelve

The lack of parental attention can take a more serious turn in some of these children who either will themselves sick or get into accidents to force parental concern. Nine-year-old Sarah spent the better part of a winter taking off her parka after she left home for school and walking barefoot in the cold in order to get sick. "I planned to get so sick that everyone would have to stop what they were doing to take care of me, like bring me ice cream and soup," she says. "But all I got was a cold. And nobody cares anymore if you get a cold."

Sarah has a lot of company. Some children of divorce not only will themselves sick, but actually do get sick; a doctor in Australia went so far as to recommend inoculations against streptococcal infections for children undergoing the stress of divorce. An unusual number of somatic symptoms emerge, such as headaches and stomachaches. One girl whose father was an orthopedic surgeon developed severe leg cramps which only he could alleviate by massaging them away.

The accident rate also rises among these children, especially boys. Though some parents attribute this increase in injuries to the child merely being accident-prone, they are often mistaken. One ten-year-old boy who lost contact with his father after divorce broke his collarbone, his thumb, and a vertebra in his back within the space of three months. Some accident-prone children even realize what they are doing. After eleven-year-old Philip broke one arm falling off his dirt bike, broke the other arm in gym, ripped the cartilage in his leg, and had to have stitches in his hand after tangling with a barbed-wire fence, he admitted, "I was angry. Maybe subconsciously I wanted the accidents to happen so they'd pay attention to me."

On a more abstract but very important level, unparented children often lack philosophical direction from their parents and may grow up with values transmitted more by their peers and television than by their families. Hectic single parent life is often reduced to the basic levels of providing shelter, food, clean clothes, and fast information for the children, with little time left for personality development. "Families have become a group of individuals who each get on their own track at 7:30 in the morning and get off it at night," observes Wayne Holder, director of child protection for the American Humane Association. "Children don't receive enough adult interaction. The face-to-face discussion of feelings, values and philosophy of life between parents and children are missed completely."[11]

At these ages, when children are still basing their own social attitudes and values on those of their parents, they need a sounding board which often just isn't there. "I feel like I have to make an appointment with my father if I have something I want to discuss," says an eleven-year-old boy. Adds a twelve-year-old girl who was disciplined for rudeness at school, "How do I know how to act? Nobody ever told me."

THE TOO-OLD CHILD

Harry is sitting on the edge of his mother's bed while she gets ready to go out for the evening. He shuffles his feet nervously as his mother tells him more than he wants to know. "He's very sexy, this fellow, not at all like your father. Remember when he used to fall asleep in his chair every night watching television?" the mother asks him. "Which do you want, Harry? A sexy girl or a girl who's going to take care of you?" Harry shuffles his feet harder. "I dunno," he mumbles. He wishes he could go do his math homework, but his mother keeps after him. "Which looks better, Harry? The blue or the red?" she asks, holding up two dresses. "They look the same," he says. His mother makes a face. "Now, come on, Harry, decide," she says. "You're a man. Which makes me look better?" Harry stares at his feet. "The red," he says. His mother brightens. "Thank you, dear. It's so hard making all these decisions alone."

Harry feels very uncomfortable. His mother has been after him more and more lately to help her make decisions, to reassure her, to advise her. When she's feeling up, she wants him to be her pal. When she's down, she looks to him for sympathy. She even cries right in front of him. He wishes he were older and knew the right things to say to comfort her. And he wishes very much that his father were around to handle it, or a grown-up friend who would understand her problems better. After all, he's just a kid. And though part of him is proud to have become so important to her, another part of him wishes she'd just leave him alone.

In psychological terms, Harry is becoming a "parentified" child. Through a role reversal that is very common in divorce, the parent becomes more dependent on the child than the child on the parent. Without adult company, the parent uses the child as a confidant, an adviser, even a therapist. Often the burden falls to a child well before divorce, when the marriage is in trouble but the parents do not want to face it. Instead they talk to each other through the child, defer decisions to the child, depend on the child to keep the family afloat. "We've treated families where the little son or daughter is actually running the family," says Craig Everett, director of the Conciliation Court in Tucson, Arizona. "In one case, no one did anything in the family without checking with the nine-year-old girl first. She was even responsible for disciplining her little brother. It was like she was thirty instead of nine. And her parents let her play that role so that they didn't need to deal with their own conflict."

Most children are flattered by all this attention and, indeed, power. Instead of being treated as dumb little kids, they are looked upon as pseudoadults, roles they are eager to assume. "In a divorce situation, the mother may begin to rely on the boy to take over the husband's role and almost be like a husband to her in a lot of different ways," says Sandra Volgy, the child Advocacy Counselor at Tucson's Conciliation Court. "The same thing applies to fathers who have custody of little girls. They'll turn them into little homemakers. She's got dinner ready for him when he comes home from the office and she's cleaned up the house after school. Children like getting all that attention and responsibility but it's not healthy for their development to suddenly be an adult at the age of nine or ten."

The more sinister aspect of parentification is the emotional web the child is drawn into—and can't get out of. "I feel like I have a responsibility to my mother," says eleven-year-old Mike, his voice trailing off. "If she's upset, I'm the one who comforts her. . . ." Such responsibility can add a layer of guilt on children who at this age want to spend more and more time with their friends but feel tugged back to the dependent parent. "My mother's not a real mother type," says an eleven-year-old girl. "I'm more of a pal to my mother than a daughter. After my father left, it did bring me and my mother a little closer because we'd spend more time together. But when I went out with my friends, I'd always feel a little guilty because she was home all alone."

Another girl, this one twelve, has in effect become her mother's mother. "She really needs someone," says the black-haired girl, whose mother has sunk into a postdivorce depression. "She doesn't take much care of her appearance. She's always buying clothes for me, but never for herself. I say 'Why don't you go shopping for *you*? Buy some nice shoes instead of sneakers.' " Molly gives a world-weary sigh. "She doesn't have a job, but she's always talking about getting one. But she never gets herself to interviews. She's always circling these things in the want ads, but she never goes to the interviews. I say, 'Why don't you go?' She says, 'I can't get it together.' "

One of the dangers for children like Molly lies in their sense of failure at not being able to fulfill the parent's needs, a syndrome often compounded by the guilty ex-spouse who delegates all responsibility to the child. "Dad is always saying to me

'Your mother is very fragile and delicate. You must take care of her,' " Molly says in annoyance. "Doesn't he think I know that? I'm doing the best I can."

Even where the child has been able to cope successfully, there is apt to be resentment. "The problem is that I'm the only man around the house," says a twelve-year-old boy. "For years I've taken charge of things that I shouldn't have. I miss not being able to just sit back and be a child. I act like my sister's father when she talks with her mouth full, for example. It's not my place to do that. I feel like my mother's husband, too, like when it's time to put up the storm windows. If there were a father here, I'd be helping, not doing. Sometimes I like the role. Sometimes I don't. My mother expects me to do things I shouldn't have to do. But then, there's no one else to do them."

A child hurried into an adult role because of divorce often suffers for it later. The effects of parentifying a child at eight, nine, or eleven, may not show until adolescence, when the child tries to move away from the parent—and can't. Realizing the overimportant role he's been handed, he gets angry. But the thought of letting that parent down by pulling away makes him feel guilty. Some stay stalled. Others, both boys and girls, become openly rebellious and defiant in an effort to extricate themselves. Still others try to replace the sort of relationship they know best with a new partner, one they can control and not get too involved with. And this pattern can follow them into adulthood. "The ones who are parentified have so many emotional needs," says Craig Everett. "They feel that the only attention and approval they'll get is by repeating the cycle, that their only sense of self-esteem is to take over the next house and run it. The loss of a childhood is a very serious thing. In later years, the parentified child becomes the overserious person, the overcompulsive person, the people who can't enjoy themselves, people who don't have any sense of themselves as spontaneous human beings."

A common—and destructive—reaction among parentified children is to escape their roles by leaving their childhoods too early. Girls may become sexually provocative and contemptuous of the parent who has been overdependent on them.[12] Boys may pull away by mimicking what they perceive to be appropriate older behavior, swaggering and strutting, often using their fists more than is necessary. Truancy, cheating, and even petty thievery are not uncommon among these children, who feel threatened by any authority. And just when these children most need adults to pattern themselves after, they may close themselves off from the adult world. "I'd like to get away from grown-ups altogether," says eleven-year-old Abe, who has already run away from home once. "I'd like to live with a friend whose parents are divorced. We would know why each other was staying, know how to cope away from a bunch of grown-ups. I'd probably make myself eat healthier meals, I'd wake up later." Abe pauses. "The ideal situation would be a coed craft camp in a different country."

THE REJECTED CHILD

Eddie is picking at his dinner, absently pushing the peas around with his fork, but not eating any. "I'm just not hungry," he tells his mother. After dinner, he develops other symptoms, a stomachache, a headache. "Maybe I'm getting sick," he says to his mother, who suggests that maybe he should stay home from school the next day. And that is just what Eddie wants to hear. Tomorrow is Father's Day at school and Eddie doesn't have a father anymore. It's been a year since he saw him, and he's only gotten a couple of postcards from him. Eddie is wise enough to know that Father's Day will be hard on him. And so is his mother.

Parents can leave their children for any number of reasons. Some feel too emotionally immature themselves to be effective parents. Others feel so depressed after divorce that they not only don't want to be reminded of their former home lives by seeing their children, but also fear that their depression will be harmful to the children. And then there are the callous ones, of course, who simply try to eradicate the past by running away from it. But whatever the reason for abandonment, be it defensive or offensive, the children left behind suffer terribly. There is no way they can escape feeling angry, rejected, and unworthy of love, no matter how hard the custodial parent tries to make up for it.

Some children of ten or twelve can mask their feelings of rejection through anger. But others get stalled in the yearnings of seven- and eight-year-olds. Ten-year-old George, for example, missed his father so much after his parents separated that his mother sent him to Cincinnati to live with his father. It lasted three weeks. "I was all happy," recalls George. "It was nice. I started going to school. I was treated really good, but after three weeks my father said, 'I can't get a divorce with you here.' Then he said, 'We're going for a ride.' I fell asleep in the car. He went in and packed my clothes and suddenly we're at the airport. I was upset. I took the plane ticket and walked onto the plane. I didn't say good-bye." George has only seen his father twice in the last year—and can't even call him up. "He doesn't even trust me with his own phone number," says the boy sadly. "He thinks I'd give it to my mother. I have to call my father's sister in Florida to have him call me. He doesn't want Mom to call him. I write letters. I have his address. But it hurts me."

Mothers on the run can be no less insensitive to their children's feelings. Joe's mother left him and his older brother two years ago to move into a commune in Los Angeles. Since then she has only seen the boys twice, even though Joe frequently goes to the commune on weekends in the hope of bumping into her. "I'm still very upset about not seeing her," the twelve-year-old mumbles. "She tries to pacify us by giving us hordes of money. I think she thinks by giving money each week, that's her contribution to me. Every Friday on the bulletin board—two twenty-dollar bills stuck on it." Joe says his mother thinks she is being altruistic in withdrawing from her sons' lives. "She told me that she thinks she's going to fuck up our lives with her nastiness. She doesn't want to start that again," says Joe haltingly. "I'd rather see her and live with it. She doesn't deal with it or us. Just give the money and run. . . ."

Being rejected outright by a parent is an extreme. More common after divorce is the slow erosion in the parent-child relationship which often leaves the child feeling just as rejected, if not more so. The noncustodial parent who makes promises then breaks them, who visits the children erratically or who shows up late can be more distressing to these children than the parent who has no contact at all. Instead of being rejected once, these children feel rejected time and again. And because fathers see their daughters less at these ages than their sons, and for shorter periods, the girls can feel particularly bereft.

The relationship between eleven-year-old Allie and her father, for example, has changed dramatically since her parents separated a year ago. And Allie, whose policeman father used to take her down to the precinct with him all the time, feels very hurt by it. Now she sees him only rarely—and erratically. "He'll call and he'll say he'll take me out on such-and-such a date. Then he doesn't show up," says the long-legged blonde rapidly. "He said he'd take us to the beach and he never called the whole summer. It gets me so annoyed. He said he would do it and he never called to even make an excuse. That makes it even worse."

When Allie does see him, the visit is inevitably a letdown. "Now he acts like all he wants to do is get through the visit and leave," she says. "He used to be all cheery and nice, but now he's nervous and it makes me feel nervous being with him. You know how it is when you first meet someone, you're a little nervous? That's how it is when he takes me out." Another girl looked forward to her birthday dinner with her father only to have it end in depression and loneliness. "When he took me out on my birthday, it seemed as though we didn't know each other," says the twelve-year-old, chewing on the ends of her hair. "I felt weird. He'd gotten me a Snoopy watch, even though I'd asked for a digital watch. And he doesn't even know my clothes size anymore. He got me a top and a jumpsuit and they don't fit. I felt terrible. I felt that I was with this total stranger that I've known all my life."

Some fathers can feel uncomfortable with their daughters after divorce, not only fearing their alignment with their mothers, but unsure how to treat them in this period of burgeoning maturity. These fathers often distance themselves in reflexive self-defense, which both bewilders and frustrates their daughters.

"My dad feels just because I'm visiting he has to take me somewhere. It's a bummer," says eleven-year-old Tina. "Sometimes I'd like to spend the day walking in the park and talking to him like we used to. But he doesn't want to get involved with me. We're always going out to dinner or to Disneyland with other members of the family. That's not a relationship. When you ask to sit and talk, he sits and watches TV. He doesn't want to get involved with *me*." Her voice rises in frustration and anger. "It's like he doesn't want to know me as a daughter," she yells.

Reluctant parents often stall the development of children who should at this point be growing away from them. Instead of dreaming about teenage rock stars or involving themselves in their own social lives, these children may remain fixated on their fathers. Eleven-year-old Susan, for example, is expending far too much energy plotting how to see more of her father and how to extend the length of his visits. "I'll ask him if he wants a cup of coffee," she schemes. "Then I'll try to get into the conversation as many things as I can, like what would happen if I ripped up my leg again. Then I'll ask him to play a game of cards to keep him here as long as possible. Or I'll ask him to play the Life game, which is the longest game we have. I'll try anything to keep him here as long as possible. So far the longest he's been here is fifteen minutes."

THE SEXUAL CHILD

Twelve-year-old Tanya and her nine-year-old sister, Lily, are rummaging through their father's bureau drawers. "Here's one," whispers Tanya excitedly, showing her sister a single earring from her father's stud box. Lily strikes another gold mine with the discovery of a nightgown alongside her father's pajamas. "Slinky." The girls giggle. Lily moves to the closet where she discovers not only a very feminine-looking bathrobe, but an improbable pair of pink silk mules. "La-de-dah," says Tanya, mincing around in the slippers. "What's this?" says Lily, opening a box from the bedside table. Tanya looks at the contents carefully. "Rubbers," she says to her little sister. "It's so when he fucks all these girls, they don't have babies."

Sex and the single parent become infinitely more complicated with children this age, especially with girls. Sexual tension grows between children and the parent of the opposite sex, while challenges are laid down between children and the same-sexed parent. Sexual jealousy runs high between preadolescent girls and their fathers' partners, making any positive relationship between the two difficult, if not impossible. The situation can become so charged that researchers warn that the ages of nine to fifteen are the worst ones in which to attempt remarriage.[13] "When remarriage had not occurred until the child was nine or ten, acceptance and a positive relationship were less likely to occur than in young children," observed Hetherington. "Children in the preadolescent and early adolescent period were less likely to accept even a good stepparent than were younger or older children."

Children of divorce grow up quickly, some too quickly, in terms of sex. Girls usually enter puberty—and a second oedipal period—around ten. (Boys usually start maturing two years later at twelve). In an intact family, the mother is a forbidding barrier between father and daughter, so the daughter's second oedipal phase is somewhat muted. But in a single-parent household, the atmosphere can be highly erotic. The children can become titillated by it, and it may either add fuel to what is really a mild oedipal phase or cause the children to become prematurely sexually active.

Boys are not immune from sexual conflicts and anxieties. But at this age they are more concerned with the ethics of conduct than with sexuality itself. Their oedipal time will come in early adolescence, when they will identify with their fathers but give their hearts to their mothers. Even then, the oedipal urge will be less severe. It is more permissible for a daughter unabashedly to love her father and to challenge her mother than it is for a son to show the same degree of affection for his mother and square off with his father.

Both boys and girls, however, want very much to avoid any proof of their parents' sexuality. "Children this age don't like to view their parents as sex objects," says Hetherington. "They don't know how to handle their own sexuality and it becomes very threatening to see Mom or Dad become overtly sexual rather than neuter." But in single-parent and remarried families, the children often can't escape it.

Just what constitutes sexuality is greatly exaggerated by the very fertile but inexperienced imaginations of children this age. The most simple and innocent displays of adult affection can send the children into frenzies of anxiety and embarrassment. Hetherington points out that if, for example, a male partner comes in at the end of the day and gives the mother a hug and a kiss, the children are wont to describe their relationship as: "They're always hugging and kissing. It's disgusting." Highly sexual themselves, children this age see almost any affectionate act on the part of their parents as a prelude to orgy. One single mother and her new companion took her two daughters, twelve and ten, out to dinner. Wanting to say something privately to her friend, the mother raised her menu to cover their faces. "Mother," her twelve-year-old pleaded in full blush. "Stop necking."

Many children will try very hard to dodge the confrontation with their parents' sex lives. "Sleeping over," which was a natural extension of friendship just a few years before, now becomes fraught with innuendo, especially for preadolescent girls. Many refuse to spend the night in the same house as a new parental partner. "When Lois is there I won't sleep over at my father's house," says eleven-year-old Annie. "Not with her there." Sexual rivalry can become so intense between the young daughter and the new female partner, who is almost inevitably younger, prettier, and sexier than the safe mother, that a good relationship may never develop. "We meet all the girls my father is dating," says ten-year-old Edwina. "I'm jealous of every one of them."

Often it is the parents who are sexually jealous of each other, and they use the children to spy on the sexual activities in the separate households. Children are constantly being grilled by one parent or the other as to just who is coming and going in the house, where they sleep, what goes on that the child is exposed to. For girls especially, a prematurely heightened sexual awareness can spill over into all aspects of their lives. At school, they can alienate themselves from their peers who suddenly look immature to these newly sophisticated eyes. No longer content with their own age group, these school-aged girls may start running with an older, faster crowd and seek out relationships with males a good deal older than they are.[14]

144

THE COMPETITIVE CHILD

Relating to the mother's new partners can be no less fraught for girls. With an unrelated male around the house, the taboo of incest is lifted. Any man is fair game to practice on, to tempt, to win. And though the girls' attempts at seduction are inept, the intent is there. Flesh may even be flashed to provoke attention from an older male. One ten-year-old girl who had scraped her thigh falling off her bike pulled off her skirt time and again to show her mother's boyfriend. Another took to showing off her gymnastics headstand in the living room—wearing no underpants. "My mom's boyfriend likes listening to my stereo more than he likes to go on walks with Mom," says eleven-year-old Toni. "But don't tell her."

Young girls do not hesitate to take on their single mothers competitively. They clash head-on over almost everything, far more than do boys with their fathers. The role of the stronger, authoritative, more intimidating older male will squelch direct confrontation between father and son in the latter's oedipal years. But nothing seems to slow down the confrontation between mothers and daughters. "What would happen if you had a boyfriend and he liked me better?" one twelve-year-old girl asked her recently divorced mother. "Why that would be too bad for both of us," her mother replied. The daughter smiled. "Maybe for you, but not for me," she said sweetly.

Divorce often exacerbates mother-daughter competitiveness with an abrupt—and unwanted—bridging of the generation gap. In the flush of freedom after divorce, a mother is apt to enter a second adolescence just as her eleven- or twelve-year-old is entering her first. Suddenly their attitudes overlap and the daughter can feel blocked in what she now feels is her turf. "I mean there's my mother at college with a new perm and listening to James Taylor," says one twelve-year-old in disgust. "We go shopping and she buys all the clothes I want for herself. She's gone crazy. That's no way for a mother to act." Another girl spent hours learning a new dance step from her mother, then announced to her friends a few days later, "You should have seen my mom trying to jitterbug. She's pitiful."

THE MORAL CHILD

Children this age are looking for structure, for a framework on which to hang the rules they've been taught. They want to respect their parents, look up to them, emulate them. On the brink of adolescence, these children study their parents very carefully, seeing them as blueprints for their own ascendence into adulthood. And often, their strict moral code clashes with their single parent's new laissez-faire attitude toward sex. Sex is reserved for marriage, these children want to believe, welcoming the excuse to postpone their own sexuality. But the activity of their parents belies that belief, threatening them even further. At this age of hard and fast rules, they are also defining the reputations of their peers as "good" or "bad." And suddenly their parents are earning all the wrong labels.

The ambiguity of many contemporary adult relationships adds to the children's toppling sense of morality. Their parents often start having affairs before they are divorced or even legally separated. The children often see this as one parent "cheating" on the other, and it reinforces their tendency to take sides with the "good" parent against the "bad."[15] Prolonged parental separations, in which the parents simply agree to live apart without the finality or legality of divorce, further tax the children's moral codes. In their eyes, the parents are still married and their sexual behavior is embarrassing at least and indecent at most. Predictably, girls are hardest on their mothers, while boys demand more of their fathers. "My mom has this boyfriend named Donald and he sleeps over," says an eleven-year-old girl. "I don't like the idea. I don't think it's right for my mother to have a man sleeping over when she isn't married to him yet. I have different rules for my mother than my father, but I don't know why." Jeffrey is equally upset by his father. "I've lost a lot of respect for him," says the twelve-year-old. "He's always been strict, he's a Catholic and he goes to Mass every Sunday. But he's living with this girl. Why should he expect me to live by rules if he doesn't?"

Sex and affection are, of course, natural conditions of life. And single parents lucky enough to enjoy satisfying relationships are not going to stop. But it is important to be aware of the children's perceptions of these relationships. The flaunting of sexuality, the rapid turnover of partners, a parent's preoccupation with sex in both conversation and attitude may either encourage a child's premature and precocious sexuality or fill the child with disgust. In one single-parent home where the mother was having a series of one-night stands, her daughter left a note on the kitchen door: "Fuck Mother."[16] Another preadolescent girl leaned out the window as her mother drove away with a date and yelled, "Whore!"

HOW PARENTS CAN HELP

Most of these children's extreme reactions to divorce will abate after a year, except for the sexual tension.[17] But there are critical areas left that, if not addressed by parents, can persist for years and actually damage, rather than merely distress the children.

Defusing the anger the child feels toward the parent he has decided is responsible for the divorce is all-important. It is tempting for an embittered parent to enlist the all-too-willing support of the child as an ally. But such vindictive triumphs, though satisfying, may not only prevent the child from resolving the divorce and moving on, but also may backfire: in adolescence, when a teenager learns to think less in black and white terms and more in adult tones of gray, he may turn on the parent who has poisoned his mind against the other. Instead of being thankful to the sacrificing, custodial parent for protecting him from the undeserving "bad" parent, he may accuse that parent instead of preventing a relationship with the other parent he was never allowed to know—or to love.

At this age especially it is important for both parents to stress the good points about the other to the children, as they still base their self-concepts largely on parental images. To say to the children after a difficult separation, "You're just like your mother" or "You hold your head just like your father" can be taken not only as an insult by the child but as a warning that he or she, too, is going to be a "bad" person, and unable to form satisfying relationships. Parents need to guard against such comments at this age particularly; the children, especially girls, are maturing rapidly, and beginning to look like mini-adults. The twelve-year-old girl in her first grown-up dress can look startlingly like her mother when the father first met her; an eleven-year-old boy can adopt a swagger that is all too reminiscent of the father. And the déjà vu words pop out of the parent's mouth without forethought. Better, then, to add a phrase or two, such as "You look just like your mother did. Very pretty"; or "You hold your head just like your father. It's one of the things I loved about him."

Boys especially need consistent and firm parenting from their fathers and their mothers at these ages, for without it the boys are prone to get into trouble. Ten- and eleven-year-old boys are singled out again and again in psychiatric studies of divorce as being more aggressive and more disobedient than boys from intact families.[18] At this age when boys may become hypermasculine and even contemptuous of anything feminine, it is more important than ever for fathers to remain involved with their sons, to serve as role models for masculine self-control.

To counter the exaggerated effect of divorce on boys this age, there is a growing school of thought that favors same-sex custody. In an ongoing study at the University of Texas, comparing six- to eleven-year-old children in mother- and father-custody homes, daughters were found to do better with their mothers while sons fared even better with their fathers. Indeed, boys who lived with their single fathers were found to be "warmer, have higher self-esteem, be less demanding, show more maturity, act more sociably and behave more independently with their fathers" than did the sons of intact families! The same held true for girls in mother-custody families, for every quality but self-esteem, which was higher among girls from intact families.[19]

On a more practical level, it is helpful for parents to think up ways to distract these children from their distress. Encouraging the children to pursue extra activities, to join the swimming team, to go to camp can help them take their minds off the problems at home and even heighten their damaged self-esteems. Because children this age are highly sensitive to feelings of deprivation, extra effort on the part of the parent can often heal a hundred slights. Dinner out once every two weeks or a regular trip to the movies *alone* with the parent can make up for many lonely afternoons and dispel the child's feelings of being uncared for.

Above all else, these children need to have their confidence restored in the world as an orderly, ethical place, and their faith in the stability of the new family structure affirmed. Without these essential securities in place, their entry into adolescence will be delayed—or dangerously premature.

TEENAGERS
The Age of False Maturity

The developmental problems that began to ripple in preadolescence now in adolescence become a tidal wave. Even in the happiest of families, the memories of living with teenaged children are not likely to be gentle recollections but vignettes of conflict, rebellion, and stormy emotions. The task is hard for teenagers, who must establish identities separate from their families but integrate family ties at the same time; few do it easily. In this adolescent period of the Great I Am, teenagers are often inconsistent, vacillating between feeling as if they are all-knowing, omnipotent beings and seeing themselves as helpless, dependent creatures. They try on different roles the way women once tried on hats, and in the process keep their families continually off-balance.

Change is the order of the day. Boys now enter their growth spurts, gaining eight or nine inches between the ages of twelve and fourteen. Their genitalia develop, their voices sink, and they slim down (unlike girls, who don't shed their baby fat until sixteen or seventeen). Teenagers are now definitely members of two different sexes, and their new sexual maturity makes them both proud and anxious. In one survey of teenage health, it was nervousness, above all other conditions, that turned out to be their number one complaint.[1]

Parent-teen relationships can become very complicated. Boys now take on their fathers, not only for possession of the female, but for their superior place in society and the order of things, while girls continue to challenge their mothers. Parents may fight back too little or too much, but the immediate results are always the same: values clash, harsh words are spoken, and only occasionally does the family get through three meals in a row together calmly.

Adolescence is not a simple condition, of course. There is a world of difference between a thirteen-year-old and a nineteen-year-old, and there are specific tasks to be accomplished on the road to adulthood. The youngest teens work hard at shedding their childhood identities and dependencies, proclaiming at every possible instant they are no longer to be treated as "little kids." By the midteens, they are at full war against the mores and expectations of the Old Guard in their attempt to extricate themselves and to regroup as the next generation of improved adults. These years see the height of nonconformity to the adult world, and of conformity to their own teen subculture: to its music, its own distinct way of dressing, its language, and its idealistic values, not yet compromised by experience. Only at the end of adolescence—during the late teens—have they tried a little of everything and finally established fairly well their own individual set of adult values and expectations.

Not surprisingly, the developmental tasks of the adolescent are both exaggerated and blurred by divorce, not only by divorce that occurs during these years, when the emergence of the second oedipal phase can make young teenagers perceive the departure of a parent as personal abandonment, and thus approach their own relationships with exaggerated expectations of rejection; but also by the "sleeper" effects of divorce that occurred during their younger years. It is during the teens, when a child begins to act and think as an adult, that the lasting effects of a badly resolved divorce—parental abandonment, inattention, or overdependence—suddenly jump to the fore.

In some ways, teenagers are luckier than younger children. Though the egocentricity of the youngest teens sees the re-emergence of blame, middle and late teens take no responsibility for the divorce and thus are exempt from the pitfalls of guilt; their increasing objectivity allows them now to recognize their parents as individuals with singular interests and needs; their extrafamilial lives are so active and full that they have countless sources of gratification to draw from to bolster their self-esteem and distance themselves from the troubles at home. And rather than being enmeshed in the distress of the present, teenagers have developed the capacity to think ahead (though not very far), to plan for their own futures, and to look forward to leaving home for college or work.

But in other ways divorce during their impending adulthood works against them; the depth of their adolescent feelings, and a new capacity for self-reflection, deepens their understandable feelings of anger, sadness, embarrassment, betrayal, and shame.[2] If their reactions are severe, they can get into very adult kinds of trouble. Alcohol, drugs, promiscuity, overaggressive behavior are all too available avenues of "escape" for the emotional teenager, and these are, of course, more dangerous *in kind* than the pitfalls of earlier childhood. Additionally, a teenager is old enough to make life-changing, practical decisions but may not have the developmental consistency to make them wisely; the impact may be felt for decades. One obvious example is offered by the high school dropout rate for children of divorce: it is over twice that of students from intact families.

Even if teenagers don't respond in palpably dangerous ways, there's an inherent psychological need that may trap them. The teenager's major task of these years is breaking away, testing himself against family limits and values, to emerge as a whole adult. In some cases, where the divorced parents are themselves entering a "second adolescence," the familiar family discipline can melt away, and their teenagers, left without limits or guidelines, may become deeply insecure.[3] For others, the loss of a stable family home can be critical if they no longer feel they have a safe harbor to run back to from time to time. The net effect is that many teenagers disengage prematurely from their families, while others do so too late—or never.

All in all, divorce is apt to make adolescence more turbulent and stressful for both generations. Sexual tensions within the family run high; money becomes a bigger issue than ever before, as teenagers come upon the exorbitant practicalities of college tuition and support; and through it all, teenagers flirt with the powers and the dangers of the adult world.

THE PSEUDOMATURE TEENAGER

Freddy guns his dirt bike, accelerating past the baseball field. Dumb ninth graders out there in their silly uniforms. He heads for the shopping center on the outskirts of town where he's going to meet his good buddies. Nervously he checks his wallet to make sure it doesn't jiggle out of his pocket. He's got cash—$50 from his latest deal—and he's on his way to buy more dope. It's easy money, dealing drugs. He's got a reputation now with juniors, even seniors at school, who know they can trust him to deliver. He's not a kid anymore. He's bigger than his mother and might even be bigger than his father, though he's not sure; he hasn't seen his father since the separation a year ago. Just think: a year ago he was playing baseball with those wimps and playing catch with his father at night. He can hardly remember being such a little kid. After all, he's fourteen now, and nobody can tell him what to do.

Freddy looks and acts older than his fourteen years. He *feels* older than his fourteen years. Most of the time. There are disturbing moments when Freddy wishes someone would stop him from getting deeper and deeper into a world he doesn't really understand or know how to cope with. When he has those moments, he wishes hard that his father would come home and start playing catch with him again, or some dumb thing like that. There are times when Freddy really wishes he could go home, but his mother is useless. All she does is yell at him for not doing the chores and for staying out so late. No wonder he is home so rarely; who wants to listen to all that nagging? Freddy feels that he's on his own now. Totally.

In adolescence, the acceleration to adulthood often goes too far too fast and then backfires. Rather than moving steadily, if stormily, through the classic sturm und drang of adolescence, part of the teenager becomes overmature, while the other part remains stuck in childhood.[4] Such pseudomature teenagers are deceptive. Grown-ups, on meeting them, will often compliment the single parent by saying, "My, how mature your son (or daughter) is." But at other times these same children will throw childish temper tantrums, act overly dependent, or seek the kind of approval a ten-year-old needs. Adolescent boys like Freddy, with no male figure to hold them in line or show them self-control, may test their masculine aggression beyond normal age-appropriate mischief. Freddy is looking for trouble, and eventually he'll find it.

For girls, the more common pattern is to become pseudosophisticated, run with an older crowd, and enter sexual activity early.[5] Fifteen-year-old Lisa, for example, got so fed up with her divorcing parents' animosities and inattentiveness last year that she dropped out of high school, moved in with another dropout, got pregnant, and had an abortion. "It was so heavy at home I just had to get out of there, but then all we did was sit around getting drunk and pretending to be grown up," says the girl, who has now returned to school. "It's a year I would rather forget."

There are dangers even for the child who doesn't go to the extremes of promiscuity or lawbreaking. Pseudomature adolescents are apt to cut themselves off from their own age groups, thinking of their peers as "babies" unworthy of their own, more mature attention. "Kids my age are dumb," says one eighth grader. "They still think Nixon is President. They like third-grade girls." Many of these young adolescents will seek out older teenagers and older life-styles: "I have a lot of older friends in college," boasts thirteen-year-old Allen. "One guy who was my counselor at camp—he's in college now. He comes to see me. And I hang out a lot with tenth graders. We mess around in a bar on Eighty-sixth and Third [in New York]." Others become loners, prematurely cutting themselves off from their families.[6] "I try to be independent," says thirteen-year-old Kim. "I try to get away from needing anybody, especially my parents. And it's better. I'm sort of all by myself."

Acting cool is the epitome of triumph for teenagers, whose emotions are anything *but* cool. "Chill out" and "cool your buns" are the common expressions of this generation of adolescents, who seem to yearn for an ice pack to reduce the heat of their feelings. But if they succeed, there is danger of cool turning to frost. Overwhelmed by their family problems, some young teenagers of divorce can become rigid in their rejection of emotional expression. They become virtually unreachable in their aloofness and view the world from an unbridgeable distance. Not only are they overcontrolled themselves, but they feel they have to overcontrol everything around them.[7] Any disorder, any peer or sibling behavior they don't approve of, any parental command can make them overreact wildly. "My Mom thinks she owns me," says one fourteen-year-old boy. "I just yell at her and tell her to fuck off."

Socially, such pseudomature adolescents tend to control

their peers and become manipulative and demanding. In some cases, they become preoccupied with their plans for the future, setting out-of-reach goals to escape the present.[8] One fourteen-year-old girl turned down all invitations during the summer so she could read everything possible about law school. A fifteen-year-old boy dropped out of all school sports so he could spend more time cramming for his college SATs—two years away.

Often these teenagers take everything too far. Experimenting with drugs and alcohol is de rigueur at these ages of derring-do, and those substances are so omnipresent in high schools that teenagers are bound to grapple with them at some point. But family disruptions, especially where the hostilities do not decrease after divorce, can cause the adolescent to overindulge dangerously in what are really emotional sedatives so that he never learns to resolve or live with conflict. "Peer-group experimentation with drugs and alcohol may become a daily attempt to hide feelings of shame, suppress anxiety, dull depression, and test the limits in the newly restructured home," wrote two doctors in the *New England Journal of Medicine.*[9] Not all children of divorce become junkies or winos, of course. But during the early and middle teen years, when feelings can run higher—and lower—than at any other age, the temptation to blot out the turmoil of divorce can be overwhelming.

THE CHILDISH TEENAGER

Pseudomaturity is probably the major danger for teenage children of divorce, but it isn't the only danger. Divorce can have quite the opposite effect on the emotional development of young teenagers. Instead of accelerating them too fast toward adulthood, divorce can either stall their progress through adolescence or regress them into the security of childhood.[10] Thirteen-year-old Annie, for example, dropped out of her middle-school dramatic club and gave up after-school soccer so she could instead spend afternoons with her mother at the latter's real estate agency. Another girl, who had started to babysit occasionally to make movie money, doubled her babysitting chores and stopped going to the movies altogether. She was seeking out the company and play patterns of much younger children, disguising her regressive need under the rubric of an age-appropriate job.

Without the encouragement of the departed parent, such teenagers can also become immobilized in decision making. Teenagers are beginning to think for themselves, to pass their own judgments, to firm up their own sense of conscience. But though they may insist dogmatically on their views, underneath they are still unsure. To buttress themselves, they bounce their opinions off their separate parents, not only for reinforcement, but to see how far they can go. When one parent is removed and the other distracted, the teenager loses the security of that sounding board and may either go too far—or not be able to make decisions at all. "Sometimes I can't even think of what to put on in the morning," says fourteen-year-old Chris. "I say to my teacher, 'What do you think—how do I look?' But he always says, 'You look fine,' without noticing what I've got on."

The relationship with the same-sex parent can also become uncommonly—and regressively—close.[11] After her father left home, fifteen-year-old Amy and her mother became almost inseparable. Amy's mother, who had always been rather childlike, became more so. She and Amy began to wear identical clothes, to giggle together over private jokes, to ape each other's mannerisms. Slowly but surely the two shut everybody else out of their lives, including Amy's friends and her father. Instead of going away to boarding school as the family had always intended, Amy decided to stay home with her delighted mother who, for the first time in years, was no longer lonely.

Instead of the two-generation camaraderie that can often develop after divorce, Amy's relationship with her mother was almost infantile. and Amy, rather than moving forward through adolescence, was in fact moving backward.

THE OEDIPAL TEENAGER

Seth is making a birthday cake for his mother. Carefully he runs the spatula, loaded with Instant Double-Fudge Frosting, around the sides, resisting the impulse to lick his fingers. "It'll give me zits," he says sorrowfully. Balloons and crepe paper hang from the curtain rods, and the apartment is so clean it looks as if it's about to be photographed for *House & Garden*. Seth has even bought daffodils for his mother, which he has arranged rather lopsidedly on her bedside table. Nervously he looks at the clock, hoping everything will be letter-perfect by the time she gets home from her public relations job. He sets the table, laying out two place mats, two knives, two forks, two spoons. "This will make her real happy, I bet," says the fourteen-year-old proudly. "A real happy birthday."

On one level, Seth is being the model son. With love and pride he has created this masterpiece for his mother, who means more to him than anyone in the whole world; no smallest detail has escaped his attention. He has even decided to wear a suit for the occasion, partly to honor her, but also because it makes him feel more grown-up. Not for the first time, Seth thinks how nice it is that his father isn't around any longer bossing everyone around. He and his mother get along just fine. In fact, they make a terrific team.

The danger, of course, is obvious. It would be far more appropriate for a boy Seth's age to be mooning over the girl who sits next to him in chemistry class, or to be keeping track of the batting averages of the Yankees. Instead, Seth is devoting far too much attention to his mother; he has become more a miniature lover than an adolescent child.

When the oedipal stage coincides with divorce, boys and their mothers may become uncommonly close. The boy may just naturally assume the father's place in the family, now that he is gone, sitting at his place at the table, acting as the mother's confidant and escort. Single-parent families lack what child psychiatrists call the "echelon structure" of an intact family. Without two parents to head the household and share decisions for the family, children move up the ladder to become, if not peers of the parent, at least junior partners. And whereas younger children often try and remind themselves of their fathers by acting out their roles, the impact on adolescents is different: many adolescent boys are delighted to replace the father altogether, to win, in the absence of competition, the generational war that breaks out when boys reach puberty. Some shrink from this scary new role, but just as many don't.

Parents often contribute to this process, for coopting the teenaged child into an adult role is an easy escape from loneliness for many single parents. Teenagers look mature, are eager to supply advice, and can be sympathetic and supportive. The danger comes when they start living their parents' lives rather than their own.

Often the egocentricity of young teenagers makes them feel that only they can restore parental happiness. Wallerstein and Kelly describe one fourteen-year-old boy who tried to rescue his mother from a chronic postdivorce depression: "Immediately following the father's departure from the household, Tom began to assume the role of a protective adult in his mother's troubled life. Soon he began to check on her social activities, to monitor her telephone calls, to sit in his father's place at the dinner table, and on occasion, to lie down on the sofa beside her to comfort her. Gradually he became increasingly preoccupied with his mother's mental and physical health. He was jealous of her other relationships, and his worry about her reached phobic proportions as he began to stay up at night to await her return. At the same time his attachments to his friends and his interest in his school activities lessened."[12]

This boy's case is, of course, extreme. But because so many children of divorce live with their single mothers, lesser variations on this theme are carried out time and again. Just as girls practice their feminine roles on their fathers, boys practice on their mothers. This syndrome is especially pronounced if the single mother encourages the boy to fill in the male void not only around the house but in her social life as well. "We got to be a pretend couple," says one mother whose thirteen-year-old son accompanied her everywhere in the year following her divorce. "Now that I look back on it, it was a bit creepy." If the boy is an only or the oldest child, the oedipal situation can intensify. "It makes me nervous now when I give him a hug," says the mother of another thirteen-year-old. "He responds more like a sort of lover than a kid. I want to show him affection and support but at the same time I want to push him away."

THE TORN TEENAGER

Molly is packing to go home from boarding school for Christmas vacation. She's planning to spend a few days with her mother and stepfather in Southampton, then a few days with her father in Scarsdale. Then she plans to visit her father's parents for New Year's because they keep complaining that since the divorce they never get to see her. Bewildered by all these moves, her roommate asks her which she considers home. Molly thinks for a minute, then replies, "School."

Molly is one of the thousands of children of divorce who spend their vacation time trekking from one parent to the other. In the routine they describe as "parent-hopping," these divorce veterans spend countless hours in bus stations, airports, and train stations, stretching to meet their filial obligations. Some resent it enormously. "You don't see the parents freezing their asses off on some train platform Christmas morning," says one sixteen-year-old who splits the holiday between his mother and father. "It's the kids who have the hassle." Others, like Molly, don't mind too much. "You get to a certain age and you can pretty well plan your own time," says the fifteen-year-old. "I try to be fair to each parent and give them the same amount of time. The rest is my own." Still others simply won't do it. Teenagers are old enough to call their own visitation shots, and many have summer or holiday jobs that keep them rooted in one place; others just state flatly that they want to stay wherever home is.

Content with seeing the part-time parent infrequently, teenagers are in many ways luckier than younger children who either yearn for their noncustodial parent or dismiss him out of anger. The visitation problem many teenagers face is the opposite one of obligation and loyalty. They are finally old enough to realize objectively what it takes to raise a child—the time, the effort, the money. By midadolescence teenagers also understand that their parents may need them as much as they need their parents, if not more. Their parents have now become recognizable individuals, with their own vulnerabilities and dependencies. And teenagers can feel a great responsibility to be good company to both their single parents, sometimes to the exclusion of their own age groups.

The loyalty dilemma can be as simple as one evening's worth of company. Sixteen-year-old Charlie, for example, spent Sunday with his father, and as the day drew to a close, his father asked him to stay on to watch a baseball game on television. His mother, however, had asked Charlie to act as bartender for a dinner party she was giving that night. Charlie felt trapped. His father was lonely and wanted him to be a baseball pal. His mother was nervous about giving a dinner party alone. And Charlie himself wanted to go to the movies with friends. Charlie solved it by going back to his mother's for the cocktail period, then returning later to his father's to pick up the game in the fifth inning. He missed the movie altogether. "It's nice to be needed and loved and all that," says Charlie, "but there's only so much of me to go around." Rather than letting either parent down, many teenagers flee to the neutral ground of friends. "My dad wanted me to spend the weekend with him on Fire Island. My mom wanted me to go with her to the Vineyard," says seventeen-year-old Mark. "I called up my best friend in East Hampton and asked if I could go there. That way neither Mom nor Dad felt I was playing favorites."

Where the relationship with the custodial parent has been overly close, older teenagers may experience more than the normal wrench at leaving home when the time comes. Lonely single mothers especially can make it very difficult for their children to leave them, even to go to college. Eighteen-year-old Nell, for example, feels so guilty about leaving her mother all alone that she is consciously doing badly in her high school work. "My grades have gotten progressively worse throughout my four years of high school," says the brown-haired teenager. "A lot of this has to do with my ambivalence about going away. By keeping my grades low I'm theoretically trying to keep myself in high school." Another college-bound teenage girl is also having mother-inspired second thoughts. "I'd planned to go to college and live with my father next year," says seventeen-year-old Beth, "but my Mom laid this big guilt trip on me. She says, 'If you move out I might not be able to get alimony.' Now I don't know what to do."

If teenage daughters have difficulty getting out from under their mothers, sons often have just as much difficulty living up to the often latent expectations of their fathers. Divorced fathers who paid little attention to their sons as young children can suddenly become demanding superfathers in adolescence. The pressure is on. The father's ego is at stake in his son's achievement, and without day-to-day contact, many single fathers pack all their need to influence and control their adolescent sons into the little visitation time they have together. Eighteen-year-old David, for example, positively dreads the weekends he sees his father, because he has to defend himself constantly. "All he does is gripe on me, and I don't want to listen to it," says the high school senior. "He wants to know why my grades aren't better, why I didn't go out for lacrosse, if I still spend too much time listening to music. If he lived at home we could have one hassle a day. Now we have to have them all in one day."

The multiples of parents and their new partners can also drag out a teenager's triumphs—and failures. Andy circulates between the homes of his mother and her boyfriend, his stepfather, and his father and stepmother. When he gets a good report card, he gets lavish praise from five different adults. But when he does badly, as he did this winter, he dreads his visitation route. "If you have one set of parents then you get one dose of yelling and it's all over," says the college freshman. "I have five people in three houses who give me disappointed looks and heavy sighs. I go through it in one house and then move on to the disappointed looks in the next. It's going to be a whole summer of sighing."

THE MONEY-WISE TEENAGER

Paula is looking covetously at a pair of painter's pants in the window of a store she passes each day on her way to and from high school. They're on sale for $16.95, but she doesn't have the money to buy them. She sighs and hurries home. She understands that since the divorce there just isn't as much money as there used to be, what with supporting two households and all that. And Paula won't bug her mother about the pants, because she knows her mother is doing the best she can. Still, she'd sure like those pants. If it weren't for the divorce . . .

Teenagers of divorce are very savvy about money. Being

halfway out of the nest and probably with some experience in a job of their own, they know just how much it costs, if not to live, at least to buy what they want. Unlike younger children, who see money spent as proof of love, who want everything shiny new instead of used, many teenagers, in self-defense, congratulate themselves on how little money they spend on themselves and point with pride to their bartered or second-hand bargains. They are forced to take money management seriously. And they are very much aware that divorce has made them poorer.

It is frustrating for teenagers to start on a course of downward mobility. In this intense period of peer conformity in terms of clothes, life-style, and possessions, teenagers are deeply conscious of how their families stack up economically against others. "We live okay and we are fed," says one sixteen-year-old. "But our parents are starting all over again while our friends' families are on their feet." Teenagers are also well aware of the costs of divorce and the games their parents play. "My father is talking about getting a divorce for *our* sakes. Bullshit!" says fourteen-year-old Abe. "It's going to cost a shit-load of money."

Continuity can be all important to the teenager who is experiencing so many physical and emotional changes in himself. And the economics of divorce can be very painful. Dividing up the spoils of marriage often means selling the family house, for example, a traumatic experience for a teenager who sees his entire history being auctioned on the divorce block. One sixteen-year-old boy took it upon himself to sort out all the remnants of the household for a garage sale, neatly tagging everything from hand-painted trays to his old tin soldiers. Over and over he chanted in his mind, "Off with the old, on with the new," to make himself feel better. A fourteen-year-old girl chose a photo essay of her house in New Hampshire for a school project, poignantly using a shot of a child's empty wooden swing for the cover with a "For Sale" sign behind it. "It really makes me sad," she says. "I don't think I'll be able to adapt very well to living somewhere else. I've lived in that house all my life. I love it. It's my home. But Dad doesn't want Mom to have the house. And she doesn't want him to have it."

Education during the teens—and getting someone to pay for it—may become a sore point. Teenagers are overconscious that they are soon going to have to answer the childhood question "What are you going to be when you grow up?" and many are nervous about the possibility that they won't have the educational background for a successful career. They may not know what they want to do, but they want to be prepared for something. And divorce often decreases the income available for the teenager's education, forcing him to go to a college his parents can afford, rather than one he prefers. This is frequently a point of bitterness among divorced kids. "I wanted to go to Connecticut College but Dad said he couldn't afford it," says an eighteen-year-old boy. "I ended up at a state university where there is far less for me to choose from, especially in business courses. If they had stayed together, I bet I'd be at Connecticut College now."

Often this newly revived anger is directed specifically at the parent who the teenager feels is willfully jeopardizing his or her own future. "I have to get financial aid for college because my father pays less than $10,000 a year in child support, even though he's a top executive at a Madison Avenue advertising agency," says a college-bound seventeen-year-old. "You'd think a father would care more about a kid's future." Some determined teenagers even take their parents to court. One young woman sued her father for not paying her law-school tuition, to which he had consented orally during the divorce proceedings. "I don't like to be suing my father, but I'm forced to," says the law-school freshman.[13]

With their rising sophistication about money, many teen-

agers think of themselves as economic hostages of their parents. To survive, they learn to adapt to the wealthier parent's
quirks, to dance to his tune, to spend manipulative effort to ensure their continuing support. As a result, in these years of high
personal standards, they feel hypocritical. "I hate the way I
have to toady up to my father, but it's the only way to make
sure he'll pay for college," says an eighteen-year-old boy. "I
even told him I'd registered as a Republican to get him on my
side." Another boy spent his whole last semester as a high
school senior commuting to his father's house on weekends. "I
cut my hair, wore buttondown shirts and even told him I liked
my stepmother," says the boy, now a freshman at the University of Vermont. "I hated myself for doing it, but you've got to
be practical. He's the one with the bucks."

Any couple may wield the power of the purse strings in order
to keep a teenager in line. With divorce, however, such money
manipulation becomes even more deadly if the separate parents hold differing expectations for the child. Alex, for example, has dropped out of college altogether and moved to San
Francisco to look for work. "Mom said she'd pay the tuition if I
concentrated on the arts," says the boy. "Dad said he'd pay
only if I majored in business. There was no way I could do both,
and besides, what I wanted to do was communications. So I just
split. I can't stand the hassle."

Money also complicates relationships between teenagers and
their parents' new partners. Teenagers often complain, for example, that their father's new girlfriend gets the presents from
him that *they* deserve. "It's the little things we want, like a
Walkman or a new pair of jeans," says a fifteen-year-old girl.
"But everything we ask for, Dad turns around and buys for her
instead." When the parent is spending more money in his postdivorce life than he did on his intact family life, teenagers feel
not only gypped but resentful. "Sue made him put in a swimming pool for her. Then he bought her a Mazda RX 7 and a

Datsun 283 for him. His is black. Hers is rust. I say that's disgusting," says fourteen-year-old Lucy indignantly. "Sue redecorated the bedroom and is putting in an entire wall of closets with mirrors on all the doors. She redid the bathroom because she didn't like the shower. She wants one big enough for two with a revolving door. God. It's like, 'Where are the tennis courts, Dad. I'm waiting for them.' "

Even parents themselves don't always escape the emotional pain of the teenagers' dollar wars. Self-serving teenagers may swing their loyalties to the parent who can benefit them the most. Whereas parents choose the custody and visitation arrangements for younger children, teenagers often choose their own, and they sometimes base their decisions on material rewards. One fourteen-year-old boy, who for three years had moved back and forth between parents in a joint custody arrangement, decided instead to move in with his father permanently. "Face it," says the boy. "Mom has one tiny apartment and one television set. Dad has a whole house, three TVs, an Apple computer, and a Betamax. My friends and I have much more to do there." Sometimes parents dangle these material rewards intentionally. "Dad said I could have my own room if I lived with him," says a thirteen-year-old girl. "My Mom said I could have my own phone. I chose the phone."

THE "MISIDENTIFIED" TEENAGER

Jack can't decide what to wear to a wedding his mother is taking him to. Should he look preppy and wear khakis and a tweed jacket? Or should he look more punk and wear a T-shirt and army fatigues? It's hard for Jack to make up his mind about most everything these days. That Vietnamese kid in his class, for instance. Should he just keep feeling sorry for him because of the war and everything, or should he let himself get pissed off because the kid keeps swiping his football pads? And what about yesterday, when a guy seemed to make a pass at Jack's girlfriend? He lost his temper completely and almost punched the guy out. But Jack thinks of himself as quite a cowardly person. Who is he really? What does he think? What should he think? More and more lately, Jack has been wondering what his father would think about all this. But since the divorce, Jack only sees his father once in a while. Jack shrugs and decides to dress punk—then puts his jacket on over the T-shirt so he won't give anyone the wrong impression.

Much of Jack's confusion is normal for a teenager. Not only is he trying to resolve just what masculine behavior means, but he is trying to sort out his social, ethical, and philosophical attitudes as well. Many of those attitudes are influenced by their acceptance—or rejection—by his peers, which puts an even greater burden on Jack's sometimes paralyzing self-consciousness. Like other teenagers, Jack is going through what psychoanalyst Erik Erikson called "identity crisis," a developmental task of adolescence so essential that if it is not resolved in these teenage years it may never be.

Parents are all important now to these teenagers who need a supportive forum to extrapolate the best from their confusion of ideas in order to form a whole sense of themselves. As they leave childhood, teenagers are intensely curious about their genetic, intellectual, and emotional heritages, which they interpret as signposts to their own impending roles as adults. Divorce considerably complicates this search for identity, especially if one parent is inattentive or entirely absent. Even if the noncustodial parent keeps in fairly close touch, the absence of day-to-day contact can make the relationship tense; the teenager may be cautious, afraid of alienating the parent, while the parent may be just as reluctant to rock a potentially loaded boat. As a result, the relationship can be very superficial just when the teenager needs something solid to butt up against. Fifteen-year-old Stanley, for example, dances between the raindrops with his father, even though they speak on the telephone almost daily. "Our relationship is skin-deep—we chat about school," says the boy. "We rarely deal with each other on a real level. Neither of us has taken the step toward confrontation." Even face to face, the two generations have not connected. "I get depressed, withdrawn, when I visit him," says Stanley. "We sort of sit around, have a Sunday dinner with lots of superficial chat, but not about anything. It's a semirelief for me when I leave." After seeing *Ordinary People,* another boy, eighteen, was disturbed by the lack of communication between father and son in the film and spontaneously called his own father long-distance to say he loved him. "What's the matter?" his father quickly responded. "Are you on drugs?"

Matters grow worse if the missing parent doesn't maintain contact. In a syndrome psychiatrists call "foreclosure of identity," children of either sex may adopt the real or imagined attitudes of the departed parent rather than struggling to find their own. Where the parent has left before the child reached five—the period of identification with the same-sex parent—the uncritical absorption in adolescence of the parent's fantasized characteristics can be destructive.[14] This is particularly severe as a "sleeper" effect, since the longer it's been since the child has known the parent, the less realistic will his memories of the parent be. If, for example, the absent mother or father has been perceived as primarily sexual, the child becomes pseudomature and sexually active him (or her) self before there is the capacity for any real affection or commitment. Or if a boy, for instance, perceives his father as aggressive, his identity foreclosure may take on a hostile tone. Such a boy is more apt to disobey any authority, and even to lie, cheat, and steal.[15] Or he might direct his anger at his mother,[16] and develop a general anger at all females. Bob's father, for example, dropped out of his life when the boy was five. Now fourteen, Bob idolizes his absent father and remembers (or thinks he does) that his father had nothing but contempt for his mother. Almost six feet tall and very skinny, Bob in his adolescence has become what he thinks his father was: a woman-hater. Of his older sister Bob says, "She's a bitch. She's full of it. I can't stand her." He has little communication with his mother. "I don't tell her anything." Even girls his own age don't escape his "father's" wrath. "The girls are all mad or they're schizoid," says Bob. "I break up with girls all the time. The best way is to call them up and say, 'Fuck you.'"

And what of children who have never known a parent at all? The adolescent search for identity often impels them, like adoptees, to try to track down their whole identities—to look, literally, for their missing halves. One boy who knew his parents had divorced because his father was an alcoholic began to make nightly rounds of different bars in the futile hope of finding him. Another boy who had endured ten years without getting a single birthday card from his father suddenly at fourteen left his mother to live with the parent he hardly knew. This last pattern is actually quite common, and such rejections can fall heavily on the custodial parent. Writer Jane Adams watched her fourteen-year-old son turn from a happy, loving child into a sullen and resentful teenager before he left her to live with the father who had paid little attention to him. "There is no anger, but that will come later," Adams wrote in *The New York Times.* "Anger that his father, with the simple words, 'I want you, son,' can do what she, who has loved and wanted him and loves him still, cannot."

As these examples—and the statistics—indicate, it is boys who most often lack same-sex role models in the crucial years of adolescence. Adolescent girls without mothers seem to have less difficulty. Not only do girls in father-custody homes see their noncustodial parent more than do their male counterparts in mother-custody homes,[17] but single fathers are far more apt to be helped out by female friends or relatives than single

170

mothers, providing an array of surrogate role models for their daughters to pattern themselves after.[18]

It is the absence of the father rather than the mother that seems most disruptive of the identity process in adolescent girls, especially where the father has left before the girl reached five. Though it is common for many daughters of divorce to become sexually aware, if not precocious, before their counterparts in intact families, daughters whose fathers left very early can at the extreme become downright promiscuous.[19] Rather than slowly establishing a sexual identity through interaction with a loving and attentive father, these girls often enter heterosexual relationships prematurely and with males a good deal older than they are. In resolving their identity crises, these girls are apt to think of themselves as highly sexual and more sophisticated than other girls their own age. But this sophistication is hollow.

THE OVERSEXED TEENAGER

Tracey and Stan pull into her driveway after the movies on Saturday night. Tracey groans when she sees a strange car parked near the back door and the lights on in the living room. "Who's here?" asks Stan. Tracey shrugs. "Oh, some new guy Mom met at work," she says. Stan laughs. "Boy, your mom sure is a pistol. Different guy every weekend. She must be wearing them out." Tracey is silent at his side. "What's the matter, Tracey? Jealous?" asks Stan. "Very funny," says Tracey, but her voice doesn't sound amused at all.

The discomfort and embarrassment that preadolescents feel at their parents' sexuality intensifies greatly during adolescence. Whereas preadolescents for the most part fantasize about sex, many teenagers are sexually active, salving their lofty and troubled consciences with the comforting rationalizations of love and commitment. But their parents' seeming promiscuity tears at the very framework they are clinging to to sanction their own sexual behavior. If sex can be reduced to an impersonal sport, an act of little meaning that bears within it none of the stuff of dreams, teenagers may panic at the loss of their illusions.

And Tracey is panicking. At seventeen, Tracey is already "playing house" with Stan. They have fumbled their way through intercourse a few times, Stan proudly wearing his newly bought condoms, and they talk about marriage, what their babies will look like, what sort of job Stan will have. But suddenly their talk seems hollow. Tracey is worried that she is fooling herself, that the example of her parents' divorce may make it impossible for her to follow through on her fantasy commitment, that her mother's frivolous attitude toward sex will become her own attitude. Tracey suddenly feels very uneasy about her future.

"Let's go to your house," she says quickly to Stan. "Will your parents be asleep?" "Probably," he says, checking his watch. "But I don't have any rubbers." "Who cares?" says Tracey.

Teenagers watch closely the perceived successes or failures of their parents and the "failure" of divorce can signal clearly to them that they, too, will be unable to sustain love and commitment. The obvious sexuality of the parent creates problems of its own. Out of a sense of competition or defiance, teenagers may feel compelled to begin their own active sex lives prematurely, or, in a swell of moral outrage, to divert their sexual energies into more destructive channels. Wallerstein and Kelly found that the behavior changes in teenagers who felt betrayed by their parents' "indecent" conduct sometimes took the form of actual delinquency, running away from home, and acute depression.[20]

There is nothing new about the well-known increase in teenage sexuality. But the children of divorce have taken sexual liberation a step farther than even today's hedonistic norm. A recent study at the University of Connecticut,[21] for example, found that students whose parents had divorced admitted to more sexual activity with more partners than students from either intact families or families where one parent had died. As noted previously, other research has confirmed that teenage girls, expecially, become sexually active at a younger age and more frequently than girls from intact families.

Early sexuality can take on all sorts of implications for teenagers of divorce. Some of them, especially girls, seek it out as a way of replacing the parent in terms of lost physical contact and comfort. "I didn't care what the guys did to me just so long as I got hugged," says one young woman who had had two abortions by the age of seventeen. At the extreme, other teenagers, again, especially girls, can try to replace the lost family unit by prematurely forming one of their own. But it rarely works. The divorce rate for adolescents married at seventeen is three times the rate for those who marry in their early twenties.

THE RIVALROUS TEENAGER

All teenagers are naturally apprehensive about their sexual attractiveness and their ability to perform. But in divorce, that anxiety can be heightened by the ever younger ages of the parents' partners. In an increasing trend, single mothers are now almost as likely as single fathers to choose younger lovers, lovers who are often perilously close in age to the children. Oedipal possibilities can reemerge. And the comforting feeling, so essential to a teenager, that the parent is of a different generation can be destroyed by the presence of his or her Puma-footed partner who has more in common with the teenager's generation than that of the parents. This blurring of the sexual age lines between parent and child, adults and adolescents, may seem heady stuff to the grown-up who wants to feel young, but can terrify the inexperienced teenager who wants to feel old—but not that old. One single mother took a twenty-seven-year-old lover, and her teenage daughter panicked when her own boyfriend quipped, "Hey, maybe I should date your mom."[22]

Divorce can also lock parent and teenager—especially fathers and sons—in a subtle sexual duel. The recently divorced adult is often just as anxious as the teenager about his own sexual allure and performance. The parent feels threatened by the sexual bravado of the teenager; the teenager feels threatened by the greater experience and power of the parent. Often the generations react by competing overtly, trying to outdo each other in conquests. "You wouldn't believe the things I've tried," one seventeen-year-old boy challenged the father. "Maybe I should give you lessons." Fathers and sons can even compete for the same women in a blatant face-off between the generations. "I never bring any girlfriend around my father," says an eighteen-year-old boy. "I've been burned. I introduced him to one girl and the next thing I knew he was taking her out. I mean, really, that's sick."

Teenage girls and their mothers are more apt to engage in a negative sexual war. Though flirting with each other's partners is a common generational gauntlet in divorce, the challenge usually stops short of seduction. Whereas the number of sexual liaisons is deemed a competitive plus between men, the same number is a minus to women. The double standard lives, especially between mother and daughter, and neither lets the other forget it. To provoke her sexually active mother, one sixteen-year-old dressed in ever more suggestive clothing until the mother finally reacted. "You look like a whore," the mother said to the heavily made-up daughter. The retort was quick. "Who do you think I learned it from?" One study of mother-daughter relationships found that the category most marked by strife was that between divorced mother and adolescent daughter, worse than the same relationships in either intact or widowed families.[23]

To avoid being unwilling witnesses to their parents' sexuality, some teenagers sabotage their parents' relationships. By exorcising the source of the parent's sexual interest, these teenagers reason, they return the parent to his or her former state of asexuality. Beyond the rage they often feel toward the new partner for causing the breakup in the first place, teenagers also see the new partner as an impediment to reestablishing a secure home base. Teenage girls tend to practice psychological warfare. "I pretend not to hear Alice when she asks me to do something," says sixteen-year-old Ellen of her father's new partner. "When she gives me something, I either say it doesn't fit or leave it behind when I leave. It'll take a while but I'll break her down." Boys are often less subtle. One teenager disconnected the ignition wires in his father's girlfriend's car and repeatedly left obscene messages on her answering machine in a thinly disguised voice. Another took to locking the back door when his mother went out for the evening, presuming that she wouldn't take a key with her. "It worked," the boy says proudly. "She had to wake me up to get in, and if she had a guy with her, just seeing me turned him off."

THE RELIEVED TEENAGER

The older a teenager gets, the less he or she is distressed by the parent's sexuality. By eighteen or nineteen, a teenager recognizes the parent's need for the same intimacy and companionship the teenager wants for himself. If the divorce has been transacted with a minimum of acrimony and the parent has not been too distracted, such support for the parent may occur earlier. And for many adolescents, a new and seemingly permanent partner for the parent is a plus. Adding a new adult to the household eases the burden on teenagers who would rather get on with their own lives. "Thank God Mom has someone to talk to now," says a sixteen-year-old boy. "I can go out at night

175

again without feeling guilty." The improved mood of the parent and the reestablishment of some sense of family routine is also welcomed by the teenager who now feels he has regained a home base. "Do you realize this is the first time in a month that we've actually all sat down to dinner together?" one eighteen-year-old boy said to his sisters, his astonished mother, and her new partner. The children all raised their glasses in a celebratory toast.

On a more practical level, teenagers can also benefit from the friends and contacts of a new parental partner, ending the isolation that often marks the single-parent family. "I've met tons of new people since George arrived on the scene," says eighteen-year-old Andrew. "He's really made an effort. I have contacts now for summer jobs, recommendations for college, maybe even some permanent jobs for the future." And the simple easing of household maintenance can be a breath of welcome air to teenagers who have been overly depended on by their single parents. "Every time Mom gets a new boyfriend I say, 'How do you feel about storm windows?' " says a sixteen-year-old.

Though teenagers are certainly more adaptable to change than younger children, they are not above the pain of numerous attachments to and separations from their parents' various partners. They may seem worldly wise and independent, yet teenagers still yearn for the security of adult love. Some distance themselves from their parent's partners to set up a defensive buffer against potential loss; others try too hard to be liked. One single mother was astonished when her fifteen-year-old son exploded into angry tears after she told him she had broken up with the man she'd been seeing off and on for six months. "Don't you see that every person you go out with I consider my possible stepfather?" he yelled at her. "With every one I try to be that much more caring so he'll like me, so we'll get off to a good start. Then you just go and split up. Don't expect me to love any other man of yours or get too close to him, because as soon as I do, you'll take him away from me!" When his rage had subsided, his mother apologized for not realizing the stake her son had in what she considered casual, companionable relationships. And both were quite relieved. "I finally realized that Mom was just going out and didn't want to get married," says the boy, "so I bagged the whole thing. I was exhausted trying to be a son to each one. Her boyfriends became just people. The whole thing was resolved by ignoring the father image and saying, 'You're just another person.' I'm relieved I don't have to make another commitment."

Teenagers often develop chameleonlike personalities, adapting to the different habits and quirks of their parents' partners. But though flexibility is a personality trait worth developing, constantly adjusting to multiple partners can take it too far. Mark and his mother, for example, lived for a year with a car-racing enthusiast, and Mark spent his fifteenth year in a grease pit at the track. When he was sixteen, he and his mother moved in with a classics professor who insisted that Mark wear a coat and tie to dinner and study Greek. Throughout the changes, Mark frequently visited his father, who lives in a SoHo loft in New York where the atmosphere is laid-back "attitude" and cocaine. "Sometimes I feel like Superman dashing into a phone booth to change clothes for the next personality," says eighteen-year-old Mark. "But I've learned to deal with people, to fit in so I won't be an outsider. In a way it's good because I can get along with almost anybody now. But in a way it bothers me because you're so programmed to change yourself to please other people that you're not quite sure who you really are yourself."

HOW PARENTS CAN HELP

Easing teenagers through the upheavals of divorce is not as difficult as doing so for younger children. If the adolescent has had a fairly stable background before entering these turbulent years, divorce, though upsetting, should not seriously disturb this last phase of childhood.

Divorce can even be positive for many single parents and their adolescent children, who often enjoy a close and healthy relationship. The emotional ups and downs of divorce can make adults sympathetic to the turmoil the adolescent is going through and vice versa. In a climate of mutual generational understanding and support, the single-parent family can become more cohesive than many intact families. If the divorce has been a "good" one, if the parental hostilities have not dominated the household, and if the children see the splitup as a reasonable solution to their parents' unhappiness, the children often benefit. "I like it this way because I get to see each parent separately," says thirteen-year-old Kim. "It's more free and closer at the same time."

Honesty on the part of both parents does much to dispel a teenager's lurking feelings of inadequacy. At this age, children are capable of understanding the gray areas of life and the ambivalence that surrounds so many of the reasons for contemporary divorce. The words "We just grew apart" or "We wanted different things out of life" ring true to teenagers who are finding those same differences in their own lives. Similarly, they can understand the more extreme reasons for divorce and welcome the relief from a family disrupted by alcoholism, mental disease, or violence. Teenagers really want to get on with their own lives, and family situations that hold them back or drain them of their energies can harm them far more than divorce. At this age especially, divorce can be seen by the children as the successful resolution of a problem that cannot be solved any other way.

Unloading too much critical appraisal of the other parent on teenagers is a temptation single parents should avoid, however. Though teenagers finally seem mature and independent, they still want to idolize their parents as role models or images to improve on in their own adult lives. The denigration of one parent by the other not only strains a teenager's sense of loyalty to both, but undermines his search for a positive identity just when the search is at its height. Just as young teenagers hunt through their parents' bureau drawers looking for clues to their secret or sexual lives, older teenagers probe the psyches of their parents to find out where they came from and where they are going. And the news should be as good as it can possibly be.

Teenagers are also incredibly sentimental about their childhoods, recognizing that the state of juvenile dependency they were so eager to grow out of is one they are now reluctant to leave. The wise parent respects that. In one of the sleeper effects of divorce, teenagers whose parents divorced when the child was much younger can suddenly express anger at an unsuspecting single parent for having denied them the comfort of intact family memories. "I can hardly remember what it was like having my Dad in the house," complained fifteen-year-old Bob to his startled mother. "I think I remember him swinging us around on the bed. But that's it from my childhood. One snap. One picture."

Though it is hardly reasonable to expect a single parent to share happy memories or leave photographs of the former spouse on the mantelpiece, making those souvenirs of childhood available to the teenager can be very comforting, especially when they include *both* parents and the child. They are proof that he or she was loved jointly by both and bounced as a baby on the parents' knees; that like other intact families, they went on picnics and to amusement parks. Proof of family solidarity, however fleeting, gives teenagers of divorce more confidence that they will be able to establish families of their own and, against inherited odds, even make them work.

It is also helpful to realize that the ease with which teenagers seem to adapt to moving from household to household is deceptive; in fact, the emphasis on what they consider to be home actually intensifies, as adolescents spend their energies experimenting with the unfamiliar outside world. Simple physical stability in the home—right down to the furnishings—can be very important to the teenager, even if it conflicts with the newly single parent's desire for change. One single mother merely rearranged the furniture in the living room, moving the father's favorite chair to the garage. Her teenage daughter was furious and promptly moved everything back—including the chair. "You just can't change everything all at once," she yelled at her astonished mother. "This is my home, too, you know."

Beyond physical mementos, teenagers crave the history of their childhoods. On the brink of severing family dependencies, teenagers want reassurance that their parents protected them—and wanted them—when they were too young to protect themselves. Such guarantees are surprisingly hard to come by after divorce, as many parents' recollections of the teenagers' childhoods are clouded with their own dissatisfaction. It is tragic that just when a teenager is struggling to build a positive sense of identity, embittered parents may seem to go out of their way to tear it down. One fourteen-year-old girl was told by her mother that she only married the father because she had to. "Mom told me she got pregnant in a boat under the Verrazano Bridge and that Dad's parents made them get married," says the girl. "It doesn't make me feel too good to know they didn't marry each other because they loved each other or because they wanted me." Eighteen-year-old Carl carries an even greater burden from his divorced parents, whose unceasing hostilities have lowered his self-esteem as far as it can go. "All the family troubles started April 12, 1964, the day I was born," he says. "My mother loves to tell me I was never supposed to be, that she had an abortion and it didn't work. My father gets his jollies by describing how my mother beat me as a baby so he had to take me away. I guess I've been apologizing for being born all my life."

Not surprisingly, teenagers of divorce often approach their own heterosexual relationships with trepidation.[24] More than children in intact or widowed families, these children need the encouragement of their parents to risk a commitment of their own. Cynicism from parents has a way of trickling down—and sticking. "Sometimes I think my parents have led me not to be serious with a girl," says fifteen-year-old Seth. "I haven't been with a girl longer than two months, sometimes only a week. I've seen so many things fall apart." Other teenagers take their lack of trust in relationships to an extreme and become obsessively possessive. "I can't stand it if my girlfriend even looks at anyone else," confesses a college freshman. "I know I'll lose her if I don't get over this possessiveness, but I keep thinking she's about to bug out on me. And I just can't take any more losses."

The subject of marriage elicits even more caution from teenagers, especially as they grow closer to the age of marital possibilities. For many, reality has replaced romance. "I won't marry until I can support myself financially," says seventeen-year-old Allison. "I've seen Mom go through that—going back to school, working, making ends meet. Nothing is guaranteed with people. I don't want to fall into the trap of being dependent and then having to dig out." Eighteen-year-old Rex is just as adamant that his future wife have a job—and a good one. "I'm not about to get saddled with alimony," he says. "I'm not going to marry anyone who isn't at least a vice-president."

Sadly, but perhaps again realistically, modern teenagers do not think of marriage as the Valentine message of lifelong love. Instead, they use the word "try" over and over again in talking about marriage, as if ordering a new dish they might not like and could send back. "I definitely think I want to try marriage," says eighteen-year-old Alice. "But I'll work at it. Divorce is just an easy way out and I'll be more aware than people who don't have divorced parents." Sixteen-year-old Laura is just as cautiously optimistic. "Just because my parents' mar-

181

riage went wrong doesn't mean mine will," she says firmly. "I'll give it a try, take my time, and make sure I really love him."

There is above all a pervading cynicism among teenagers, a sense of resigned inevitability that though they may enter marriage with the highest of hopes, these hopes are doomed to be dashed. "I'll probably get married, and I'll probably get divorced," says fourteen-year-old Peter. "Everybody does."

STEPLIVES
Pitfalls and Failed Expectations

The setting is perfect. The man has brought his two teenage sons, the woman her ten-year-old son and eleven-year-old daughter on a skiing holiday in Vermont. Together they've rented a big log cabin, complete with fireplace, deep couches, a closetful of Scrabble and Monopoly. The kids take lessons in the morning; they all ski together in the afternoons, and devour vats of spaghetti in the evening. Everyone's getting along famously—just as the father and mother had in mind. Tonight's the night, they decide, to tell the children that though they have come on this vacation as separate families, they will soon be a united one. "We have something to tell you," they say to the children over dinner. Forks are suspended in midair as the children brace for the words they already know are coming. "We have wonderful news," the parents push on. "We're getting married. We're all going to be one happy family."

The children, old enough to know what politeness demands,

try not to let their respective parents down. "Congratulations," the oldest boy says to his father. "That's nice," says the daughter to her mother. The other children remain silent, staring at their plates. "Come on, now, let's celebrate," the father insists. "Let's have some champagne." "No, thanks, Dad," his younger son says. "I'm beat. I think I'll turn in." "Me, too," say two of the other children, leaving the table. Only the youngest remains. "How much change do you have, Mom?" asks the ten-year-old. "I better call Dad to tell him the bad news."

Remarriage has become an accepted—and even expected—ritual of American life. Some 1,300 recycled couples with children under eighteen retie the marital knot *each day* now, bringing the total numbers of the country's steppopulation to 35 million adults sharing between them 7 million children. One child out of every six now lives in a stepfamily.[1] So common has remarriage become that it even has its own jargon. Trying to get away from the negative stereotyping of the prefix "step," which in Old English meant "bereaved orphan," such families are now called "blended" or "reconstituted" families. But simply updating the words does not make the situation easier. That the situation *isn't* easy is reflected in the statistics on remarrying: for all that five out of six divorced men and three out of four women remarry within three years, the divorce rate is higher for second marriages than for first marriages. This may be partially explained by divorce veterans' being more apt to divorce again; but more than one school of thought attributes the increased marital fallout rate to the problems inherent in trying to make one family out of two.

Juggling the needs of his, hers, and eventually their children can add unendurable stress to a new union whose promise for the future seems sandbagged by the past. One study found that couples with children on both sides, whether the children lived permanently with them or "visited" on weekends and holidays, were the most likely to report high rates of marital conflict, disagreements about child rearing, dissatisfaction with the

spouse's parental role, and problems with the differential treatment of natural children and stepchildren."These parents complained that so much time was being spent working out the
stepparent role that there was little time or energy left to resolving marital difficulties," the study concluded flatly.[2]

Often, the happy newly married couple is unaware of the
pitfalls that lie immediately ahead and promptly falls into them.
Increasingly, they are discovering they are not alone. Workshops and self-help groups for stepparents and even entire
stepfamilies have sprung up all over the country. The Stepfamily Association of America now offers solace and advice to
2,000 members and sends out a quarterly newsletter, "The
Stepfamily Bulletin," filled with tips on family life the second
time around. How-to books for adults, with variations on the
word "step" in their titles (*Stepping into Stepparenting, Living in Step, How to Win as a Stepfamily*), get checked out regularly from library shelves, while children's fiction now includes new titles such as *Me and Mr. Stenner,* about an
eleven-year-old girl and her stepfather, and *Out of Love,* the
story of a thirteen-year-old boy and his stepmother. Stepfamilies have even become a subspecialty in family therapy. Before
treatment can even begin, mental health professionals often
have to make up "genograms," which map out the complex
ranks of stepaunts, uncles, brothers, sisters, and grandparents,
as well as the child's biological relatives. But still the divorce
rate for second marriages climbs.

The multiples of personalities and their individual needs in
stepfamilies make the solutions to their problems particularly
elusive. The variables are so many, the influences so diffuse
that no matter how much an observer may want to break down
cause and effect into tidy packages, the pieces rarely fit. Many
of the tensions in stepfamilies are born in the original divorce
or even marriage and carry over to the remarriage. The ages of
the children, not only at the time of their parent's remarriage,
but at the point of the divorce, can be indicators as to whether

the new blended family will "take." And the personalities and expectations of all members of these instant new coalitions, family groups created out of marriage licenses rather than blood and shared history, can either clash or merge to form a cohesive and positive support group.

What *is* predictable in stepfamilies are the areas of potential conflict. Many stepfamilies seem doomed to thrash about in a morass of failed expectations on the part of the stepparents, of the biological parents, and of course of the children. Structure and hierarchy in a stepfamily are often blurred by the confusion of its members, whose ways of doing things and whose positions in their original families inevitably clash in their new families. And competition can become intense and destructive, not only between the children and their step or half-siblings, but between child and stepparent, stepparent and counterpart biological parent, even between the newly married partners. Their multiples of new "family" members, bound together not by blood or choice, but by the marriage of only two of them, can make their relationships far more reactive than those within intact families. There is no shared family history, no continuity of memory, and often the differences rather than the similarities between stepfamily members are emphasized. The predictable patterns of stepfamilies, then, are particularly difficult to break down into individual responses, as each is so dependent on—and reactive to—so many others. It is not only fairer, then, but more practical to listen to the respective grievances of all "blended" family members rather than isolating the children. And the depth of those grievances are often determined by just who these new family members are.

THE CAST OF CHARACTERS

The probability of problems varies with the cast of characters joining an established single-parent family. As the vast majority of mothers have custody of their children, the stepfather is most often the new addition. And his family circumstances define both the best and the worst possibilities. The best and most successful stepfamily is one in which the stepfather has no children of his own. The worst and potentially the least successful occurs when he not only has his own children but brings them with him permanently into his new marriage. The most common and middle-ground arrangement, which has particular problems of its own, involves the stepfather whose children live with his former wife and who are "visiting" children.[3]

The problems can intensify when a woman without children moves into the household of the custodial father. As women continue to have more day-to-day responsibility for child care and household responsibilities, the stepmother's role becomes far more visible and influential than that of the usually more distanced stepfather or even that of the biological father. Whether the woman inherits live-in or visiting stepchildren, the possibilities of sabotage or failed expectations multiply.

The sex of the children also plays a major role in the acceptance or rejection of the new stepparent. Though very young boys are apt to welcome a stepfather, older boys often do not. Since the behavior of boys living with a single mother is often undisciplined, the arrival of an authoritative stepfather can bring an inevitable clash of same-sex wills. Determined to shape up the boy, a stepfather may impose rules and standards that only make the boy more rebellious. (One adolescent boy in New York threatened his stepfather with a harpoon gun when the stepfather berated him for coming home late after a newly imposed curfew. Another in Connecticut ran away from home when his stepfather handed him a list of chores he expected the boy to perform regularly.)

Girls are often even more reluctant to accept a stepmother. And because girls are prone to express their anger or disappointment by taking it out on their families, the relationship between the two generations of unrelated females can be particularly cruel. Resenting the stepmother for usurping the mother's rightful place, and jealous also of the father's newly directed attention and affection, girls can be merciless in their revenge. One twelve-year-old girl chose her father's remarriage as a theme paper, carefully detailing all the reasons she hated her stepmother. When she got a high mark on the paper, she showed it to her stepmother on the pretense of eliciting praise for her academic achievement.

The ages of the children, not only at the time of their parent's remarriage but also at the time of the original divorce, is another factor determining how well the new "family" will take. When parents divorce during a child's first oedipal phase (three to six) or second (nine to fourteen), the child may bear a residue of guilt for causing the breakup. To relieve that guilt, the child is often determined to break up the parent's new marriage in order to have a better chance of getting his real parents back together. The departure of the opposite-sex parent during these oedipal periods can also be felt very deeply by children. Having been burned once, the child will be less likely to risk emotional investment in a new stepparent. No matter how affectionate the stepparent may be, the child may keep his distance or even ignore the stepparent altogether. The child's stage of sexual development can also burden a new stepfamily. As we have seen, the reluctance of children between nine and fifteen to view their parents as sexually active can cloud their willingness to accept a stepparent of either sex.

The merging of stepsiblings and eventually half siblings under the same roof, either on a permanent basis or in a visiting situation, adds yet another potential time bomb. Parents often naively think that children will automatically like each other just because they belong to the same age group, but quite the opposite is usually true in stepfamilies. Overnight, the children find themselves sharing a room that was previously their own, sharing a bathroom with someone who hogs the shower, sharing even the hard-won attention of their parent. And rather than becoming one big happy family, the stepfamily household can break down into intensely warring factions.

Even the extended families of this new union can present problems. Suddenly there is a bewildering number of aunts, uncles, cousins, and grandparents whom the child is expected not only to keep straight, but to respond to as if they were blood relatives. Where these new relatives go out of their way not to discriminate between their blood and inherited family members, the children can benefit. But often—not unnaturally—the reverse is true, and the unrelated children may feel left out and increasingly insecure in the extended family structure. Even when instant "relatives" bend over backward to include a stepchild, he or she may still feel odd man out. "My stepfather's family were all blue-eyed, blond, jut-jawed people, and here I was, an olive-skinned, black-eyed surprise in their midst," recalls one stepdaughter. "They always made me feel like a Gypsy changeling, though it was never anything they said or did. It was just a feeling I had. And I resented it enormously."

Girls more readily accept stepfathers than stepmothers, and boys have difficulty accepting either. But there are variables within this framework. Often, the degree of success or failure of the relationship between child and stepparent depends on the relationship of the child with his natural parent of the same sex. If a boy continues to have a warm, supportive relationship with his own father after his mother's remarriage, he is far more apt to be receptive to a stepfather.[4] The same is true, though less so, for girls. Stepmothers and their stepdaughters often eventually make their peace, but the road to mutual acceptance seems fairly independent of previous relationships.

FAILED EXPECTATIONS

Many stepfamily problems are rooted in the original divorce. Few children, especially younger ones, wanted their parents to divorce in the first place, and most feel helpless and frustrated at not having been able to prevent it. Faced with a second marriage in which they have equally little say, their frustration escalates. Their reconciliation fantasies are strained, if not dashed. Still angry at the natural parent who they feel either allowed or caused the divorce, or, afterward, deserted them, they may redirect that anger toward the new "parent" in the house, even if he or she has done nothing to deserve it. And even where the premarriage relationship with the children has been good, the unsuspecting new stepparent can suddenly find the door slammed in his face.

At the extreme, the children's displaced anger can be almost pathological. In two badly handled divorces in California, which merged into one disturbed stepfamily, the mother's teenaged son refuses even to acknowledge the presence of his stepfather, while the father's teenaged son is equally distant toward his stepmother. And they all live under one explosive roof. "My stepson won't talk to me," says the stepfather. "If I speak to him directly, he'll answer me only if his mother is here. My own son isn't any better. He says he hates his stepmother and can't even stand the sight of her. He goes into his room as soon as she comes home from work and won't come out. She hasn't seen him in three weeks, even though we're all living here together."

The expectations of natural parent and child are often at loggerheads during remarriage. The parent, understandably, is happy at the thought of a new beginning, often a new and better home for the child, a new parent figure to help share the load, and a future holding few memories of the past. The child often wants exactly the opposite. He or she doesn't want to lose the close relationship with the parent that often follows divorce, to move to an unfamiliar neighborhood and new school, to be bossed around by someone who acts like the missing mother or father, to lose the pervading and often comforting hope that time might be turned back and the parents reunited.

The parent then feels betrayed by the ungrateful and selfish child. And the child feels betrayed by the parent who, by remarrying, is obviously seeking his or her own happiness without regard for the child's.

The child often has a point. Remarriage is apt to rekindle the same problems the child had at the time of the divorce. Once more the household is thrown into confusion. The child gets less attention from the parent, who is concentrating on the new spouse. Having lost a parent once through divorce, the child can become convinced he is losing the remaining parent to remarriage. Often, too, he has stepsiblings to contend with. And the child isn't sure where he belongs or even if he belongs at all. Nightmares can return, along with the old array of somatic disorders such as headaches, stomachaches, and, in some cases, insomnia.[5]

To forestall a pending marriage, the child may try to prevent it, or afterward, to bring it down by playing on the parent's vulnerable marital history. One eleven-year-old girl kept pointing out to her mother that if she hadn't been able to hang on to her father, why did she think she could hang on to her new husband? A twelve-year-old boy whose mother had left his father because he was an alcoholic began to count the number of drinks his mother's fiancé had every evening. "You don't really want to get into all of that again, do you?" he asked his mother. Sometimes children will try to pit the new partners against each other. Involved in a business problem, one new stepfather was late to dinner four nights in a row. When the teenaged daughter pointed out that her father had used the same ruse to cover up an affair, the mother confronted her new husband. To the daughter's delight, the adults got into a row. To the daughter's disappointment, they made up.

Though the tactics of these children may seem Machiavellian, often in remarriage their most dire fears come true. When the custodial parent remarries, the children, temporarily any-

way, lose much of that parent's attention. When the noncustodial parent remarries, they often lose much of that parental
attention also. One study found, for example, that after noncustodial fathers remarry, they see far less of their children,
especially their daughters, and for shorter periods of time.[6]
And even the visitation time left takes on a new and less rewarding nature for the children.

At issue is the private and often very personal world the
children and the single parent have created in the wake of divorce. Remarriage means that children face the loss of a one-
on-one relationship with the parent, and that they also have to
adjust to sharing visitation time, not at Dad's "place," but at
Dad's "new home." The difference may be subtle to the adult,
but it is blatant to the child. "After Dad got married, it was
awful visiting weekends," says seventeen-year-old Nora. "I had
a little room in the house—I always had a little room in all
Dad's houses. He told me, 'Always consider my home as your
home,' but it never, never was. I felt I was being pushed out
by my stepmother. Her being lord over the house was upsetting to me. Two or three times we went to a family therapist.
I resented it. 'Hell,' I thought. 'I'm not part of *this* family.'
I felt abandoned. My father had no time for me. Eventually, I stopped going there. I just announced it when I was sixteen."

Paradoxically, getting along too well with a stepparent can
make the child's problems worse. Remarriage often presents
children with loyalty dilemmas they are too unsophisticated to
solve. If they find themselves liking the stepparent, is that disloyal to their natural parent? Or worse, will they lose the love of
the natural parent if they accept the new parent figure? Faced
with this quandary, the child most often chooses to remain loyal
to his natural parent, shutting out the stepparent, even though
he or she may be warm, affectionate—and there. "The child
sees what adults don't want to see, that a man can have a new

wife, a woman a new husband, but that he, the child, cannot have a new parent. There is no such thing as an ex-mother or an ex-father," wrote A. W. Simon in *Stepchild in the Family.*[7]

The higher the expectations on the part of either the stepparent or the child going into remarriage, the greater the risk of disappointment. When it comes to raising expectations, it is sometimes lamentably fair to point the finger at the wicked stepparent. Just as the adults court each other, the soon-to-be stepparent may woo the children. Often, however, the real motive is to please the natural parent and to win the children over so they won't interfere with the adults' courtship. In such cases, the rules often change after the marriage has taken place, and the children, quite naturally, feel duped. "It was very different before we got married," one "wicked" stepmother confesses. "We all went on trips together, we sang and danced, and I promised them each a pet. After we got married I wanted nothing more than to go away with my husband alone. I'd leave them a list of chores and finally told them I hated gerbils." The children are quick to pick up on such hypocrisy. "My stepmother's character changed after she married my father," says one sixteen-year-old boy. "Before she was almost obsequious. Unlimited Cokes, lots of food, very disposable things. Whatever you like, dear. She went way overboard trying to win us over. After the marriage I suddenly had a ration of Cokes and she was far less willing to drive us anywhere. And it's gotten worse. As soon as we sit down at dinner now she'll tell me I'm to clear the table, and that my sister is to put the dishes in the dishwasher and bring out the dessert. I think she's having trouble adjusting to household chores now that she has no incentive to do it. She's won. And she no longer has to make any effort on our behalf."

Even where the stepparent is genuinely eager and willing to take on responsibility for the children, it may not work; while the stepparent may want a child, the child may not necessarily want a stepparent. The harder the stepparent tries, the more he or she can be stonewalled by the child. An enthusiastic new stepmother, for example, can plunge into her role with the highest intention—and overattention—toward the child. His wish is her command and she becomes superparent, chauffeuring him to activity after activity, fixing him his favorite meals, buying him presents. But the child may feel uneasy at being the center of so much attention and frightened by the sense of power he has. He may rebuff the stepparent to get out of the spotlight, and the stepparent, in turn, will feel hurt and rejected when the child doesn't acknowledge or appreciate her extraordinary efforts on his behalf.

Positive expectation can turn quickly into negative expectation for the rebuffed stepparent. Another example is the father who had only sons of his own, and who therefore looked forward to life with his new stepdaughter. But the honeymoon was short-lived. "She is mean to her mother. Really mean. But when I speak to her about it she says it's none of my business. Her favorite line is, 'You're not my father, you know,' " says the stepfather. A formerly enthusiastic stepmother now dreads the visits of her new husband's sons. "It's gotten so bad that I find myself saying Thank you when one of them at least takes his plate from the dining room into the kitchen," she says. "I know that teenagers are all basically slobs. But these boys won't stop punishing me for marrying their father."

The natural parent can also be disappointed by the new spouse if he or she doesn't take a deep interest in the children. One of the greatest pitfalls for stepfamilies is the expectation of the natural parent that the stepparent will automatically love the children the way he or she does. The realization that the stepparent doesn't can be profoundly depressing to the parent. "I was so hoping he'd grow to love the kids, but he hasn't," says one woman of her new husband. "He's nice to them and all that. But he's just not into fixing bicycle gears or leaving work early to get to the school concerts. Sometimes I feel more alone as a parent now than I did before we were married." Unrealistic expectations of parental love from a nonparent can form real tensions between the new couple. "I didn't marry him for his children. I married him for him," says a woman who inherited two teenagers. "We've got two kids of our own now and instead of spending time with them I have to keep dealing with these other kids who hang around the house messing it up and expecting to be fed all the time. I resent it. I really do. I keep looking at them and thinking 'these are my husband's relatives, not mine.' "

The situation isn't any easier for the stepchild who wants to establish a parent-child relationship with a stepparent who is either inattentive or withholds affection. Here, too, a cycle of unfulfilled expectations can take hold. George, the stepfather of a young boy, purposefully held back in his involvement with him, fearful of usurping the natural father's role. The boy, on the other hand, who was three when his mother and stepfather married, spent extraordinary amounts of energy trying to elicit George's love and attention. The more he tried, the more the stepfather held back. Now eighteen, the boy still hasn't given up. "I always considered my stepfather my real father and Dad someone I visited on weekends," says Allen. "I found myself saying, 'My father does this and that' and meaning George. I tried hard to be his son, like writing his name on the back of my life jacket at camp one summer. I've always considered him more my father than he has considered me his son. But I don't think he ever understood that. It took me until this year to ask him if I could call him Dad, too. And he said no."

It is the fate of many stepfamilies to be filled with failed expectations on everyone's part. And often there is nothing that can be done about it. Where the child has been hurt by a parent long before the stepparent arrives, a relationship of accommodation and even friendship can evolve, but rarely a relationship of great depth. And perhaps it shouldn't. The most successful stepfamilies are the ones in which the child looks to the stepparent as an intimate friend and supporter. Boundless love and affection can pass between them. But a stepparent can never really take the place of a biological parent, no matter how much the child wants it or how hard the stepparent tries.

FORMLESS FAMILIES

Stepfamilies are further handicapped by the ambiguity of the role of each family member. Whose job is it to discipline the children? The parent with the blood tie or the stepparent? Whose side should the parent take? That of his own children, his stepchildren, or his new wife? And where does the new stepchild fit into a family of stepsiblings? This confusion of clear roles can create havoc in a "blended" family, which often turns out not to be blended at all, but broken down into blood ties that often strain the survival of the entire unit.

Stepparents, for example, may feel uncertain about the amount of discipline they should hand out, or even the amount of involvement they *want* to invest in somebody else's children. Children are equally confused about how they should regard a stepparent. "It makes me confused," says ten-year-old Adam. "Sometimes I think of her like a friend, sometimes a sister, sometimes an aunt. I don't know what a stepmother is supposed to be."

The demands on a stepparent are also complicated by the risk of being seen by the children as usurping a natural parent's role. Children simply will not stand for that. "She tries to pretend she's our mother, but she's not," says ten-year-old Meaghan. "She tries to do anything to make us happy, but she can't make us. She wants us to call her 'Mother.' I won't. I just call her Maryanne. That's what her name is. I'm not calling her something that isn't true." Stepfathers are less easy marks for such criticism, since they are usually less visible in the day-to-day dealings in a family. But they do not escape altogether. "I like everything about Bob until he starts telling me what to do, like clean up my room," says eight-year-old Robbie. "Then I get mad because he's acting like my father and he's not."

The chain of command that subtly characterizes natural families breaks down (or is never established) in the stepfamily. When the natural parent is present, the stepparent often defers to him or her. When the natural parent isn't around, the stepparent takes over. And the children can balk at this inconsistent seesaw of authority. Worn down by trying to discipline increasingly resistant children, the stepparent may give up and defer all responsibility to the natural parent. Called the "Bypass Pattern" by stepfamily specialists, this avoidance of confrontation between stepparent and child often escalates into a total breakdown of discipline. "The stepparent doesn't want to discipline the child. She doesn't want to risk jeopardizing whatever relationship they might have tentatively built," says Dr. Janice Nadler, who heads a stepparents' counseling group in Los Angeles. "She also feels she doesn't have the right and that the father won't support her anyway. Instead, she tells the father, 'Your child is acting terribly. I want you to speak to him.' But the father gets caught up in protecting the child and doesn't say to her, 'Go, you do it.' It puts everybody in a very tight, constrictive bind."

Sometimes the situation is reversed: the stepparent wants to discipline the children, but the natural parent blocks him. Whether out of the sheer habit of being totally responsible for the children, or protectively, to relieve the stepparent of responsibility, the natural parent often interferes. This not only weakens the stepparent's position with the children, but further clouds just what role belongs to whom. One stepfather, who had no natural children, was scolding his stepdaughter for leaving her bike out overnight in the rain, when the mother came across them. Immediately she took over the scolding, leaving the stepparent just standing there in left field. "This shouldn't be your problem," she said to him. The stepfather shrugged in frustration. "How can you expect me to help you with the children if you won't let me?" he retorted. "If I didn't want it to be my problem, I never would have said anything in the first place."

The situation can be compounded when it is the mother's children who live in the house and the father's children who "visit," the most common custody arrangement following divorce. The father feels guilty for leaving his own children in order to live with unrelated ones, while his children are angry that they have to visit their father when these other children get to live with him. And the stepmother becomes the scapegoat. Refusing to see any flaw in his own children during visitation, the father lets them get away with murder. The stepmother tries to discipline them but the father blocks her, insisting in his guilt that they are perfect and that she, by inference, is imperfect. With such clearly drawn lines, his children ignore any request from the stepmother, which in turn makes *her* children furious. And so it goes, until these visitation nightmares—weekend after weekend—bring the beleaguered adults to the point of divorce. "I thought I was going to be a wonderful stepmother and the children would call me blessed," says one stepmother with two children of her own. "Then crash. Boom. Bang. My husband wouldn't back me up on weekends when I asked his boys to take out the trash or to clean up their rooms or to just plain pitch in. Hell, no. Whenever there was a problem, the ex-wife, the children, and my husband would all line up on one side and that was that. There was no support for me. I almost pitched it in several times."

This lack of family structure, which children need more than adults, can quickly lead to anarchy if it is not resolved. Children's tendencies in any new situation are to challenge authority, to test the boundaries of the new structure to see how far they can go. It is the parents' role, be they natural or step, to define and enforce those boundaries. In the process of over-compensating to avoid stepping on anybody's toes, wishy-washy parents can instead let the formless family drift into failure.

THE NAME DILEMMA

The tenuousness of stepfamilies is exemplified by the collection of different last names its supposedly cohesive family members collect. In this case, the answer to the poetic question "What's in a name" is: a lot. To young children especially, having a different last name from the rest of the family, even their mother's, is not only confusing, it compounds the common feeling in a stepfamily of being an outsider. Defensively, many young children want to take the names of their stepfathers. "Nobody knows who I am," one eight-year-old girl said tearfully to her mother. "At school nobody even knows that I'm sister to Carrie and Sue [her younger half siblings]. It's like I'm a stranger."

Older children seem more practical than emotional about the need to have the same name as the rest of the family. One fourteen-year-old girl became increasingly upset as the time for her mother's marriage came closer. Finally she told her mother that she, too, wanted to change her name, even though she was very close to her natural father. Why? "Because no one will know how look me up in the phone book," the girl confessed. The situation was quickly resolved by listing the girl's own name in the telephone book as a separate entry.

Other name changes become more complicated, even to the point of creating a neurotic lack of identity. One boy, torn by his loyalty conflict between his mother and stepfather and his father and stepmother solved it by using the last name of the stepfather during the winter when he lived with him, and the name of his natural father in the summer which he spent with him. This transferable identity came to a head when the boy enrolled in college and had to choose one name or the other. Choosing the name of his stepfather, the boy became increasingly upset and guilty and finally dropped out of college and into therapy. "All adolescents go through an identity crisis, but this boy had been having one for years," says his therapist. "He literally didn't know who he was."

In this era of multiple marriages, a child can also find himself bearing the name of someone to whom he really has no connection at all. Often stepfathers adopt their young stepchildren, especially where their natural fathers have deserted them. But if that second marriage breaks up too, the child is set adrift with no true identity. Mark, eighteen, was adopted by his stepfather when he was three and a half. That marriage broke up two years ago. Now Mark alternates between living with his stepfather, his natural father, who is on his third marriage, and his mother, who has taken back her maiden name. "The name I've got out of the whole group is the only person I'm not related to," says Mark. "I keep fantasizing about being taken unconscious to a hospital where they track my name on a computer and start treating me for some rare blood disease that runs in somebody else's family."

There is, of course, no rational solution to the name problem. So many families these days are composed of his, her, and their children that multiple names are commonplace. Nonetheless, the confusion to younger children, especially, warrants some creative thinking. As marriage seems so perilously fragile these days, and as mothers nine times out of ten retain custody of the children, perhaps both mother and child should bear the mother's maiden name. In stepfamilies, the children then would at least have the same last name as one of the adults.

INSTANT SIBLINGS

When parents remarry, children can suddenly inherit a whole set of "brothers" and "sisters." And the children start to move back and forth now not between parents as they did after divorce, but between established homes. Fitting in and staking out a secure place in multiple households filled with people with whom they are expected to have instant sibling relationships can be both bewildering and taxing. Overnight, for example, the birth-order hierarchy can shift. The child who has always been the oldest is suddenly bumped by an older stepbrother, or the "baby" is replaced by an even younger step- or half-sibling.

Often the children are ill-prepared for this extraordinary upheaval in their lives. Just as parents may suddenly split with no real warning to their children, a parent can decide just as quickly to remarry. And the children are expected to rejoice not only for their parent's newfound happiness, but for the addition of a family of "sisters" and "brothers"—whom they often haven't even met. One mother told her two daughters, eight and ten, at breakfast that she was going to get married, and that their new family was coming to visit in an hour. "We were dumbfounded," recalls one of the daughters. "We'd only met the guy once and never even knew he had any children. It turned out he had four. When they arrived outside our house in a big brown station wagon, his kids refused to get out of the car and we refused to come out of the house. There we were, peering out our windows and them peering out of theirs. Our parents stood in the middle on the sidewalk, each frantically waving at their own kids to come out. We finally did."

In stepfamilies, the assorted children line up in any number of ways. Sometimes it is by blood, other times by sex. Curiously enough, in several stepfamilies the best arrangement turned out to be cross-sex. In one, a nine-year-old girl bunked in happily with her seven-year-old stepbrother. In another, an eleven-year-old boy became a great comfort to his six-year-old stepsister. In other families, neither blood nor sex but age becomes the criterion. "It was the biggies against the littlies," says one stepdaughter, whose family suddenly swelled to six children. "But it was tough. We tested each other a lot. Not only were we supposed to be brothers and sisters, but friends, too. And we didn't even know each other."

Stepfamilies are launched at full speed with little or no breaking-in time and with no sense of shared family history, and the simple act of having dinner can turn into a bewildering battlefield. Children are persistent creatures of habit about their seats at the table, for example, and the feathers can fly when a newcomer takes over an accustomed place. Food and eating habits can clash, as the two family histories merge into one. Annie loves carrots. Stepsister Susy hates them and has never been made to eat them. Rufus likes his bacon lean. Stepbrother Andy likes his fatty. Susy and Andy have been allowed to drink soft drinks with dinner. Annie and Rufus have been forbidden soft drinks and served either milk or orange juice. One family has watched television during dinner. The other has not. And suddenly they are all stuck at the same dinner table, not just for the evening, but presumably for life. With stakes that high, compromise is low, especially among younger children whose competitiveness is still more home- than outside-oriented.

Visiting stepchildren can have a particularly tough time, especially when the parent's remarriage has brought new siblings into their old house. Chores that seem simple to the adults can take on all sorts of reverberations for the visiting children. One twelve-year-old boy regularly refused to do his prescribed jobs on visitation weekends. "Why should I lug out the garbage *they* made and mow the grass *they* walk on," he says about his stepsiblings. "They live in my father's house. I don't."

The jockeying for position in the stepsibling hierarchy is also exaggerated by its lack of day-to-day continuity."I had a lot of catching up to do in the household," recalls one fifteen-year-old girl who spent every weekend with her father and new stepfamily. "I had to make my own space every time. There was a whole household going on all week and I was coming out on the weekends. I had to either change the routine or fit into it." The sense of dislocation is no less for the custodial children, who feel their home is invaded every weekend by the visitors. "There was always trouble, kids yelling at each other, parents yelling at the kids," says sixteen-year-old Ned. "My stepbrother bunked with me and used to pull all my stuff out of the bureau so he could put his in. Then I'd throw his out. It wasn't my house. It wasn't his house. It was nobody's house. I didn't feel it was my home until all my stepbrothers and sisters went away to boarding school and we were alone with Mom and my stepfather."

Not surprisingly, the rivalry between stepsiblings, especially younger ones, revolves around their respective natural parents. Often the children compete for attention, for little extras, to prove to their stepcounterpart that their parent loves them more. The use of a parent as a weapon is also a favorite among stepsiblings, especially the ones who are least in favor of the new marriage. "There is a lot of 'My mother's better than your mother' and 'Your mother stinks,'" says one girl of her stepsisters, who bitterly opposed their father's remarriage. "We wait until no one can hear us at night and then we go at it. We're very protective of our mother knowing how much they hate her." The rivalry is exacerbated, as always, by the natural parent favoring his or her children over the stepchildren. "If we don't make our beds, we're little schmucks," says the twelve-year-old girl with remarkable sophistication. "But if they don't make theirs, they're big schmucks."

Growing up with a stepsibling of the opposite sex can also

create confusion, especially if they get along too well. The children live together in close proximity and the atmosphere in a newly remarried household is apt to be just as sexually titillating as that in a single parent home. With the taboo of incest lifted, the whole thing can get very tricky. Among younger children, it can be as simple as playing Doctor. "It's pretty hard not to notice each other if you share the same bathroom," says one fourteen-year-old girl who has a stepbrother a year older. "When we were five and six we used to spend a lot of time groping each other, pretending we were my mom and his dad in the next room. And even then we realized we weren't really related, which made it more exciting—and scary." With older children, the stakes are higher. Fourteen-year-old Marjorie began dating her eighteen-year-old stepbrother after their parents married, making her mother very uncomfortable. "Clara looks just like me and Terry looks just like his father," the mother said. "It was a little creepy, as if they were copying everything we did in a shadow dance. It got to the point that I didn't even want to leave them together in the evening watching television. I sent Clara away to boarding school."

Even where the stepfamily becomes healthily close and supportive, a charge can remain between stepsiblings. Ella, for example, grew up with her stepbrother, and even shared a room with him as a little girl. Now twenty-three and twenty-four respectively, Ella and her stepbrother are still very close even though he has married and moved far away. They make great efforts to see each other on vacations and during holidays and the atmosphere surrounding those meetings is apt to be highly erotic. "I look at him now and think, God, what an attractive man," says Ella. "He's funny and intelligent and he's got the right kind of background. But I also realize that that sort of thing doesn't happen. But then, of course, it could."

The addition of a natural child for the newly remarrieds also creates a strain for the children of the former marriages. Not only is there yet another threat to securing parental love, but common sibling rivalry is intensified by half versus full blood. Ten-year-old Mike, for example, straightforwardly hates his two-year-old half brother. "It's no good," says the boy angrily. "He gets all the attention. I get none. He's an idiot. I feel like creaming him but when I smacked him once I got grounded for two days. When he's seven I'm going to beat him up."

To make sure of staking out a secure claim on a parent, some half-blooded children invest far too much effort. Fourteen-year-old Stuart, for example, openly competes with his two much younger half sisters for attention from their father, his stepfather. "He has no blood commitment to me and I can't stand it," says the boy, who lives with his mother and stepfather. "I try extra-hard to stand out from my half sisters, like sending him two cards on Father's Day and buying stereo parts for him. I like to put out so I can try and equal my sisters. I know I won't be able to ever, but I can more if I keep doing things extra to show him I really care."

Even where parents are very careful to treat children equally, there simply *is* a difference between children born of the existing union and children born of a prior one. "I do wish I had a real brother instead of a half one," says eleven-year-old Susannah of her brand-new baby half brother. "In a way I envy him that he's going to grow up with a mother and father. Like when I visit my stepmother and father now, it's different. She's going to feel more comfortable with him than with me."

The rivalries and insecurities of unrelated or semirelated children all living together usually smooth out in time. Though some stepchildren seem predisposed to make life just as miserable for their siblings and stepparents as they possibly can, the stepparent can defuse at least some of that anger by treating all the children with impeccable equality. And if a stepfamily can survive the childhoods of its children, it can survive anything.

WAR GAMES

Remarriage of a former spouse can open old wounds, even when single-parent life has settled down to a comfortable routine or the parent has remarried. One researcher found that mothers, especially, reexperienced the feelings of depression, helplessness, anger, and anxiety they had had at the time of the divorce.[8] In this climate of heated emotions, disagreements long since settled about visitation and child support become sore issues again. Remarriage even spawns new child custody fights, especially after the noncustodial father remarries and then feels he has a "family" to raise his children in.

The motives behind these custody switches, however, are not always in the child's best interest. One such custody switch in Arizona involved a man who had had a vasectomy following his divorce, his new young wife, who wanted her husband's children if she couldn't have her own, and his parents, who felt they had lost their grandchildren to their custodial former daughter-in-law. The court decided against the father. "It was a very unpleasant, nasty situation," says Craig Everett at Pima County's Conciliation Court in Tucson. "I'm not sure the father wanted the children for himself at all, but to settle his marriage problems and appease his parents."

Short of custody fights, remarriage seems to breed a new animosity—and often an unhealthy sense of competition between the two new sets of parents, especially between the women. Men seem more comfortable with their ex-wives' new spouse, and on occasion are even grateful to them for fathering their children. Former and present wives, on the other hand, are far more apt to square off with each other and become openly competitive, if not downright hostile. In one study of remarriage, fully 50 percent of the men reported approval of the ex-wives' new husbands, while fewer than 25 percent of the women expressed approval of their husbands' new wives![9]

Where there is animosity between the two mothers, it simply has to spill over onto the children. If one constantly or even occasionally bad-mouths the other, the children get caught squarely in the middle. The children who want to like the step-mother—if for no other reason than to keep the peace—feel disloyal to their natural mother if they do. They quickly learn to fib, to tell little white lies to their natural mother, downplaying their affection for their stepmother. "I liked Sarah from the beginning, but I knew my mother didn't like the idea of my father having a new wife," says eleven-year-old Ellen. "So I felt very uncomfortable being with Sarah, like on a ski trip, knowing that my mother didn't like her. But at the same time I didn't want to be mean to Sarah. My mother would say to me, 'Do you like Sarah?' and I wouldn't know exactly what to say. I felt like I had to be on my mother's side in a way, but I liked Sarah anyway. So I said to my mother in a dumb voice, 'Well, I like her,' but I didn't exaggerate or anything."

When the stepmother in turn bad-mouths the mother, the children feel even worse. Comparisons are often drawn between different criteria for disciplining, different tastes, even different ways of running a household, from setting the table to making (or not making) the beds. The child often unwittingly provides clues to the ex-wife's habits, the habits the husband lived with in his prior marriage, and the stepmother is quick to jump on them. One little boy proudly made salad dressing in his stepmother's house and then, like his mother, put it in the freezer. The stepmother was furious. "She yelled at me. She said, 'I don't believe your mother puts the salad dressing in the freezer!'" the boy reported. "Then she said, 'I knew your mother was peculiar, but not that peculiar.'" A ten-year-old girl, visiting her father's new home, left her bed unmade one morning and quickly invited her stepmother's wrath. "She told me, 'Your mother may let you live in a slum, but I won't,'" says the girl. "She said it real soft, but I was supposed to hear it."

When the father has remarried and the mother has not, money can also become a double-edged sword between the child's two households. The new wife and stepmother often begins to resent the amount of money her present husband is spending on his former family, and often does her best (or worst) to stop it. Even where there is ample money on both sides of the family, the sabotage can be subtle but cruel. "I really can't believe her comments," says a fifteen-year-old boy of his stepmother. "She says things like 'Are you being fed all right in New York?' as if my mother was starving us, or 'Maybe I should be the one to buy your clothes,' when I show up in something she doesn't like. Last week she bought me a pair of corduroys which I don't like, then said my mother could certainly afford to pay for half of them what with all the alimony my father was paying her."

Often the financial duel goes both ways. The new wife will launch an unsubtle campaign to marry off the ex-wife, not only to reduce the financial hold on her new husband but to sever the emotional one as well. At the same time, the ex-wife may postpone or avoid marriage altogether in order to keep the alimony checks coming in. And the children learn tactical life lessons that do not bode well for their own future honesty. "My Mom lives with Steve, but she says she doesn't want to marry him because then she'd lose her alimony," says a thirteen-year-old girl. "My stepmother says my mother is doing it just to spite her so she can't have the nice things she wants. They're all just using each other because of money. It makes me sick." Where the mother has no active social life and therefore little opportunity to find a new partner, the child can feel the weight of the stepmother's impatience and become very defensive. "She's so snoopy. She's always saying to me, 'Has your mother met somebody nice?' or 'Do you have something to tell me about your mother's love life?' " says a fourteen-year-old girl. "It makes me feel bad for Mom. She'd love to have a man, but there aren't many around."

Men's habits with money in these situations is less calculating, but can be an equal or greater source of bitterness if the family pie has to be divided into smaller and smaller portions. Whereas women are more apt to compete for emotional control of their families, men are more apt to compete—or withhold—financially. After remarriage, the father is likely to spend more money on his present union than on his former one, and a deep resentment can set in. "I visit Dad, and my half brother has the ten-speed Peugeot I asked for and goes to private school," says a twelve-year-old boy. "I want to say to him, 'Hey, Dad, I'm your son, too,' but I don't dare." Fathers, natural or step, can in fact be quite insensitive when it comes to dealing out cash. "My stepfather can't imagine how it feels when my half sisters get all these new clothes from him while I struggle along on the measly clothes allowance I get from my own father," sighs a fifteen-year-old girl. "They shop at Bloomingdale's. I go to the thrift shops. I drop little hints to my stepfather and he says it's terrific I'm learning to budget. Oh, those girls are so spoiled. I really hate them."

Quick to pick up on their parents' competitiveness, many children use it to their advantage. It is one thing to learn how to "butter up" people in childhood to gain an end. But children of divorce and remarriage truly become expert at the devious game of manipulation and artfully play one parent off against the other. Older children often wield this weapon to get money. "I wrote two letters at the beginning of the term to my father and stepfather," confesses one college freshman. "I told Dad that my stepfather hadn't come through with the allowance he'd promised, and I told my stepfather the same thing about Dad. Bam. Two checks arrive and I was good until Christmas." Younger children, especially girls, wage a more psychological warfare. Facing down her mother, who wouldn't let her go to the movies, one girl said, "My stepmother is much nicer to me than you are. She's like a real friend. She took me to two movies last weekend and bought me ice cream afterward."

Her ploy worked, and her mother sent her off to the movies.

Parents and stepparents often encourage this deadly game, competing through the children themselves. "Winning the children over" becomes the Golden Fleece to protagonists whose ulterior motives have less to do with the children than with beating each other out. "My mom bought me a sweater," says one thirteen-year-old girl. "I wore it to my dad's, and my stepmother went right out and bought me a windbreaker. I wore the windbreaker home and my mom went right out and bought me a down vest. I didn't dare wear that back to my dad's in case they felt they had to buy me a fur coat."

Not all the stakes stepfamilies play for are material ones by any means. Lurking beneath these more blatant forms of competition are emotional needs for reassurance, acceptance, and security. Often an innocent stepparent takes the rap for children who feel insecure about their relationships with their parent. In noncustodial situations particularly, where the parent-child relationship is almost always more fragile, the stepparent can become the fall guy.

Twelve-year-old Ralph, for example, blames his stepmother for taking his father away from him, although the father paid scant attention to him even before he remarried. Ralph has persuaded his father to consider his birthday a "free" day which the two of them can share on any day of Ralph's choosing—alone. This year they spent the day skiing at a local mountain. Ralph has bigger plans for next year because his father was "busy" and missed his tenth and eleventh birthdays. "I get to add those," says Ralph. "I've been saving free days for so long to go *alone* with him on a nice trip. When Judy comes it isn't fun. Nobody laughs anymore. She's never satisfied. She's always screaming or whatever. Or unhappy. I just try to avoid her."

In a curious twist, the stepparent can also become the fall

guy for a parent who doesn't want to become involved with his own child. The stepparent might be forced to become a buffer between them, and not daring to admit his rejection by the parent, the child's full load of competitive anger lands on the stepparent. "I want to have time alone with my father," says thirteen-year-old Fred. "But every time I want to go alone for a ride with him, no, *she has to go with us*. She's protection for my dad against me. He's afraid to be alone with me. Maybe he thinks I'd start asking him if he would come back."

Adolescent daughters, especially, can display their competitive insecurities about their fathers through almost ruthless treatment of the stepmother. Some will be sullen and rude to the stepmother when the father isn't around, then turn all sweetness and light when he is. When the stepmother complains to the father about the daughter's treatment of her, the father will protest, saying he's seen no sign of it at all. "You're so hard on her," one father told his new wife after the stepdaughter had called her a "frigid bitch" behind his back. "She's trying so hard to please you so you'll love her."

Other teenage girls use sex as a weapon to enrage the stepmother, a weapon many fathers don't—or pretend not to—see. One sixteen-year-old girl often donned see-through clothing and put her arms around her father while they watched television, totally shutting the stepmother out. When the stepmother later pointed out this seductive behavior to the father, he not only laughed it off, but said he was flattered by all this female attention. "In an intact family, if a mother were to say 'I think Mary is a little too old for that, it's too seductive and I'm getting pissed off,' the father has to deal with it as a mother's interest," says psychiatrist Frank Williams in Los Angeles. "When a stepmother says it, he feels this competitiveness on her part and can criticize her for it, saying, 'You want to separate me from my daughter.' "

ONE NO-WIN STEPFAMILY

For all the best intentions on the part of the parent, the step-parent and the children, some stepfamilies are doomed to disappointment. One such stepfamily in Colorado incorporates all the failed expectations and cruelties of stepfamily war games.

To look at this family, you would think them the model American stepfamily, a bright eleven-year-old boy, a softly pretty thirteen-year-old girl, a hard-working, nurturing father, and a dedicated young stepmother. The modest Colorado ranch house they have lived in for seven years is squeaky clean, centering around a circular gas fireplace. On the wall-to-wall carpeted living room floor, the boy, Ned, is neatly folding his newly washed underwear into threes, supervised by his super-tidy stepmother, Nancy. And because the stepmother, whose face looks too pinched for her twenty-eight years, is so articulate, as is her stepson Ned, who drums his fingers nervously on the kitchen table during the interview and whispers so she won't hear, their versions of the same story follow just as they told them.

Nancy: "After we got married their mother went away for nine months and didn't see the children at all. Just sent them occasional postcards. They were only five and seven then, and they finally admitted they didn't even remember what she looked like. Now she lives in Pennsylvania. At twenty, I became an instant mother and the supplier of all their needs. Their mother refuses to think she has caused them any grief. We have confronted her and said, 'Look, they really feel bad.' And she says, 'Oh, no, they don't. They are perfectly adjusted. They have no problems.'

"She's never shown one iota of concern for either of her children. She's full of protestations of deep love for them, 'My

212

darling, I love you so much. I miss you terribly. I can't wait till
we are together,' but it's been over a month now since she has
even called. It's terrible. The children naturally want to believe
what she says, but she doesn't back up anything that she says
with anything she does. I wish she would die a very long, miserable, gruesome death.

"I don't know whether it's her fault or whether my anger is
misplaced, but I feel that her presence and her involvement in
our lives has been a big, giant sore. And I am resentful. I ended
up with her responsibilities and yet she is trying to collect all
the rewards and goodies for things she never does.

"Basically, I'm a mother at heart. But it's turned out to be an
extremely disappointing situation for me. The whole experience of being a stepparent has just beaten down my self-
confidence about being a parent myself. I feel like such a failure that I think I don't want my own child. I'd be a horrible parent because I've done all the things that I am supposed to do,
the right things, and my kids don't love me, they don't respect
me, they treat me like dirt, and I end up of course hating them
and being resentful of them and I don't want to feel that way
about my own.

"I have become the psychological parent because I am here,
I am stable, they know they can turn to me. I am not threatening. They can be nasty and mean to me and I will still love
them. Well, they have a lot of sadness and anger inside them toward their own mother that they have been unable to date to
express to her. Any time they have even hinted at expressing
their feelings toward her, she rejects them. And it's not very
subtle. Ned has tried to tell her how he feels, and she responded by only writing letters to her daughter. She just cut
him out. And it was real painful for him.

"After that, he did what his sister Laura does, which is real
kiss-ass. Laura still is so desperately afraid that her mother
won't love her, she'll do everything she can to try and please

her. She still calls her 'Mommy,' a girl who is madly in love, wants to wear makeup and high heels and who only sees her mother two or three times a year. Laura thinks she is seventeen but she acts like a three-year-old.

"They fight with me like crazy, and I'm the bad guy. I'm the really horrible person because I make them eat right and clean their rooms and brush their teeth. I make them have concern and consideration for other people's feelings. We have rules in this house, maybe more than we need. But I'm the authoritarian figure, the disciplinarian because their dad's at work. They've really used me, I think. I'm the convenient scapegoat for them to dump their frustrations on, because it's too threatening to dump them on their mother or father. They already feel, I think, that they've lost their mother and they're afraid of losing their father so they're real nice to him and they give me all the shit.

"What really hurts me is when they are angry at me, they will destroy things that I have made for them in front of me. They will deliberately try and show me that the things I have done and the time I've invested has meant nothing to them. And they choose to say things like 'I can't wait to go see my mother' and 'you're not my mother.' We've tried to have an honest relationship and I have told them what hurts me. But when Laura gets angry, the very first thing she'll do is use the deepest things I've shared with her against me. That just wrenches my heart right out of my chest. It betrays all the confidence and trust that I have had in our relationship.

"My husband does recognize that basically I am a good parent and that I have brought them up with concern. But he does find it difficult that I don't have the unconditional love for them that he has. And I don't. Especially after the way they've treated me. I think at one point I wanted desperately to be their real mother. But I've been trying to deal with giving up that fantasy and to deal with that loss because it's never going to happen. They don't feel that way about me no matter how hard I try.

"Do this all over again? Hell, no. I love my husband dearly and I wish that things could have been easier for us. But we lose out so much when we're in conflict over the kids. I would say that over 95 percent of our fights are over the kid situation. One on one, we're very well matched, we're very compatible, we have a good time together, but when they're around, the fur flies. I could have a much better marriage if it weren't for the kids.

"It was finally essential to my mental health to start being honest. I had to tell the kids that I didn't think their mother was in any way deserving of their affection. I had swallowed my feelings for too long. I was in fact feeling suicidal. There were several times when I was ready to end it all, and other times when I was ready to leave my husband because of them. I got a lot of negative vibes from my husband, who would say, 'They are going through something difficult,' and I would think, 'Goddammit, I'm going through something difficult, too. What about me?'

"Really, I can't think of any stepfamily that functions better than we do. My husband and I have managed to keep the marriage going, the kids do well at school, they're not into drugs or vandalism. A happy stepfamily. I think the stepfamily part of it is almost always the unhappy part of the marriage. The rest of it can be all right."

Ned: "I don't see my mother a lot. She lives in Pennsylvania. I guess I live with my father because my mom didn't want to take care of us. She still likes to see us and stuff. She didn't just take off. They got divorced—and she gave us to my dad. I didn't really understand it then, but when I got old enough, yeah, it made me sad. Kind of. Kids in school say, 'Where's your mother?' and I say, 'Pennsylvania.'

"She wanted to be on her own and to travel. She didn't want us to go to a lot of different schools. Sometimes I think she's wrong, because I could have gone traveling with her.

"So then Dad married Nancy. We have fights a lot. I guess we get along pretty well, but it's not the same as with my mom. I don't think of Nancy as my mom at all, but she tries to be.

"We fight about chores, mostly. It doesn't have much to do with whether she's Mom or not. But when she tries to be my mom, I get mad. I rip things and break things, jump up and down and run down to my room. I get paper to rip up and sometimes I rip posters that they gave me, or pictures of them. One time I broke a sword they gave me out of wood from Mexico. I broke that. It was terrific. I have a picture of my mom in my room. But I'd never rip that up.

"I'm not mad at my mother. She's really wonderful most of the time. I miss her a lot except around vacation times and there's nothing to miss because we'll be seeing her. I don't do anything when I miss my mom. I just miss her. I just keep on going like usual. I don't like writing letters much, but she writes letters and I write back and she calls. I talk with her a lot, unless I'm mad and I don't talk to her. Then I call her back. Sometimes I don't like to talk on the phone, like when I'm in trouble. Then when she's hung up I start crying and call her back. Maybe I'm trying to get back at her a little by not talking to her, but then I end up crying.

"My sister gets along worse with Nancy than me. She was older when it happened. I think she's taking it worse. Her relationship with Nancy isn't good at all. They're always fighting. I guess my sister likes and wants to be with my mom all the time. Her and Nancy fight about what she wears, whether she's ridden her bike so she can get exercise, what time she goes to bed, when she doesn't wash the dishes very good. Nancy's very neat and she makes us all be. When we get really mad we just look at her and say she's not our mother. We just look at her really hard and say that.

"I'm not that much mad at my father. I should be, I guess, but I'm not. If I'm mad at my mom sometimes, I should be mad at my dad. They should be the same. I don't feel that way about Nancy though, because she isn't part of the family. Well, she sort of is. I don't see my mom that much, and Nancy has lived with us over half our lives. But it doesn't make too much difference because I want to get my mom back.

"I have other friends who have stepmothers. And we talk about them sometimes. We say, 'Our stepmothers are tight,' and if we get mad at our stepmothers, we say, 'Would your real mom do that?' It doesn't really help or make a difference having friends with stepfamilies. Not that much. Kids with moms and dads have it better than us. They probably fight a lot too, but I think there's more fighting here. We get just as much loving, I guess. But there's more trouble going around. Those kids don't have to go on vacations and go someplace and child support and all that. It's better to have a normal family.

"I'll probably get married when I grow up. And I'll probably get divorced because a lot of people are now. I'd feel sorry for my kid to have to go through what I am, but if we get divorced, it's because I wouldn't like whoever I was married to. That's more important than the kids. We wouldn't stay together because of the kids. My mom and dad sure didn't."

MAKING IT

Divorce wars are bad enough. Wars between and inside stepfamilies are even worse. The multiples of people generate even more expectations that may fail, more confusion and displaced anger, more hurt to both parent and child who would seem to have experienced enough. Though it is extraordinarily difficult for new partners to recognize and accept the ties a parent has to a former union, they simply must. It is all part of the stepfamily package. No one can undo the past; the solution is to learn to live with it.

In spite of the tensions, many stepfamilies do manage to get it together—and stay together. If the divorces that preceded the new union have been successfully completed emotionally, the adults can bring enthusiasm and maturity born of experience into the new alliance. Some cut off all ties with the former spouse, as if to start from scratch with the new partner; other remarried couples, especially those with children, keep up a close partnership with their former spouses.

And if it all works, it can work very, very well. Children stand to gain an additional "parent," another concerned adult, whose presence not only relieves the load on the single parent, but brings positive attention to children who can't seem to get enough of it. "She does all the things mothers do, like sew on my buttons and change the sheets," says one nine-year-old boy of his stepmother. "I kind of like it." Boys, especially, can benefit from the atmosphere in a warm, supportive stepfamily. After remarriage, mothers are apt to become not only more firm and more consistent in dealing with their sons, but more loving as well. And stepfathers can become close to their stepsons. In turn, the boy's whole attitude can change, resulting in more mature and controlled behavior both at home and in school. The six-year follow-up of one ongoing study of stepfamilies found that where the natural parent had encouraged the involvement of the stepparent, where the stepparent was not only authoritative but warm, and where the children's natural parents maintained close relationships with them, the children were functioning better than those in either single-parent families or conflict-ridden intact families.[10] When all is said and done, the success or failure of a stepfamily depends on the natural parent and the person he or she has chosen to marry.

Even the extraordinary numbers of natural, half and steprelations that overwhelm some families can strengthen others. Some sociologists go so far as to suggest that multiple marriages and the "kinship networks" they create have actually rescued the nuclear family from its isolation and reproduced a modern form of the extended family with all its inherent supports.[11] "I have two stepsisters, a half brother, two new aunts and uncles, and eight grandparents," says one seven-year-old boy happily. "I get Christmas presents from all of them except my baby brother, who doesn't know how to buy things yet."

What is essential for the child's adjustment in a stepfamily is the cessation, as always, of warfare between his natural parents and now his stepparents as well. An about-to-be-married parent can also relieve a lot of the child's anxiety about the stepparent by playing down the importance of the child-stepparent relationship. The new couple, after all, has chosen to love each other, but the child often feels he has no choice. The child will feel immensely relieved if his parent allows him *not* to love the new stepparent and assures him he will not risk losing the natural parent's love if he doesn't. This clears the way for the child to strike his own relationship with the stepparent without pressure or interference from the natural parent.

To prepare parents for the complexities of stepfamily life, some professionals advise counseling sessions for all couples about to embark on such a predictably fraught course. And the success rate is astounding. Out of the five hundred couples counseled at the Step Family Foundation in New York, only four went on to divorce. "We teach them the expectations they can have—and not have," says Jeannette Lofas, executive director of the Foundation. "You can't expect an elephant to jump a five-foot fence, or a truck to act like a Ferrari."

Above all else, the children should not be allowed by either the stepparent or the natural parent to victimize the stepparent. Children will test and test again to find out just where everybody stands. When served dinner, for example, the child might say to the stepparent, "My mother/father cooks better than you," and then wait to see the reaction. Both the natural parent and the stepparent should respond calmly, pointing out the child's rudeness and saying that yes, the other parent does cook very well, but that in this household they do things a little differently. And he is welcome to eat his dinner or not. The stepparent, in particular, needs the support and backup of the natural parent to build a framework that will support all the new family members and help prevent it from breaking down into blood alignments.

When all is said and done, however, few children are really happy at the thought of their natural parents marrying someone else. Their original family unit gets stretched farther and farther apart and the hope of restoring it becomes dimmer. Though adults may benefit from changing partners, their children often see remarriage as the death of the only real family they will ever have. In time, usually the same three-year period it takes a family to adjust to divorce, the children may not only come to accept their new family forms but to be enhanced by them, but the beginning may be very rough.

It is common now at weddings for the flower girl toddling up the aisle to be the bride's daughter rather than her little sister or niece, the nervous best man to be a gawky son rather than a brother or college roommate. And for all the joy that may be fluttering in the hearts of the newly reweds, they should bear in mind that their children's hearts are apt to be more clouded.

Some children distance themselves emotionally. "I was the best man at my father's wedding and I felt . . . detached," says fifteen-year-old Max. "I have been looking on at a distance at my ex-parents all the way from the divorce to the remarriage." Another boy, this one thirteen, weighed his father's request to be his best man for two months before accepting. "Dad getting married to someone else. That was hard," the boy confesses. "I didn't even say 'Congratulations.' You can't say *that* when your father left your mother to marry another woman."

Witnessing the ceremony proved too much for a ten-year-old boy who refused to go, even though he had "a chance to get out of school." "I would have said when the guy says, 'Is there any-one who objects to this marriage?' 'Yeah. Me! I don't want them to get married!' " A fourteen-year-old girl nearly solved her conflict by staying too long at a neighbor's house on the morning of the wedding, but the justice of the peace waited till she showed up. Then she took it all in defensive stride. "It didn't bother me watching them get married," she says. "The way I look at it, I'm supposed to have a tough exterior, so that's the way I pretended to feel. I personally think it's the best way—not to show the way you feel."

DIVORCE AND THE SCHOOLS
The Second Family

Emily was six the year her parents separated, the same year she entered first grade. At home, the situation was terrible. Her father kept leaving, then coming back only to fight viciously with her mother and leave again. When her father wasn't there, Emily's mother was so depressed she often wouldn't get out of bed all day. When Emily's father was there, he and her mother would scream at each other and sometimes even throw things. Emily was quiet as a mouse all year at school and was no trouble at all to the teacher. And because no one at the school had known Emily before then, they didn't know that she had grown unnaturally quiet.

By the time Emily was in the second grade, her father had finally left home for good, and cutting himself off from his past, never saw Emily and her brother or sent any money for their support. Their mother tried to get a job, but found that she had no salable skills. Relatives helped out financially, but the mother's depression continued to spiral. She started drinking, and sometimes Emily would come home from school to find her mother passed out in front of the television set. Emily's brother, now in fourth grade, was behaving very badly. Friendless, he would fly into rages in the classroom, bully his classmates, and eat by himself in a corner of the cafeteria. One day when the teacher asked him if he'd finished the project she'd assigned, he hit her.

Emily's brother was sent to a special school for disturbed children.

Still, nobody noticed Emily at all until she entered the third grade, when it became increasingly difficult not to notice that she had a problem. The other third graders were beginning to pay attention to their clothes and their appearance; Emily's clothes were dirty and rumpled, her hair uncombed. She began to steal her classmates' belongings, a notebook here and there, a pencil case, a hairbrush. Her classmates taunted her, accused her of theft, and ostracized her, calling her "el disgusto." Emily never said a word, and in fact even stopped responding to her name. She seemed to want to be abused by her classmates. Her teacher didn't know what to do. She called Emily's mother for a conference, but Emily's mother didn't show up. The teacher talked to the principal and he tried to locate the father but couldn't. Desperate, the teacher spoke to the school psychologist, who recommended psychiatric care for Emily. But when the teacher called the mother again, the mother said there was nothing the matter with Emily, and anyway they didn't have any money for doctor's bills. The teacher then called the local family counseling agency, but their funding had been cut back and they were so understaffed that there was a three-month waiting list. Even the local church was uninterested in the problem, as Emily's family were not church members. And so Emily moved on to fourth grade. And her third-grade teacher heaved a sigh of relief that Emily was someone else's problem now.

Just whose problem is Emily, anyway? Her mother is obviously so overwhelmed by her own problems that she cannot respond to the warning signals Emily is sending out. The school is caught in the bind of neither wanting to interfere in family affairs on the one hand, nor to see a student drop by the wayside on the other. And even if the school knew its role clearly, it is ill-equipped in terms of staff and expertise to help Emily.

As the rise in divorce rates is steadily matched by a decline in the influence of such traditional institutions as the church and the family itself, schools are increasingly faced with a dilemma of national significance. The pressure on schools to act as second parent to its students has been growing constantly since the sixties when the drug and sexual revolutions spread to school campuses. Often, at that time, the schools chose to act as go-betweens in the conflicts of parents and students, trying to bridge what became known as the generation gap. In the era of abandoned formality, teachers began to be called by their first rather than last names, and became as much mentors and confidants to their students as they were teachers. Now educators and school administrators believe that disruptions in family life have replaced the social turmoil of the sixties with a far more fundamental impact. And the schools are more involved than ever. "Children have two basic homes, their own and the school," says Dr. Maurice Vanderpol, director of the Institute for School Consultation at McLean Hospital in Massachusetts. "When something goes wrong in the home, they look for help at the other."

Whether they get it is the nub of the present dilemma. "Since the late sixties, parents and professionals have been tugging and pulling to redefine what each is supposed to do," says Joseph Featherstone, a professor at the Harvard Graduate School of Education.[1] Some educators remain resolute in their

refusal to involve themselves in anything outside their academic responsibilities. "It is just not the school's mandate to
keep on providing programs for students with nonacademic
problems," says William Woessner, superintendent of schools
in Southampton, N.Y. "Our duty is to educate, not counsel."
Others disagree, seeing the school as an all-encompassing institution mandated to fulfill all the students' needs. "You can't address the academic issues if the kid's bouncing off the wall because of a family crisis like divorce," says Eric Rofes, a teacher
at the Fayerweather School in Cambridge, Massachusetts, and
editor of *The Kid's Book of Divorce*. "It's very important for
schools to deal with divorce, in a very direct manner."

Though the attitudes of educators may be polarized, the impact
of divorce on children as students is distressingly clear. During
the upheaval of divorce, children's academic achievements are
more apt to become losses. Their grades go down, their homework assignments are completed irregularly, if at all, and their
attention spans lessen, along with their ability to concentrate.
Sometimes preschool and primary school-aged children just
plain go to sleep in class, exhausted by the stress at home. Like
seven-year-old Johnny, who took it upon himself after his father left to stay awake guarding the house for burglars, or
eight-year-old Kate, who suddenly had to take almost total care
of herself, the children of divorce can be simply worn out. And
symptoms show up in the classroom.

There seems to be no age limit to poor performance in
school, though gender does seem to be a factor. One highly
touted study found that from elementary school right through
high school, boys from single-parent homes were more often
classified as "low achievers" with grades of D and F than children from intact families. At the other end of the bell curve,
more boys from intact families were classified as "high
achievers," with grades of A and B, than were boys from sin-

gle-parent families.[2] Only girls from high-income single-parent homes seemed exempt from the problem, showing better grades than boys in similarly affluent two-parent families.[3] The adverse effects of divorce on academic achievement are corroborated by an informal survey of 200 students at a public high school in Braintree, Massachusetts, which found that the vast majority of low reading scores came from the test papers of kids from single-parent homes.

The youngest children more openly display their problems in the classroom, not being old enough yet to differentiate between the separate worlds of home and school. Preschoolers often become regressively confused, forgetting the names and functions of familiar objects. The cognitive confusion about their parents' splitup, which leads some preschoolers to think that the loss of one parent signifies the imminent loss of the other, naturally affects them and their learning abilities. In one study, teachers' reports on preschoolers whose parents were divorcing included such academically inhibiting behavior as high restlessness, distractability, fear of failure, excessive daydreaming, and clinging to the teacher.[4]

Though luckily the preschool years are not as important academically as the higher grades, a pattern can start here that will be hard to break. The play patterns of preschoolers are a subject of great fascination to child development researchers, as it is the child's unself-conscious behavior in fantasy and imaginative play that determines his cognitive development and level of maturity. And here the children of divorce are handicapped yet again. One classic study found not only that the children of divorce played for shorter periods of time and were more apt to be onlookers than children from intact families, but that their play patterns were less socially and cognitively mature as well. They were apt to play less imaginatively and, in fantasy play, to be narrower and more rigid. Boys, particularly, seemed less able to move from the "I" phase to assuming another role in fantasy play, a transition that usually occurs between three and four-and-a-half.[5]

Often the personal needs of preschoolers derail their new gratification in learning and achieving. Many cling excessively to the teacher, seeking both affection and reassurance against abandonment, instead of working in the block corner or putting together a new puzzle. They don't learn from their classmates, either. Instead of peer education through cooperation and interaction, little boys, especially, often alienate their classmates by overaggressiveness and bullying, while girls can become just as isolated by withdrawing. Though these disruptions in the child's learning process are usually short-lived, leveling out within a year or two after parental separation, these children's first experiences with school are apt to be dominated by their emotional distress rather than by progress in cognitive function and the ability to learn.

Children who are elementary or secondary school age when their parents split up experience many of the same classroom problems as younger children but on a more sophisticated level. Restlessness, inability to concentrate, and increased daydreaming interfere with their academic progress in both study periods and classroom lectures. "All the time at school I kept daydreaming," says seven-year-old Beth. "I couldn't see the words on the page and sometimes the teacher would get mad at me because I couldn't hear her." The severity of this classroom daydreaming at these ages seems to depend on the degree of distress witnessed in the parent at home. If it is high, girls seem to spend their classroom time dreaming about reconciling the parents or the return of the absent parent to the home, whereas boys tend to day-worry rather than daydream about the depressed parent's well-being.[6]

At these ages the children's behavior at school and at home is often contradictory. Old enough now to comprehend fully the different settings of school and home, children can safely act out their angers and fears in the classroom and on the playground while being exceptionally good at home so as not to alienate the parent.[7] Conversely, a child can act overmaturely at school while continuing to throw tantrums at home. Children's schoolwork can be just as variable. Though most show lower levels of achievement, some children go to the top of the class through almost obsessive absorption in school work. "School has actually saved my life," says twelve-year-old Sally, who is the center of a custody battle. "My grades have gone way up. I'm spending more time on my work now so I don't have to think about all this trouble. I spend all night in my room doing homework."

The upheaval in a divorcing household, however, does not make it easy on any school-aged child. Just getting to school can present a problem. According to one national study, the children of divorce are more apt to be late, to be late more often, and to miss school altogether. Children from single-parent families are absent on an average of four days more per semester than are children in two-parent families, and they are twice as likely to spontaneously skip school as are their counterparts in intact families.[8]

Their workloads can also seem overwhelming. One nine-year-old boy, at the center of an angry custody fight, fell apart when he received an incomplete on a school paper and actually ran out of the school and across a nearby field, screaming all the while, "I won't do it."[9] Other children can temporarily buckle under the loss of the parent who had been very involved in the child's academic progress. "I'd been used to going to my father for help with my homework and I missed him terribly," says one boy whose parents separated when he was eleven. "For months afterward I'd say, 'Okay, I don't understand this problem, I'll go ask' . . . and then there'd be the realization. My marks went way down at school. It was the continuing realization that got to me."

Socially, the breakdown in peer relationships can also divert these children from their studies. As children of divorce are inevitably unhappy and as a result more vulnerable to teasing during the period of their family's breakup, they are grist for any meanie's mill. Though many school-aged children are sensitive to the family problems of their schoolmates, some aren't, and it takes just a few jibes to make a child miserable. "They keep asking me why my father doesn't come to Father's Day and what awful thing I did to make him go away,"says one eight-year-old girl tearfully. "They're just so mean." Another eight-year-old has become such a target for taunting that he has begun to get sick every morning before going to school and to get into fist fights when he does get there. "They say things like 'Your mother eats Kibbles 'n Bits' [a kind of dog food] and sometimes they call me an 'orphan boy,' " says the boy, who lives with his single father. "I just hate them all so much. I want to knock them all down to the ground."

For these tormented children, changing schools might be a relief. But too much changing causes problems of a different sort. Divorce often sets the single-parent family on the road, either out of a parent's urge to start over again somewhere else or, most commonly, out of financial necessity. Though the common belief is that children adjust quickly to change, the period of adjustment can nonetheless be very difficult for children eight to ten years old who are just establishing firm friendships for the first time. At these ages, they neither want to give up old friends nor take up with new ones. Ten-year-old Brandon, for example, has gone to three different schools in two years. "I feel weird," says the boy. "The kids aren't really good friends, just people. When you go to a new place, everyone's looking, saying, 'There's a new kid.' When you've adjusted it's okay, but you're never adjusted if you have to keep switching around."

And many children of divorce do have to keep switching

around, changing schools three times as often as children with two parents at the secondary school level, twice as often during the primary school years.[10] Eleven-year-old Walter went to six different schools in seven years, alternating between living with his mother, his father, and his grandparents. His favorite, he says, was the Dalton School in New York, where he actually spent two consecutive years. "I got to know the last names of everyone in my class," says the boy, who describes himself as a loner. "It was nice. But I never got good marks. Everyone was going on from where they left off last year." Thirteen-year-old Jenny, who has been to schools in Rhode Island, Chicago, and New York while moving back and forth between parents, does get good grades, but that isn't enough. "Everyone has best friends and I don't," she says. "Instead I'm a good student and have an A average. I think my grades are that high because I spend the extra times I would spend with a best friend on my school work. I'd rather have a best friend though. Everyone has one but me."

For older children, divorce during the high school years can be critical to students whose grade averages cannot bear too precipitous a drop if they want to go on to college. And often, in the shock and shame that engulf adolescents at their parents' separation, the marks are the first thing to go. "I mean, like how can you get too involved in the significance of the carpet-baggers if you're not sure you have a home to go to after school?" says a tenth grader, expressing the perceived loss of family structure so characteristic to teenagers of divorce.

Beyond the same classroom problems of inattention and lack of concentration faced by schoolchildren of all ages, teenagers face a far more serious academic threat. The loss of faith in their parents' ability to fulfill the commitment of marriage can swell to include the loss of faith in every institution, particularly school. Just when the educational stakes are highest in these last years of formal schooling, teenagers of divorce are more than twice as likely to drop out of high school as are students from two-parent families.[11]

A close and supportive relationship with a teacher often determines a teenager's ability to separate his family problems from his school life and to get on with the latter. Teenagers have less access to a single teacher as they travel between many teachers in high school, yet time and again, they cite a specific teacher, counselor, or athletic coach who helped them through the stress of divorce and served as a role model when all their filial role models seemed to be crumbling around them. "I was just going to pitch it all in one day when I bumped into Mr. Marx in the hallway," says one high school senior whose behavior and marks had deteriorated to the point of expulsion. "He took me outside and showed me a stew bum sleeping on the school steps. 'There's your choice,' he said to me. He was being pretty dramatic, of course. But it must have worked, because here I am."

It is a new fact of single-parent family life that the teacher is often seen by both the student and the parent as the one stable and consistent person in their lives. Drawn into a role that bridges home and school, the teacher becomes "coparent" to the parent, and "family" to many distressed and lonely kids. It is more than a full-time job. "More and more I have teachers who'll get called by kids all hours of the night," says Isa Zimmerman, principal of a high school in Wenham, Massachusetts.

Though many teachers respond to the increased needs of these children, they are often uneasy about it. Their training has been academic, not psychological, and frequently they face situations they are ill-equipped to deal with. Teachers these days encounter a puzzling array of divorce-generated behavior in their classrooms that ranges from disruptive bullying to sullen withdrawal, from obsessive students to failing students, from attention-craving students to hostile, rejecting ones.

231

Many manage only by sheer intuition. One mother in New York was summoned from work to school, where her six-year-old daughter had suddenly started smashing toys. She arrived to find her daughter crying in the teacher's lap. "The teacher sat and held my daughter until I got there, and during that time she was crying and making up various excuses," the mother said. "But [the teacher] knew enough to help her get out what was really on her mind—that she wanted to see her daddy."[12]

The sheer number of students going through the disruption of their families has brought a new awareness and sensitivity to teaching that goes far beyond the three R's. Preschoolers often look to their teacher as surrogate mommies and daddies. School-aged children look to them more as mentors and protectors in a world over which they suddenly have little control. "The nuns knew about it when Dad left. They were nice," says nine-year-old George. "Say I got a fifty on a test. They'd give me a seventy-five. They told me to tell them when things were bothering me." More and more teachers are even extending themselves to help their students outside the academic environment. "She's been really nice," says thirteen-year-old Nancy, whose parents are contesting for her custody, of her teacher. "She gave me Judy Blume's book *It's Not the End of the World* to read. And she told me that what my parents are doing should not give me a bad attitude about marriage."

The complications of divorce have forced many teachers to assume ever more custodial roles. It has become their responsibility to keep track of just who is allowed to pick up the child after school and who isn't, to prevent the child from being kidnapped by the noncustodial parent. Time and again, teachers are called upon to straighten out the complexities created by divorce and a student's two households. Books, homework assignments, sports equipment are apt to be left at one parent's house or the other, causing the child to arrive at school unprepared and upset. "I send notes to both sets of parents asking them to check their children every morning," says one teacher. Where there is just one note sent home with the child, it is often delivered to the wrong parent. One little girl gave her note explaining what she needed for Field Day to her mother on Tuesday. But Field Day was Thursday, the day reserved for her father, and the note was not passed along. "She arrived at Field Day without a picnic, without either parent, and wearing her school uniform while everybody else was in jeans," says her teacher. "It seems like a small thing, but to her it was very big. She hid behind the bushes and cried until I found her."

Some teachers have even adjusted their daily curriculum to counter the pressures of divorce. Fridays and Mondays have become especially difficult days for students who are torn about leaving one parent for the other at the beginning of the weekend and just as torn about coming home Sunday night. "We do more calming activities those days," says one teacher. "We leave time for the teacher to help the kid who's going to start crying in the middle of the day or be really upset. It's happening in schools all over the place."

Divorce has also changed—and complicated—what used to be straightforward communication between teacher and parents. Simply scheduling parent-teacher conferences, for instance, can become a logistical nightmare. Some parents come together, some demand separate meetings, sometimes only the custodial parent comes, sometimes one parent asks that the other not have conferences with the child's teacher at all. One teacher, who had scheduled a conference with a student's mother, received a call from the noncustodial father, who said he wanted a conference, too. The mother hit the roof, thinking the teacher might say something negative to the father about the child's care. She called the principal to protest, and because the mother was paying the tuition, the principal asked the teacher to cancel the father's conference. The teacher was disgusted. "It's just not my job to deal with all these angry parents," he says. "All I want to do is educate the child and keep both parents informed."

Increasingly, teachers are being asked to leave the classroom for the courtroom to testify in custody proceedings. Like doctors who feel torn between helping accident victims and facing possible malpractice suits, teachers are torn between supporting the child's best interests and getting overinvolved in a family's private affairs. Playing God is not a criterion for tenure. One teacher in New York has been asked to testify in court in four different cases but agreed to do so only once. "It was an out-and-out case," she says. "The father was on drugs and never knew if the child was in the house or not. The other cases were more complicated. Both parents were good enough. The children wanted to live with both of them. And I was not about to take that responsibility." Another teacher echoed the same reservation after sitting through three days of court testimony, relieved at not being called. "I'd been saying up till then that teachers had to stick up for the rights of children," she says. "I'm not so sure now. There's no way of predicting that the predivorce relationship between the parent and child will be the same as the postdivorce relationship."

There is no doubt that teachers are, in many cases, the unsung heroes of divorce. Whether they welcome it or not, teachers have become the safety net for many children and their single parents who have no one else to turn to. Lonely children often arrive at school early, hoping for some time alone with a favorite teacher, and hang around after the final bell to eke out even more time and attention. Single parents, too, depend heavily on the teachers to fill in not only the gap of the absent parent but often their own absence as well. Preoccupied with the demands of work and single-parent life, many custodial mothers and fathers gratefully and even callously relinquish their responsibilities as parents to the sacrificial teacher. And time and again, teachers pick up the single-parent slack.

It is little wonder that some teachers can feel as burdened by their students' divorces as do the families themselves, and some resent their inherited roles. "It's extraordinary to have to deal with all the extra problems of divorce as part of my job to keep this classroom going smoothly," says a former nursery school teacher. "It took more than a little rethinking on my part not to make me angry." But even the most enlightened and supportive teachers sometimes do feel angry. Male teachers, especially, can feel an unwelcome responsibility to fill in as surrogate fathers to children without them. "I'm often the only man in their lives and the kids bring me the incredible needs that wouldn't be there if there were a father present," says one teacher, who regularly takes his students camping, to the movies, on bike rides. "I feel a tremendous responsibility to them and a tremendous anger toward the fathers. I cannot believe the number of fathers who refuse to parent, either through desertion, neglect, or the withholding of affection."

But for every sensitive teacher, there is one who is not. And for every teacher who tries to help the children of divorce with their special problems, there is a school whose policy frowns on it. Teachers are increasingly being caught in the Laocoönian struggle between conservative taxpayers, special-interest children, and their budget-squeezed school administrations. The dilemma is far from being resolved.

For all that schools have become increasingly important as the influence of other institutions has diminished, many are resisting the changes their new role demands, especially with regard to divorce. Clinging to the fading image of the two-parent family, many schools simply ignore the special needs of their single-parent students, as if to pretend that this trend, like others, will pass. To be sure, the money crunch in school budgets these days is very real and not conducive to special student programs. But at heart, the resistance in schools is based more on

235

the reluctance to deal with social issues in the classroom—or even the corridors. At one school in New England, the administration insisted that the name of a divorce-counseling group be reduced to an acronym, so that the word "divorce" would never be announced over the school's public-address system.

Why is divorce such a touchy issue? Some schools feel that by acknowledging its tenacity, they are condoning it. Dependent on the support of parents, schools are also anxious not to alienate either partner in a splitting couple or, worse yet, to get caught in the middle of parental wars. Others see the schools' acceptance of divorce-related problems as a prelude to falling heir to all other social problems. And the schools neither want them nor feel able to afford them. "There is a growing sense that public education is failing," says John LeRoy, principal of a Massachusetts high school. "Yet we not only have to deal with education, but family and social matters as well, even special-need kids from the courts. We don't have the time or staff to deal with them."

Where there have been changes, they are primarily bureaucratic. Student information sheets and application forms now regularly leave spaces for both parents' names and business and home addresses. Some schools routinely send out duplicate report cards and notices to both parents. Others do so only at the request of the custodial parent or the student, even though existing family law holds that both parents shall have access to the child's records unless specifically barred by the court. But many schools tend to ignore that law, considering the relationship between school and parent more private than public. Instead, private schools tend to favor the requests of the parent who is footing the tuition bill, while public schools favor the custodial and more involved parent. This subjective—and illegal—handling of student records can put a school right in the middle of the battle it most wants to avoid—the war between the parents. "We had two divorced parents here recently, both claiming their rights," says John LeRoy. "The father wanted access to his child's record, but the mother, the legal guardian, told us not to give them to him. Eventually, we had to deal with two sets of lawyers, riled up families, even the grandparents. It was a pretty bad scene."

On a more practical level, many schools now schedule parent-teacher conferences early in the morning or in the evening to better accommodate the working parent, single or not. In an effort to defuse their divorced students' anguish at being unparented at the traditional school rites of Father's or Mother's Day, more and more schools are not holding Parents' Day instead, where either parent is welcome. But in these days of working parents, even this device doesn't always work, and more enlightened schools now hold Friends Day or an open house to which anyone close to the child is invited. "For the first time I had somebody," says a third grader. "Our housekeeper came and brought us all cookies."

A few schools have hit the problem of divorce head-on and are beginning to include courses on divorce in their curriculum. The Mildred E. Strang Middle School in Yorktown Heights, New York, for example, offers eighth graders a highly popular course called "Who Gets Me for Christmas?: A Course on Separation, Death and Remarriage." The interest in the subject has grown beyond the sixty-six junior high school students who first took the course, generating small discussion groups and a weekly parents' meeting. To buttress the raised consciousness of the teachers who have chosen to sit in on the course, the co-founder of the program has distributed suggestion sheets to the faculty entitled "Helpful Steps Teachers Can Take." "Avoid biased language such as 'broken home,' " reads one example. "Single-parent homes are as 'whole' as two-parent homes."

In order better to understand the pressures on their students, many teachers are themselves going back to school. A typical program is offered by Wheelock College's Center for

Parenting Studies. Much of the curriculum there is practical, from counseling referrals to a review of the current popular literature on family and children, but the thrust of the course is for teachers who are scared or confused about families in transition. In California's Marin County, the Center for the Family in Transition conducts six-week workshops for staffs in twenty-one schools, sets up peer-counseling groups and advises schools in divorce-related curriculum. But the future of this ambitious project is jeopardized by the budget-strapped public school system and by the reluctance of school administrators.

Fed up with adult apathy and indecision, some children are taking the issue of divorce into their own hands. The trend-setter was the Divorced Kids Group, a peer-counseling group at the Lexington High School in Lexington, Massachusetts. "There were umpteen million support groups for women. But for the kids, there was nothing," says Lexington's then guidance counselor, Howard Schofield, who started the group. The public airing of their frank discussions and single-parent family secrets on the radio, in newspapers, and finally on *20/20* and the *Phil Donahue Show* brought criticism of Schofield (one school administrator sneered that the group had become "That's Entertainment") and an avalanche of queries from other schools. The peer-group concept had obviously struck a national nerve, and soon children's own counseling groups had sprung up in secondary and high schools all over the country.

Overnight, it seemed, children of divorce started to talk about it. Meeting weekly and informally under the supervision of guidance counselors, the children of divorce began to let it all hang out in after-school classrooms all over the country. These divorce veterans at last began to confess their fears, their problems, and their anger into strongly sympathetic ears. Often it was for the first time. "Before, I didn't talk about the divorce to anyone," said seventeen-year-old Cathy during a meeting of KIDS (Kids in Divorced Situations) at the Dover-

Sherborn High School in Dover, Massachusetts. "No way I'd talk to a teacher. And with my friends, I'd try to explain my situation but they really didn't know what I was talking about."

Even when the situations that come up at these no-holds-barred meetings are chilling, students find a knowing ear. At one group, a thirteen-year-old confessed she had come close to killing herself the day before her custody was to be decided in court. When she heard "Yeah" and "I've been there" from the rest of the group, she relaxed and smiled. Because their members have so much in common, these groups usually become very close and supportive. When a fourteen-year-old girl walked into the weekly meeting of KIDS and announced breezily, "My Mom won everything on the alimony appeal," the group cheered.

Beyond unloading their particular emotional problems in the security of their peer group, most of these informal divorce groups also learn the nuts and bolts of divorce. Divorce lawyers, court psychologists, even judges come to speak to them. And the kids go to them. The Divorced Kids Group at Braintree High School, for example, sat in on a divorce court hearing and went together to see *Kramer vs. Kramer.* Counselors also lead various groups in therapy exercises. In one drawn from Erik Erikson, for example, the students are asked to complete sentences that begin "I wish my father would . . ." or "I wish my mother could . . ." and to act out various family complications through role-playing, the student taking the part of the offending parent. A "simulation game" orchestrated by a visiting psychologist was a highlight at Dover High School. "He tied us all up with a rope," says eighteen-year-old Cathy. "One person would represent the mother pulling one way. Another would be your father pulling his way. Then there was a boyfriend, a teacher, and so on. It was incredibly vivid."

For younger children, counselors use various games to help them work out their feelings about divorce. Nursery and elementary school children often play out their anxieties with puppets and dolls, putting their own fears into the mouths of the toys. Dollhouses and houses built out of blocks easily become their own houses in their young imaginations as the children painfully build them—and often destroy them. There is even a divorce board game devised by child psychiatrist Richard A. Gardner, called "Talking, Feeling, Doing," that helps young children of divorce articulate their feelings. Other programs are more complex. In Warsaw, Indiana, a six-foot, orange, furry character named Orby is making the rounds of the elementary schools, animated by an education specialist and made to speak by a story-telling therapist from the Otis R. Bowen Center for Human Services, Inc. Through pantomime, songs, stories, dances, and games, first graders help Orby solve his problems with divorce. "We try to get the children to accept that they can have a positive input where their own feelings are concerned," says Orby's coordinator, Barbara Bontrager. "While the children may not be able to change the circumstances of their parents' divorce, they can change their own feelings and/or responses to the situation."

For all the benefits and supports children seem to draw from these programs, surprisingly few take advantage of them. Out of a school population of 2,300 in a Boston suburb, only ten students attended the peer-group sessions. Counselors at two other schools have discontinued the peer-counseling for divorced kids they started just a few years ago. Counselors at both schools predict the groups may be revived. "But," says one, "I don't think it's something you can sustain on an ongoing basis. You need a lot of students making a public commitment."

The reality is that many children simply do not want to talk about their family problems, especially as they grow older. Instead they do their best to forget them. "It was such a relief going away to boarding school," says a student at the Choate School in Connecticut. "It's easier on me here. The demands are simple—homework and staying out of trouble. At home the whole situation is more complicated and sticky." Day students, especially, often look at their school life as a surcease from the turmoil at home. One girl at the Fayerweather School in Cambridge participated in writing *The Kids' Book of Divorce,* but outside of that refused to talk about her parents' divorce. "I'm dealing with it all the time, every minute I'm at home," she told her teacher. "I need a place I can relax and not have to deal with it."

Parents have also registered apathy toward, if not opposition to, many of these peer-counseling groups. Understandably, they are nervous about the airing of their dirty family linen in public, feeling it is no one's business but their own. They are also curious about what their children are saying, and sometimes put the school guidance counselors on the spot. Soon after Kids in Divorced Situations began to meet in Dover, Massachusetts, one mother dropped by the school to ask if there was anything her daughter had said that she should know about. The counselor replied that he could not betray any of the students' confidences. But he was concerned. "I can understand the parents' fears," says counselor Ron Dumont. "In a way, it was like I was looking at their laundry."

School administrators are close behind with their own criticisms. Though many in both public and private schools were willing to experiment with counseling groups for their children of divorce, they now feel it has gotten out of hand. "We must spend 30 percent of our time dealing with this [divorced] group of kids," says one high school principal. "We're a large school, with lots of different needs. And I don't think we should do this." Stigmatizing the children of divorce is another opposition voiced by some schools. "We try to be sensitive to the problems divorce creates," says Vice-Principal Henry Bedford at Phillips Exeter Academy in New Hampshire. "It is an issue, and a serious one. But we don't label it, any more than we label counseling for minorities. You don't go into one infirmary door because you have a broken ankle and into another because you have menstrual cramps."

For all that most schools make a genuine effort these days at least to recognize their students' emotional needs as well as their academic ones, often they fail. Sometimes the reason is lack of money. But just as often it is insensitivity. In spite of the number of students whose parents are divorced, school curricula often still present the concept of the nuclear family as the only shape of family life. These schools stubbornly stick to outdated attitudes and textbooks that drum the "Mommy and Daddy" norm into their students' heads (though, granted, this is as much a sin of omission as of commission—textbooks are costly to replace). For the children of divorce, who sometimes represent the majority of students in a given classroom, this attitude reinforces their feeling of being different and abnormal. "Even now in school they'll talk about what families do together," says eleven-year-old Christine, 40 percent of whose classmates come from divorced families. "They'll tell stories about families going camping or going to Mass. They asked us in a discussion group what our fathers do. I felt bad because I had nothing to say."

It is possible, of course, for schools and teachers to become oversensitive to the family problems of their students, to lay all blame for their misbehavior or academic laziness on divorce. Such a convenient crutch not only gives the student an excuse to make less of an effort, but also prolongs his preoccupation with the divorce. One boy whose parents split up when he was in kindergarten was still being treated with deference in the fourth grade. "Every time some little thing goes wrong, he's supposed to see the school psychologist. It's a cop-out," says his mother. "His father and I finally had to sit down and tell him that though the school blamed all his acting out on the divorce, it was time for him to take some responsibility for his actions himself."

Though the balance may be delicate between over and underattention to the students of divorce, their teachers do need to be kept informed about the out-of-school stresses on their pupils. And too often the rigid hierarchy in many schools prevents such personal information from getting to the teachers who need it most. "Privileged" information often trickles down slowly—if at all. And the children suffer for it. One sixth grade teacher was looking forward to having a boy in his class who had been described to him as bright, popular, and a natural leader. But soon after the fall term began, it became apparent that the boy was none of these things. Not only was he doing badly academically, but his obnoxious behavior toward his former friends was hurting him socially. Only after the puzzled teacher went to the principal did he find out that the boy's parents had separated during the summer. But such information, the principal said, did not belong in the classroom. "I was forbidden to let the boy know I knew about his situation or tell his peers even though they would probably have understood him better if they had known," says the teacher. "The boy was totally isolated in the situation."

Schools cannot afford to duck the issue of divorce, no matter how strict their budgets, no matter what political or parental influences are brought to bear, no matter how uneasy they are at the ever growing numbers of single-parent students. The argument that divorce does not belong in the classroom is really moot. The issue is there, sitting at the neat rows of desks starting with the first bell in the morning and often, now, continuing well past the last bell in the afternoon. School is central to every child's life. And in this day and age, it is sometimes the only consistent thing a child has.

As in most areas of life, the dilemma faced by schools is largely related to money. If funds were available, counseling groups for every sort of distress could exist. But in these times of critical cash flow, schools seem to be spending their money on things that show quick results rather than on the behind-the-scenes services that can turn a troubled child's life around. Almost every service can be cut, it seems, as long as a school still has a football team.

Too much of the support for single-parent children now comes arbitrarily from individual teachers who choose, out of selflessness, to act as surrogate parents for children who have already lost one parent and only seem to have half of the other. But rather than rewarding these teachers, we penalize them by decreasing money allocated for public education. Not only do the teachers suffer; so do their inherited wards. With the cutback in teaching staffs across the country, it is the younger, more flexible members of the faculty who invariably get the axe.

There is a critical need for programs for these children of divorce, special supervised programs to help them sort out their feelings and reestablish a sense of trust in what will eventually be their adult world. School counselors are invaluable in drawing out these children, whether in peer groups or in one-on-one discussions. Where the budget will not allow more than one counselor, trained volunteers can be enlisted to help these children before their problems grow insurmountable. One such program in East Hampton, New York, worked wonders with kindergarten through fourth grade students in the throes of divorce, though the counselors were paid a pittance. The school is the logical setting; even though some of these children may feel stigmatized, they are very unlikely to find their way to outside facilities. The use of the school not only legitimizes counseling, but provides access for the students.

Teachers, too, need training. Even a one-day workshop conducted by a child psychologist or divorce specialist can point out the particular danger signals these children are sending out and help teachers to understand when a child is just too distracted to perform academically. And to match the important stature they assume in a child's life during divorce, teachers also need up-to-date information from the school administration and from the parents themselves about any changes at home.

Beyond their emotional needs, children in working single-parent families need company and something to do after school that will keep them from going home to an empty house. It is estimated that there are now 5.2 million children under thirteen on their own after school. Not only is it a lonely life, often it is downright dangerous. One recent study found that one out of four fires in Detroit and one out of six in Delaware were started by children at home alone after school. Only 100 public school districts presently have before-and-after-school programs—a drop in the unsupervised bucket.[13] Where school budgets cannot stretch beyond the school day, local community groups, merchants' associations, or volunteers could run afternoon programs at the schools for children who otherwise have no safe place to go.

On a more basic level, school curricula should be expanded to include courses for children in child care, emergency health procedures, and even nutrition. Increasingly, single-parent children have the responsibility of looking after their younger brothers and sisters, as well as themselves, with no adult supervision. Schools should also update their curricula and choose textbooks that include various forms of the family rather than just the traditional two-parent home. Reluctant as they may be to face it, schools have to recognize that female-headed families are increasing ten times as quickly as are two-parent families.

All this is a heavy yoke to put on the schools, which are al-

ready stretched to the limit and cutting back on the very programs that should be expanded. But this is the real world. Em-
bracing reality means recognizing that too many children these
days are essentially growing up unparented, learning far below
their academic potential, and living dangerously unsupervised
lives. Taxpayers and various branches of government should
make a wiser use of their money where these social and academic problems are centered and can be eased. Schools should
shed their reluctance and instead face their students' problems
in the eighties. And teachers, above all, should be compensated
for their increasingly responsible roles in the lives of their students. The cutting back of support systems for school children
just when they need them most is not only shortsighted, it can,
in the long run, be tragic.

CUSTODY AND THE COURTS
God on the Bench

The desert sun is low in the sky, making the cheerful blue rug seem even brighter, the green leaves of the many plants even greener. A low, round, plastic table sits in the second-floor room, surrounded by tiny blue and red plastic chairs knee-high to a five-year-old. Under a big pot of paper daisies are neat stacks of comics and children's magazines along with a mini-library of children's books. But the titles of the books belie the sunny atmosphere of this room. Instead of *Curious George* and *Rin Tin Tin,* these bookshelves hold such titles as *Where Is Daddy? The Story of a Divorce.* And the poster of shiny balloons on the wall that reads "May beautiful things happen to you," seems more a poignant comment than a promise. For this is a room in the Conciliation Court in the Superior Courts Building in Tucson, Arizona, where children and their divorcing parents who can't work out their own custody arrangement come to have it worked out for them.

The very term "Conciliation Court" suggests the new acceptance of divorce in contemporary law. Besides attempting reconciliation, specialized courts like this one in Tucson also stress working out deadlocks over custody and visitation with the help of clinical psychologists, counselors, psychiatrists, and social workers. Instead of the more traditional adversarial contest between opposing lawyers who are determined to "win" custody cases for their clients, the purpose of conciliation is cooperation and peaceful negotiation between the parents to determine, *en famille,* just what is in the best interest of the children. And it seems to be working. In Los Angeles, well over half of some 2,300 custody and visitation disputes were settled in Conciliation Court in 1980. In San Francisco, prior to the establishment of a Conciliation Court, Judge Donald King of Superior Court had fifteen custody disputes a day on his calendar call, and spent two or three afternoons a week hearing custody trials. During all of 1981, the entire court heard only three custody cases. "We have fewer in a year than we used to have in a day," says King proudly.

Though the courts and the entire legal system have traditionally been notoriously slow to catch up with societal changes, the legal establishment is becoming far more sensitive to the pain divorce can inflict. Out of resignation or, more probably, from a sense of practicality, legal institutions are now more interested in lessening the antagonism between a divorcing couple than in pitting one partner against the other. At least fifteen states now have statutes that provide a mediation structure to sort out parental antagonisms in custody disputes. And children themselves are beginning to be recognized as interested parties in the breakup of their families. Two states, Wisconsin and New Hampshire, now require that the children themselves have legal representation ("guardians ad litem") in custody and visitation disputes, and many other states give judges the discretionary power to appoint them.

At the center of all this divorce reform lies an increasingly controversial issue: custody. And contemporary judges have quite a confusing selection of kinds of custody to choose from.

Sole custody (90 percent) remains the most common, with visitation rights going to the noncustodial parent, but all legal and ultimate decisions resting with the custodial parent. *Divided* or *alternating* custody breaks custody down into a sort of time-sharing between parents where each has full jurisdiction over the child during his or her time slot, that is, the school year versus vacation time. *Split* custody entails awarding one or more of the children to one parent, the remaining children to the other. But though more and more families are informally divvying up the children in terms of age and sex, the court frowns on it. "A family unit is struck a vital blow when parents divorce; it is struck an additional one when children are separated from each other," reads one court's denial of split custody.[1] By far the most adventurous—and most controversial—form of custody these days is *joint custody*. Known also as "joint parenting," "cocustody" and "shared custody," this seemingly radical approach to custody treats the parents as if they were still married in terms of the children. Both parents share legal, and often physical custody of the child and have equal rights without one being more equal than the other.

Ninety percent of custody arrangements are worked out between the parents and their attorneys. The 10 percent that end up in court battles, either as direct actions or as a result of failed mediation, can be vicious in their content and time consuming to civil court dockets already overfull. Paradoxically, it is the easing of divorce laws that appears to have intensified the tenacity and the bitterness of custody fights. All but two states, South Dakota and Illinois, now have "no fault" divorce decrees, which do away with the legal necessity of making one partner prove the other in the wrong. Other states have either communal property laws, which simply cleave the spoils of marriage, or equitable distribution laws, which use time, effort, and money as the formula to divvy up postmarital property. With less to haggle over, it is custody that has now become the primary battle ground.

Custody used to be simple. Just one hundred years ago, children automatically went to the father: not only was the father seen as more capable financially of supporting them, but they were considered his economic property. An 1824 decision in Rhode Island explained that the father's right to custody "is not an account of any absolute right of the father, but for the benefit of the infant, the law presuming it to be for his interest to be under the nurture and care of his natural protector, both for maintenance and education."[2] An 1860 New Hampshire opinion stated that "It is a well-settled doctrine of the common law, that the father is entitled to the custody of his minor children as against the mother and everybody else: that he is bound for their maintenance and nurture and has the corresponding right to their obedience and their services."[3]

So ingrained was the father's absolute right to the services of his children that even if he deserted his family and the custody went to the mother, he was not bound to contribute in any way to their support. Child support is a modern invention. "When a divorce is granted to a wife and as a consequence of it she has committed to her the care and custody of her minor child, it follows that the father becomes entirely absolved from the common law obligation which previously rested upon him to support such child" a Maine court wrote as late as 1895.[4] A father's legal obligation to contribute to a child's welfare did not begin to appear in law until the early 1900s.[5]

The tide began to turn as women gained more stature in society, and were able to own property and to work for wages outside the home in a newly industrialized economy. Inside the home, their maternal role was also elevated. By the end of the nineteenth century, women were regularly—though temporarily—awarded custody of very young children "of tender years." A three-year-old girl in Virginia, for example, was awarded to her mother, but at four was reawarded to her father. "The tender nursing period has passed by," the court wrote in 1872, "and the time for moral training and impressions has arrived."[6]

The "tender years presumption" in custody cases (which usually applied up to the age of seven) grew along with an almost maudlin reverence for motherhood. In a societal shift, women began to be seen as nonpareils in the moral order and therefore the only fit guardians for a child. By the 1920s, mothers were in and fathers were out. "For a boy of such tender years, nothing can be an adequate substitute for mother love," read a 1921 custody opinion. "For that constant ministration required during the period of nurture that only a mother can give because in her alone is duty swallowed up in desire; in her alone is service expressed in terms of love. She alone has the patience and sympathy required to mold and soothe the infant mind in its adjustment to its own environment. The difference between fatherhood and motherhood in this respect is fundamental."[7] In the thirties, one court's image of motherhood had surpassed the sappiest of Hallmark cards: "There is but a twilight zone between a mother's love and the atmosphere of heaven, and all things being equal, no child should be deprived of that maternal influence unless it be shown there are special or extraordinary reasons for so doing."[8]

Such gushing bias toward the mother became ingrained in law and in societal attitudes for the next forty years. As late as the 1960s, one judge wrote: "That there is no substitute for the love, companionship and guidance of a good mother hardly needs any argument."[9] Mothers continued to have to go to extraordinary limits to be declared "unfit." Faced with a possible custody fight, one mother in the late seventies was advised by her lawyer that only if she and a man rolled naked around the living room floor smeared in peanut butter, in front of the children, would she risk losing custody.

The "tender years" presumption began to lose weight, however, as social change escalated. The women's movement launched an all-out attack on sex discrimination of any sort, both in the marketplace and at home. The automatic awarding of children to the mother was perceived by fathers as sexist, and in states that had passed the Equal Rights Amendment, the "tender years" presumption became downright illegal.[10] Women forgoing the diaper pail for an office desk further strained the ideal of the nurturing mother-at-home.

With parental roles beginning to blur, the courts turned to the child's rights instead. Now the quest in custody decisions has become which parent will better serve the child's "best interests," a phrase usually credited to a Kansas judge of the 1880s who awarded a five-year-old girl to her grandmother, who had raised her, rather than to her father.[11]

Though mothers still get sole custody more than 90 percent of the time, it is most often because the fathers don't want it. Where fathers dispute the mother's right to sole custody, they are now winning a resounding 63 percent of the time. In a highly publicized landmark case in 1975, child psychologist Lee Salk was awarded custody of his children over his wife, Kirsten, not because she was "unfit," but because he was deemed "better fit."[12] Visitation and support rulings also showed this major philosophical shift in favor of the children and, more often than not, their fathers. A New York court recently ordered a successful neurologist, who had remarried and moved to Florida with her six-year-old daughter, to pay more than $4,000 a year in travel expenses to her ex-husband so he could continue his monthly visits. And a mother in New York was precluded from moving to Las Vegas with her son to start a singing career because the distance would interfere with the father's visitation rights.

The courts' move away from a female bias has caught many women by surprise. One mother in New York worked to support her children and out-of-work husband while he stayed home and took care of the children. When the marriage ended in divorce—and a custody fight—the court not only awarded the children to the husband, declaring him the "psychological" parent, but ordered her to pay child support as well. Other women are giving up custody voluntarily, a new phenomenon that raises societal eyebrows past the hairline. The rejection of motherhood is still seen as a sin beyond comprehension. To counter the stigma attached to the growing numbers of women who have either lost their children in court or voluntarily given them up, women's groups such as "Mothers Without Custody" are springing up around the country. "Most women without custody have never met another woman living apart from her kids," says Ellen Kimball, coordinator of "Mothers Without Custody," which has chapters from Boston to Hawaii. "She's stigmatized . . . ostracized. Family and friends are always asking why she abandoned her children."

So far some 700 women have joined Kimball's national organization, 85 percent of whom, like Kimball heself, willingly surrendered custody. "The average person still perceives motherhood as a twenty-four-hour-a-day job. Anything less than that makes you a freak," says Kimball, who pays child support and sees her kids every three weeks in the winter and for eight weeks in the summer. "It's not as if I sent my children to an orphanage or abandoned them. They went to live with their father, who is a very good parent. But there's a terrific double standard. A lot of our members don't even admit they have children to their coworkers. It is the last closet feminist issue."

Though serving the best interest of the child is undeniably a worthy and noble goal, just how are the courts supposed to go about determining "best interests?" With all these "fit" parents running around vying to better serve their children, the checklist for determining custody has become increasingly confusing and subjective. The spotlight on the "best interests of the child" has brought with it as many variables as there are cases. In Minnesota, for example, a 1978 custody statute reads:

> The best interests of the child means all relevant factors to be considered and evaluated by the court including:
>
> (a) The wishes of the child's parent or parents as to his custody;
>
> (b) The reasonable preference of the child, if the court deems the child to be of sufficient age to express preference;
>
> (c) The interaction and interrelationship of the child with his parent or parents, his siblings, and any other person who may significantly affect the child's best interests;
>
> (d) The child's adjustment to his home, school, and community;
>
> (e) The length of time the child has lived in a stable, satisfactory environment and the desirability of maintaining continuity;
>
> (f) The permanence, as a family unit, of the existing or proposed custodial home; and
>
> (g) The mental and physical health of all individuals involved.
>
> The court shall not consider conduct of a proposed custodian that does not affect his relationship to the child.[13]

The courts clearly needed help in meeting criteria that were founded more in child psychology than in jurisprudence. ". . . In most instances the issue of child custody between two competent parents cannot be litigated effectively," the West Virginia Supreme Court noted recently.[14] And a marriage was formed between social science and the law. Terms like the "psychological parent" and "primary caretaker" began to creep into court records, along with the threat of a "parentectomy" if one parent were legally excluded from a child's life. Child development specialists and professionals set up shop in courthouses, and judges began to listen more closely to mental health experts than to divorce attorneys.

In Tucson, for example, the court employs a Ph.D. in marriage and family therapy as director of the Conciliation Court, a Ph.D. in clinical psychology to act as a child's advocate and two counselors to sort out all the relationships and influences in a child's life. Between them, they interview the child's teachers, parents, friends, and grandparents, the parents' live-in girlfriends or boyfriends, even the children of the parent's new partner, to determine their own impressions of the child's best interest. Then they send their recommendation to the judge. "After we pull all this together, we have a pretty good picture of how the whole family is functioning, not just where the child is or what the divorce issues are," says Craig Everett, director of the Conciliation Court. "We can't really put the family back together, but we can make a better judgment as to where the child is going to prosper better." And the judges, for the most part, are relieved. "Next to sentencing, custody decisions are the hardest thing I have to do," says Judge Norman Fenton, presiding judge of Pima County's Conciliation Court. "You have to play God. And after all, we're just humans doing God's work."

One of the greatest legal reforms in the area of divorce has been the courts' efforts to prevent custody and visitation disputes from reaching court. Divorce's newest industry is the practice of mediation. The methods of getting parents to mediate custody disputes varies from state to state, even from county to county. In Arizona's Pima County, for example, using the Conciliation Court is optional. In California, the laws are much tougher: all contested custody cases are ordered to Conciliation Court, at least for a while. In San Francisco, warring couples get six sessions with one of the five court-employed mediators. If they still haven't worked out an arrangement, the mediator will give the judge an evaluation of the case and it will go to court. In Los Angeles, the efforts at mediation never find their way into court records. Confidentiality is the key to this mediation process, which requires couples to enter marathon bargaining sessions. "Our concern is to promote family self-determination," says Hugh McIsaac, director of the Los Angeles Conciliation Court. "If parents come to us perceiving that we are going to make a report to the court at some later point, they might either hold back information on their own or on the advice of their lawyers." (With more than a touch of irony, the cost of negotiating custody cases at Conciliation Court in Los Angeles—which saved over 600 days of court time in 1981—is borne by appropriating $5 out of every marriage filing fee and $15 of every divorce fee.)

If warring couples can't negotiate peace in the Los Angeles Conciliation Court, they go either to trial or to a growing mini-industry of hard-core mediation centers. The Thaliens Community Mental Health Center at Cedars-Sinai Medical Center and the Center for Legal Psychiatry in Santa Monica, for example, take on much of the fallout from the Los Angeles Conciliation Court. "If they look like they're going to take too long or there are real struggles, we get a good share of them," says Frank Williams, director of family and child psychiatry at Thaliens. Other couples are referred to Thaliens by attorneys. "Though the common stereotype of attorneys is for them not to like the new divorce laws because they won't make as much money, usually the opposite is true," says Williams. "Custody cases drive them crazy. Some of these parents expect their attorneys to be Solomon and psychiatrist and judge and jury. Nobody needs that kind of money. A lot of divorce lawyers were relieved to have us move in with the parents."

It is not an easy task to defuse the hostilities and betrayals many divorcing parents feel. And most mediators don't try; they concentrate on working out the present instead of dredging up the past, and they aim for imaginative solutions. One particularly stormy custody case involved a movie mogul father in Hollywood, a mother who wanted to marry an attorney in

New York, and a battle for their two children, ten and thirteen, which had already cost upward of $50,000. Ordered out of the court and into mediation, the former couple brought their unresolved hatred to Thaliens. "She was screaming, 'You fucking bastard, you've never given me anything and you've kept me frigid for years,' and he was screaming, 'You're sick and you're not going to take those kids away from me,' " recalls Williams. "I told them, 'There must be a spark of cooperation here. You both did like each other once, so let's see what we can work out so your kids don't lose one of you completely.' " After six sessions, the parents worked out a joint custody compromise, which included the father's taking money from their community property settlement to pay for a monthly flight to New York and two hotel rooms to see the kids; the kids' receiving money for vacations and ten weekend flights, plus Christmas and Easter, from New York to California to see the father. "Any judge would have said there's no way in a million years these people are ever going to agree so we've got to give custody to just one," says Williams. "It was one of the toughest cases I've ever had."

Other cases are not so extreme. Often it is visitation, not custody, that sends parents first to court and then into mediation. Typical of visitation conflicts, says Nancy Weston, director of the Divorcing Family Clinic at the Center for Legal Psychiatry in Santa Monica, is a lack of communication between all the family members. The father leaves and doesn't come back to visit his children for a while because seeing them in his old house, perhaps with a new "father," depresses him. But the child feels rejected. The parent finally kicks himself and says, "What am I doing? I want to see my son." So he goes to see his son, but the boy is now hurt and angry that the father hasn't been there before. And the mother is still hurt and angry because of the divorce. So she says to the son, "Well, you can see your father if you want to," which makes the boy feel he is betraying her. And so he says, "I don't want to go with him, Mom," and then she says to the court, "Well, I can't make him go."

So there they are in court, where one parent must be judged right, the other wrong. The father blames the mother, saying she's "brainwashed" the child. ("They love to say that," says Weston.) The mother then cries and the little boy feels even worse. But it's all more complicated than what is said—or not said—in court. "In mediation, we would try and get them to talk," says Weston. "Mother could say, 'Well, we felt terrible when you left us. It was just awful.' And he could say, 'Well, I didn't mean to hurt you so badly. I was just so depressed I had to make a new life for myself. For a while I was still so depressed I thought I was going to die.' And she begins to understand that he was in pain, too. And gradually they learn to talk to each other and, most importantly, to the child, so he'll understand that Daddy didn't abandon him after all."

Though more and more courts and even attorneys are seeking out mediation, it isn't a panacea for all custody and visitation disputes, and it can be complicated for lawyers. Where attorneys themselves are asked to mediate, for example, they may risk violating their bar association's Canons of Ethics, which preclude attorneys from representing both sides in a dispute. The incorporation of mental health professionals into what is basically a legal decision also causes problems for mediation lawyers, who are barred from entering into partnership with anyone in a nonlegal profession. But so many lawyers are practicing mediation anyway that some state bar associations are offering guidelines for their members. The New York State Bar Association, for example, supports mediation only if the attorneys remain impartial and, at the first sign of an adversarial situation, withdraw and advise their clients to seek the advice of separate attorneys. In most places, the mediator can never participate in a court hearing if the mediation fails, and both parties must agree that anything learned in mediation is privileged and cannot be used as trial ammunition.

Mediation can also be tricky for the parents. Some legal experts caution that unsuccessful mediation can backfire. The failure to resolve conflict peacefully can further divide a warring couple. "There is a very significant risk that its use in any given case will fail and, in failing, compound and exacerbate the problems rather than alleviating them," says Samuel Schoonmaker III, a Connecticut attorney and president-elect of the American Bar Association's Family Law Section. The outcome of a successful mediation can also be tipped toward the more articulate partner. "The better-educated, more knowledgeable and better-informed spouse has an inherent advantage in mediation," Schoonmaker warns.

Where mediation is successful, it is often extremely successful. The Divorce Mediation Center in Charlotte, North Carolina, compared adversarial and mediated custody disputes and found that fully 93 percent of the mediated group expressed satisfaction with the result, compared to only 56 percent of the adversarial group. And the difference in the type of custody that resulted was just as marked. Fifty-two percent of the mediated custody disputes resulted in joint custody, whereas only 3 percent of the winner-loser adversarial proceedings ended in shared parenting responsibilities. Clearly, the ability of parents to negotiate successfully what will be in the best interests of the child is far more beneficial to all family members than battling it out in court.

But battle some parents do, often using vicious tactics to win the children. The 10 percent minority of cases that end up before the bench can inflict irreversible damage on the child and break down forever the possibility of communication between the parents. "Once parents get into court, it's like breaking a thermometer and then trying to get the mercury back in," says

Hugh McIsaac of the Los Angeles Conciliation Court. "You've already damaged the system. Things are framed in time and magnified and said before somebody with a robe on, and that really gives it a lot of weight."

Many parents try to spare their children the trauma of having to appear in court themselves, or of sitting through the proceedings. But a surprising number of parents insist the children be present. "They want their children to hear all the dirty linen," says one attorney. "They want their children to know just how much of a shit the other parent is." But more often than not, children in these fights end up with contempt for both their parents. "I really hated them both for bringing me into court," says one young woman, now twenty. "I still hate them for it, but it's more underneath now."

Some children have to face the incredible humiliation of learning in court that neither parent wants them. "I treated a woman's three children—each from a different marriage," says John Tedesco, chief psychologist at the Des Moines Child Guidance Center. "The first two recalled being treated and bargained for like a car or a house—you take the car, I'll take the children. That was the one thing that both of them had remembered about the divorce five years before." Others have to listen to checklists of their expenses as their parents haggle over support payments. "When they write out checks, they always put down exactly what they bought for you," says an eleven-year-old girl. "Once, in court, my dad told the judge how much sugar we eat."

Most judges these days interview the children in their chambers, instead of the more intimidating atmosphere of the courtroom, in an effort to find out which parent the child wants to live with. But though judges in eighteen states have to take into consideration which parent the child prefers, the judge is not bound to honor the child's choice. (Only Georgia gives children fourteen and older absolute choice, and even there the court can overrule if it deems the parent unfit. Other states give children as young as twelve a chance to state their preference, but no legal clout.) Not unnaturally, children resent being asked which parent they want to live with—and then being awarded to the other. "The judge took me into the chambers and asked. I said I wanted to live with my dad," says a twelve-year-old California boy tearfully. "Then the evaluator, he asked me, 'Where do you want to live?' I said my dad. 'Okay, I'll see what I can do,' he told me. But I went to live with my mom. Why did they ask me in the first place if they didn't want to know?"

Though it seems cruel not to heed a child's wishes, it can be just as cruel to place such a heavy decision on shoulders too young to bear it. Choosing one parent over the other often seems an unforgiveable act to children whose feelings and loyalties are already rubbed raw. "It took me a whole summer to decide," says eleven-year-old Candy. "I loved both my parents. If I moved in with my mom, my dad would think I didn't like him. I finally told my father I'd chosen Mom. He said, 'If you're going to be happy with your decision, then I'll be happy.' I wanted to believe him but I still have this feeling that he might not like me because I chose to live with her."

Though on the surface parents seem to be fighting for their children in custody fights, often they are simply fighting each other with the most lethal weapons at hand. So intent are they on beating the other parent out that they resort to bribery to win their children's choice. Some promise pets, trips, adventures, or a child's own phone, treats that rarely materialize after the child is won. "My parents kept asking, 'Who do you want to live with?'" says one fifteen-year-old girl. "I didn't know. I wanted to live with both of them. But I had to decide. My mom said, 'I'll buy you a TV.' So I chose her, and then she told me she couldn't afford a TV. She tricked me."

With court calendars so full in many states, some children have to wait for months, even years, to find out which parent is

going to get them, And the waiting can be intolerable, bringing
out the absolute worst in every family member. There is no escape from the psychological warfare, charges, and counter-
charges that escalate as the time nears for the family's day in
court. Twelve-year-old Beth, for example, has been living
through her parents' very messy divorce for six months waiting
for their case to be heard. And she is almost at the end of her
endurance. "It's terrible at home now," says Beth, her freckles
standing out against her pale face. "I argue with my mother all
the time and we get into big fights. Then she says the reason
we're fighting is my father. I tell her, 'Be quiet!' I don't want to
talk about it or them anymore. Sometimes I feel more grown-up
than they are."

At issue in Beth's case is the ownership of the house and the
custody of Beth and her fourteen-year-old sister, Anna. Their
parents have separated and gone back together four times in
five years, but this separation seems doomed to succeed, as
each parent now has a new partner. Still, the parents can't let
go of each other—or the children. "My father wants me to live
with him," says Beth. "He keeps telling me that if I choose to
live with my mother, her boyfriend will try and take over and be
my father. My mother says the same thing about his girlfriend.
It seems that my parents should be able to make up their minds
about who gets us, but they keep asking us instead. If I don't
tell and if they can't decide, then the court will pick it. I feel
sort of scared about that. It's none of the court's business."

While Beth feels helpless in this parental tug-of-war, sister
Anna is using this pretrial period for everything she can get.
Children are not above waging psychological warfare themselves, playing one parent off against the other to their own advantage. "My sister has already made up her mind, but she
hasn't told them which one she's picked," says Beth, nervously
chewing on the end of her hair. "Anna's really taking advantage. She's telling them to shut up, like really rudely, and say-

ing, 'I want a ride to the movies or to my friends—*Now!*' She tells my father to get up and give her a ride somewhere even when he's lying in bed. And he does it. It's like he's scared of her."

Beth thinks that her sister is going to choose her father, a decision that will force Beth to stay with her mother. "My mother has already lost my sister," Beth continues. "Anna thinks it's all my mother's fault. So all my mother has got is me because I can't leave her, too. So all at once I'm going to lose my father, my house, and my sister. That doesn't make me feel too good."

Beth's decision to stay with her mother by default is precisely the reason many mental health professionals think children should not be involved in their own custody decisions. "Children who are asked to make a choice between parents do one of two things which are equally destructive," says Hugh McIsaac. "One, they choose the wrong parent. Often the child and parent reverse roles, and the child will choose the parent he or she feels sorry for, or the parent who needs them more. And two, they'll choose the parent they feel closest to—and always feel guilty about making that choice. The whole thing is really loaded. Kids have two choices—to fight or to abdicate, both of which are equally destructive."

The age of the child and his ability to make a choice are obviously factors in self-determined custody decisions. But even teenagers are apt to be short-term thinkers and to place too much emphasis on the wrong areas. "Adolescents may say one thing with words and another with behavior," says Dr. Lee Haller, a child psychiatrist and member of the ABA's Child Custody Project. "For example, a child can say he prefers living with Dad, because Dad gives him more freedom. But actually the child may not be able to function without the structure of Mom's discipline."

The tensions of the average custody situation—in which the

children live with the single mother—and of the rarer cases where they live with the father have been documented throughout this book. An arrangement of increasing popularity is joint custody. As of this writing, some 27 states now have provisions allowing for or encouraging joint custody, while eight states have actual laws declaring joint custody to be the best alternative in every case where both parents are seen to be fit.

There is much to be said in favor of joint custody. The child continues to have direct involvement with both parents, a formula that is more apt to encourage continued child support payments and mutual sharing of parental responsibilities. But joint custody also requires a great deal of cooperation and contact between adults who, after all, have not divorced out of love for each other. "Where it works it is very good. But relatively few parents—maybe 10 percent— are capable of it," says Judge King in San Francisco. Joint custody is also very demanding of parents who are trying to start new lives. "Transfers, remarriage, personality, are all reasons against it," King continues. "Joint custody requires that the top priority in a parent's life has to be the children. And for a lot of people that's just not true. Their jobs, their new spouses, may be more important at times."

But in an avalanche of hope and perhaps avoidance on the part of courts, which find it increasingly difficult to choose one "fit" parent over the other, some states are taking joint custody to an extreme. In the states where joint custody is presumed to be the best custody arrangement, it can be awarded *even if only one parent requests it.* Realizing that it is difficult, if not impossible, to legislate parental responsibility or cooperation, however, the governors of at least two states have vetoed these "presumed" joint custody laws. In 1982, Governor Hugh Carey of New York said no to joint custody preference laws, even though both houses of the state legislature had passed such legislation for two years running. Carey argued that such presumed joint custody laws could actually enflame the antagonisms between divorcing parents, who, if one or the other of them didn't want it, would have to prove the basis for sole custody. Awarding joint custody to a parent who doesn't even ask for it is another cause of legal concern, and no less a knowledgeable person than the chairman of the American Bar Association's Child Custody Committee is dead against it. "I greatly oppose foisting this arrangement on an unwilling parent because I think it will never work," says Dr. Doris Jonas Freed bluntly.

But some idealistic judges persist, even, in one recent case in New Jersey, imposing joint custody on a family where no one had asked for it. Presiding over a division of property dispute, the judge took it upon himself at the same time to order joint custody for the couple's two teenaged daughters, even though custody wasn't an issue. The mother didn't want joint custody. The girls didn't want it. Only the surprised father thought it might be a good idea and consented to it. But it didn't work. In spite of the well-meaning orders from the bench, the girls spent only four months of court-ordered time with their father and then returned to their mother—for good.

So powerful has the concept of joint custody become that it influences judges' decisions in awarding sole custody. The new criteria for selecting one parent over the other in states where joint custody is deemed preferable now include consideration of which parent appears to be the friendliest toward the other and therefore more apt to promote the child's continuing contact with the noncustodial parent. The "friendly parent" clause assumes that the parent most sympathetic to the spirit of joint custody is the better parent.

Not surprisingly, the friendly parent clause has drawn a great deal of fire from opponents, especially women's groups. Men can turn the friendly parent clause to their advantage, for example, by threatening to seek joint custody if the mother doesn't accept lower child-support payments. Moreover, the clause can serve as a subtle trap for women and children who have suffered family abuse. A woman who has been mistreated by her husband or whose children have been abused often does not admit it, according to Joanne Shulman, staff attorney for the National Center on Women and Family Law. But if that same woman doesn't agree to joint custody and therefore to continuing contact with her (and her children's) tormentor, she will be deemed the "unfriendly" parent and risk losing custody altogether. Judicial bias toward joint custody has even become a hot political issue. In New York, one of the stated reasons Governor Mario Cuomo won the endorsement of NOW in the 1982 election was his position against forced joint custody.

While the politics of joint custody rage, there is also an emotional debate centering on the well-being of the child who has to shuttle back and forth between parents. Though current evidence emphasizes the benefits to children who have continued contact with both parents, the antishared-custody school of thought holds that such children are actually harmed by the inevitable constant separation and reattachment.

Albert Solnit, director of the Child Study Center at Yale University and banner-bearer for sole custody, believes that the conventional custodial parent should have even more—indeed, exclusive—control over the children to avoid what he calls "devastating consequences." "Children have difficulty in relating positively to, profiting from, and maintaining the contact with two psychological parents who are not in positive contact with each other," Solnit writes in his influential book, *Beyond the Best Interests of the Child*. ". . . A 'visiting' or 'visited' parent has little chance to serve as a true object for love, trust and identification, since this role is based on his being available on an uninterrupted day-to-day basis." To Solnit, part-time parenting is potentially so injurious to the child that it should be declared downright illegal. ". . . The noncustodial parent should have no legally enforceable right to visit the child, and the custodial parent should have the right to decide whether it is desirable for the child to have such visits," states Solnit flatly. His priority is "to protect the security of an ongoing relationship—that between the child and the custodial parent."

The children who live this joint custody life, however, are not so dogmatic about the virtues or "devastating consequences" of having to move back and forth between parents. As with any compromise, joint custody is bittersweet to the children who actually live with it—and poses particular problems. In one study of thirty-two children in the San Francisco Bay area, whose logistical arrangements ranged from switching parents weekly to switching every day, a whole new set of pros and cons was revealed. On the positive side, the children, whose ages ranged from four to fifteen, retained a high sense of self-esteem and were gratified by the efforts their parents were making on their behalf. To keep his ten-year-old son in a good school, for example, one San Francisco father, during his "week," drove the boy to and from school in an out-of-town suburb every day, and back again to soccer league games on the weekends. Another father who had remarried told his city-tired new wife that they couldn't move to the country until his seven-year-old daughter grew up.

But the study also found that such altruism on the part of the parent often became a burden to the child. These children felt a "hyperloyalty" toward both parents, who were so obviously sacrificing on their behalf. Nine-year-old Patty felt that if she kissed her mom, for example, she'd have to kiss her dad; if she were nice to one she'd have to be equally nice to the other; and she wished that a week could have eight days in it so her time could be divided absolutely fairly between each. Other children, especially four- and five-year-old girls and seven- to nine-year-old boys, expressed confusion and anxiety over their schedules, anxieties that spread throughout their whole unordered little worlds. Nine-year-old Josh, who lived alternate months with his mother and father, became so preoccupied with keeping track of things that his marks at school fell along with his self-esteem. "The big problem with joint custody is that you have to remember where the spoons are," Josh said, wrapping up all his insecurities in one image. Geographical distance became the issue with other children. While one nine-year-old who switched parents weekly had no difficulties at all, because he often made the separate two-mile journeys from school to either home by bike and knew exactly how to get to his destination, another nine-year-old boy, who lived three days a week with his mother and the rest with his father, was totally overwhelmed by the same two-mile distances because he made them by bus. Having no clear sense of the location of his parents' homes, he worried about his personal safety and was frightened of getting lost or going to the wrong house. These fears, like Josh's worry about the spoons, distorted his perception of reality. Asked what advice he would give to another boy in the throes of divorce, this nine-year-old said, "Tell him that his mother and father might live close together and then he could go and live with the other person and get to see them. That never happened to me."[15]

To ease the stress on the children who shuttle back and forth in joint custody, some judges are directing the children to stay at home while the parents do the shuttling. Called "birdnesting," such an arrangement forces the parents to alternate between living on their own and living in the original family home. In northern Michigan, a circuit court judge recently awarded the custody of the family home to three adolescent boys—and ordered the parents to move in and out on a monthly basis and pay the bills. Both parents and children were said to be "delighted" with the decision.

But most birdnesting arrangements are unrealistic and short-lived. Beyond the extraordinary disruptions in the parents' lives, it costs a lot of money to maintain separate residences for the mother, the father, and the children. And the emergence of a new partner for either parent understandably confuses the arrangement. It is one thing to expect a parent to keep changing homes, but it is another to expect a new partner to keep tagging along. Mobility is also greatly restricted. One half of a birdnesting couple in New Hampshire was recently offered a far better job in New York and an insoluble dilemma at the same time. The parent faced either relinquishing his birdnesting role altogether and leaving the children behind, or moving the entire entourage, including his ex-wife, to New York, where they could once more start rotating between three apartments. Birdnesting is no less perplexing to the children who keep having to adjust to different parental schedules and peculiarities in the one place that was supposed to remain stable. "My mother puts the TV in the bedroom. My father puts it back in the kitchen. My father says we should cook our own meals. My mom won't let us use the stove," says thirteen-year-old Alice. "It's supposed to be our house, but it ends up being nobody's house. It's all so confusing."

As the courts struggle to keep up with rapidly changing social mores, more and more parents are deciding to bypass the court altogether and simply take the law—and their children—into their own hands. "Childsnatching" is the court of last resort for desperate parents who will stop at nothing to get hold of their children. And the number of cases are growing. Though many parents don't report a childsnatching to the police, fearing indifference, experts say that up to 100,000 children a year are snatched or hidden from one parent by the other. Seventy percent of the snatches occur before custody has been settled. And the children are most often too young—between three and seven—to know how to get back home or even to make a long-distance phone call.

Needless to say, the trauma for children is great. "In most

snatches, there's no warning," says Dr. Lee Haller, a member of the ABA's Child Custody Project. "It *is* kidnapping, and often not by the parent but a hired stranger." The child is quickly fed a story to sever his allegiance to his custodial parent and to switch it to the new parent. "The kids are told all kinds of lies and half-truths," Haller continues. "They heard one thing from the custodial parent, now another, like, 'I love you; your mother doesn't want you,' or 'Your mother is dead.'" Often the parent goes on the run with the child, changing names, changing locations, closely guarding the child in case of a resnatch. "Often they're told to lie about their names in school or kept out of school altogether," says Haller.

The details of childnappings often sound more like the stuff of daytime soaps than real life. But to the participants, they are deadly real. Timmie, for example, was snatched by his noncustodial mother when he was six, snatched back five months later by his father, then resnatched by his mother, who promptly disappeared with her son. Frantic, the father and his new wife tried everything to locate them, from talking to psychics to watching the TV news to see if they could spot him in a crowd. Finally, through charge-card records, they tracked the mother to Florida and, with the aid of a detective, to Miami, where the mother had reregistered Timmie in first grade to avoid having his records sent from his old school. The boy had refused to change his name.

Convinced by the private investigators not to resnatch Timmie, his father went to court in Florida, but the judge decided that Timmie should finish out his school term and could only visit his father for the weekend at his motel. Stunned by the decision, Timmie's father and stepmother smuggled him back to New York and the next day were slapped with a felony warrant by the Florida district attorney. It cost the father $7,500 to get the warrent held while they appealed the Florida decision. Timmie's father finally won the appeal, but at a high emotional cost to the boy, and at a financial one to the father—$34,000 borrowed at 18.5 percent on credit cards and bank and personal loans.

Now ten, Timmie still has occasional crying jags and feels both betrayed and abandoned by his mother, whom he adores in spite of it all. At least he can talk about his kidnapping now, having remained mute through sessions with five different counselors. "I was mostly confused," says the towhead, squirming in his chair. "I figured Dad would find me after a while, but I thought maybe he would have given up. I asked my mother if my dad would give up and she said he already had. Sometimes I felt like crying, but it's all over now."

At least Timmie's story has a somewhat happy ending. Many children never surface again, or if they do, have a less than happy reunion with their searching parent. One mother in Washington found her fourteen-year-old daughter after seven years only to discover she was an alcoholic and had been arrested for prostitution. Another mother in New York found her daughter after ten years of searching, but the daughter wanted nothing to do with her. "Sometimes the child blames the custodial parent for letting it happen," says Haller. "Parents are supposed to be all-knowing and all-protecting. The kids ask, 'Why didn't you save me?' And 'Where have you been all these years?' "

And Timmie's father, believe it or not, got off cheaply. John Gill, president of Children's Rights, Inc. (CRI) in New York, which acts as a clearing house of information on parental kidnappings, says that some parents spend $100,000—and never find their children. In this era of specialization, the number of parental kidnappings has even bred its own elite corps of professional kid finders. In Fairfax, Virginia, private detective Don Uffinger makes upward of $300,000 a year locating missing kids, but won't reveal his methods. "Everybody's for sale at a price. I buy my information," growls Uffinger, who estimates

271

he's found 350 children in the past twenty years. His workload is not only increasing, but getting more difficult. "It's getting harder and harder to find them," says the detective. "People take them out of the country more."

In an effort to link up missing children and left-behind parents, a nonprofit organization called Child Find, Inc. circulates pamphlets carrying photographs and descriptions of the children to schools and police departments across the country, as well as school posters bearing a toll-free number for children to call. Since 1980, Child Find has located and recovered more than 185 children, who had been abducted either by their parents or by strangers. "Any missing child is a child in danger," says Kristin Cole Brown at Child Find headquarters in New Paltz, New York. In a chilling testimonial to the number of children at risk of being snatched, Child Watch advises parents to keep footprints, fingerprints, and dental records of their children, to have preschoolers photographed four times a year, and to have children wear bracelets with Child Find's toll-free phone number (1-800-431-5005)* engraved on the underside. "Teach him that this is where all children call when they are lost," Child Find advises. Laws are also being tightened to discourage parents from kidnapping their own children, and to punish them when they do. But because legal institutions are still wary about interfering in family affairs, the bills are being implemented very slowly or ignored completely. Under the 1980 Parental Kidnapping Prevention Act (PKPA), for example, childsnatching, which was specifically exempted from definition as a federal crime in the Lindbergh kidnapping statutes, was elevated to a state felony in thirty-nine states, though it remained a misdemeanor in most other states. The good news is that in states where childsnatching is now deemed a felony, the Fugitive Felon Act can be activated, and that brings with it au-

* Except in New York State.

tomatic federal involvement and the grudging services of the FBI; the act's authorization of the Federal Parent Locator Service to help track down child snatchers is less cause for celebration. Originally formed to locate child-support payment scofflaws, the FPLS uses social security numbers and tax returns to locate recalcitrant parents. But these methods proved practically useless in pinning down childsnatchers because so many change their identities or fail to file tax returns at all.

With more teeth, the PKPA ordered states to close a loophole in the Uniform Child Custody Jurisdiction Act, a 1968 law designed to limit custody jurisdiction to the home state of the child and prevent childsnatching parents from pursuing new and more favorable custody rulings in a different state. The problem was that though thirty-nine states had enacted the UCCJA by 1980, eleven hadn't, creating custody havens for parents on the run. Now all states, whether they have enacted the UCCJA or not, are bound by the Parental Kidnapping Prevention Act to honor the custody rulings of their sister states.

Even better news is the recent signing of the Missing Children's Act into law. Prior to the act, the FBI had refused to get involved in parental childsnatching unless the left-behind parent could prove that the child was in immediate danger of physical abuse or serious neglect. The new act allows left-behind parents to register their snatched children on the FBI's national computer network and even to check to make sure local police departments all over the country are cooperating in the search.

More and more childsnatching parents are neatly circumventing these new domestic obstacles, however, by smuggling their children abroad. But even the avenues of foreign escape are being closed. In a gesture of international cooperation, uniform laws and policies are being drawn up to discourage the increasing numbers of multinational childsnatchings. The pending Hague Convention on the Civil Aspects of International

Child Abduction proposes to set up central authorities in each
country to process requests for assistance in locating—and returning—snatched children under sixteen. So common has jet-
age childsnatching become that some countries, such as Mexico and the Bahamas, now require a parent traveling alone with
minor children, even on vacation, to file a notarized letter of
travel permission from the other parent before admitting them
inside their borders.

These new laws and attitudes on the part of the courts come
after the fact, of course, to children whose parents continue to
battle and to use them as bait. Children who are kidnapped by
one parent from the other, who are asked to choose one parent
over the other, who are forced to testify in court for one parent
and against the other, are broken in ways that may not show up
for years. They have learned fear, anger, betrayal, and a sense
of abandonment from the very people they look to for protection and love. Of all the ills that may stem from divorce, pitting
children against their parents exacts the greatest toll.

Sam, now eighteen, was twelve when he went to court to
choose his father over his mother. "It was nerve-racking," says
Sam, who has decided to go to college as far away from home
as possible. "I had to memorize lots of material to reel off to
tell the lawyers why I should not live with my mother. It was
tense the day it was going to be decided. We got there first. My
mother came in and came over to me. She was trying to be nice.
I was nervous. Here you are, face to face with a person you're
going to go against. I thought of her as the enemy. She was the
person who was going to try and make me unhappy. I didn't
look at her. I ignored her. I thought, 'Will you go away?' My
parents nodded at each other like boxers shake hands before
the fight. Then I really gave it to her lawyers. I told them to
stop wasting their time. I didn't know I was being rude with
them or overstepping my boundaries. But I knew I didn't want

to give them one chance to make me live with my mother. And it worked. Then I went to the men's room and threw up."

No child should have to go through what Sam did. And with the increase and success of mediation in settling custody cases, it is to be hoped that parents will grow more sensitive to what is best for their children, rather than wanting to exact a bitter victory over the opposing parent. The concept of court-ordered mediation, held either in a specialized branch of the court itself or in subsidized mediation centers, not only saves initial court time and costs, but greatly reduces the number of times embittered parents return to court to reopen old disputes.

Joint custody remains the best alternative to a supportive intact family. Though the children may experience some confusion and disorientation, as they grow older they will not be burdened, as are so many children, by feelings of abandonment or by indifference on the part of one of their parents. The pendulum swing to forced or presumed joint custody, however, brings with it more reservations. Making a child live with a parent who doesn't want to live with him, or making a parent remain in contact with an abusive or manipulative ex-spouse, prolongs the very tensions that brought a couple to the point of divorce in the first place. Joint custody is best suited for parents who can cooperate and be reinforced by the support of one for the other. Where it works, it works very well: in a study of 414 custody cases in Los Angeles over a two-year period, there were half as many relitigations in joint custody arrangements as there were in sole custody decisions.[16]

But still parents go to court. And though many courts have become more sensitive to the trauma children go through in dealing with the legal system, there is much more that can be done. All courts hearing custody cases should have child counselors trained to communicate with children at their level. Often it requires "props": the Support Center for Child Advocates in Philadelphia, for example, has produced a coloring book for children that depicts judges, lawyers, and courts and explains what each does. So successful has the coloring book become in defusing children's anxieties and confusion that many family court jurists keep a supply in their chambers.[17] In the Los Angeles Conciliation Court, children even have their own book, *My Mom and Dad Are Getting a Divorce,* written by a senior marriage and family counselor with the court. It, too, can break through the terrors some of these children feel. "Some children are shy or defensive. They don't want to talk. They don't want to draw. So I read to them from our book," says author Dr. Florence Bienenfeld. "I remember one sad little girl—her eyes got wider and wider as I was reading—and finally she smiled and said, 'This book is about me.' "[18]

Parents, too, need to be educated about the repercussions of divorce on their children. And just as schools are the logical place to focus special programs for the children of divorce, courts are the logical places to corral divorcing parents. Many courts already had out booklets to parents bearing such titles as "Parents Are Forever" and "Guidelines for Divorcing Parents—Helping Children Through the Trauma of Divorce." Some courts, big and small, go further and order parents of minor children into divorce programs. In two rural Illinois counties, all parents filing for divorce are required by the court to attend a two-hour meeting with staff from the Children of Divorcing Parents Program in Divon, Illinois. All courts, not just a few, should mandate such programs for parents.[19]

The court system should also be strengthened and streamlined in the way it deals with families. As it is now, judicial services are so fragmented that one branch of the court often doesn't know what the other is doing. In Michigan, for example, divorce is heard in one court, cases of juvenile delinquency in another, enforcement of child support orders in a third, assault and battery in yet another. Judges are then forced to make decisions on custody and support without all of the information available. "A judge is not likely to know what is really happening with the family unless the parties tell us," says probate and juvenile court judge Alexander T. Strong.[20]

Even where there is a strong and separate family court, often the judges who are rotated through are young and just getting experience before moving on. The result can be a lack of understanding of the sensitive issue of custody—and a short-termers' attitude. Instead there should be more specialty courts like Conciliation Courts, presided over by career judges trained in the social sciences. The presiding judge in Pima County's Conciliation Court in Tucson, Arizona, for example, started out as a social worker. "Before we had a Conciliation Court, judges had no time or empathy for the hurt and trauma kids go through in divorce," says Judge Norman Fenton, who has been at the court for ten years. "They were more concerned with the mechanics."

Where attempts at mediation fail and custody disputes go to court, time is of critical essence to the children. It can take as long as two years for custody cases to be decided, not counting the months of the pretrial process and the several weeks it may take the judge to render a decision. For this whole period, the child sits on a powder keg of uncertainty and lives in a household almost surely filled with tension. Four months in court should be the absolute limit, according to Stanford law professor Michael S. Wald. Yale's Albert Solnit brings it down to a two-month limit for children under five, and six months for school-aged children, with only a two-week time period for the resolution of an appeal.[21]

There is no doubt that the courts and legislatures on both state and federal levels are finally responding to the social epidemic of divorce. That there is still a long way to go is obvious. And the sorry fact remains that when a family ends up in court, when parents abuse or manipulate laws as they do now in some joint custody and child support cases, where parents even

277

break the law by kidnapping their own children, the children will suffer. Courts, after all, are designed to settle disputes that people can't work out for themselves, to enforce laws to keep people from hurting each other. The fact that so many children of divorce end up the subject of these hurtful courtroom dramas is a disheartening comment on the parents of the eighties.

CHILDREN OF THE EIGHTIES

In many ways we are all prisoners of our childhoods. Though events and decisions along the way move our lives in uncharted directions, our attitudes are nonetheless tempered by responses learned in childhood. In Anne Tyler's book *Dinner at the Homesick Restaurant*,[1] the repercussions of father desertion follow three children into adulthood. Cody, the eldest, is rigidly controlled and suspicious of his own wife and son, waiting for them, too, to desert him. Twice-married Jenny, the middle child, has learned to laugh off anything of importance, distancing herself from any more hurt. And dreamy Ezra, the youngest, tries to create the family life he never had by opening a restaurant for homesick people. Though their scars may be their strengths, they are scars just the same and part of their life's skin. "He thought of how it would be if his father returned some time in the future when Cody was a man," writes Tyler of Cody at fourteen. " 'Look at what I've accomplished,'

Cody would tell him. 'Notice where I've got to, how far I've come without you.' Was it something I said? Was it something I did? Was it something I didn't do, that made you go away?"

Though divorce has become an everyday event in American life, it is extraordinary how ignorant many of us are of its consequences. Caught up in the urgency and turmoil of the moment, we don't—or can't—see that divorce goes on and on and on, both for ourselves and for the children. Divorce is not a single event, but a series of events, just as a marriage is made up of what happens after the couple has walked back down that aisle. Yet few divorcing parents are really aware of what lies ahead, the complications, the compromises, the burden, and the loneliness, until a new and more satisfying life presents itself.

No matter how much we'd like to, we cannot minimize the effect divorce has on our children's lives. These effects are not necessarily all bad, of course, but there is no question that their lives are altered. For the short term, the child's world turns topsy-turvy. Not only does he lose one parent from the household; he often loses both when the remaining parent has to go to work. He may have to move, change schools, cope with the new responsibilities and demands of a single-parent home, adjust to seeing the departed parent part-time or even not at all. In the longer run, divorce invariably breeds financial complications, loyalty conflicts, pressure on the child to maintain close ties with both parents, and the strain of sorting out relationships in a stepfamily. Divorce even colors his own selection of friends, as he often seeks out those with the common background of divorce, while the pool of adults in his life is also affected by the now single parent's life-style. For some children, these changes may be rewarding; for others, exhausting. One way or the other, divorce sets off a chain reaction which the child has to deal with for the rest of his life.

Childhood is a special time which, though it may seem lazy and self-centered to the hard-pressed parent, is an essential period of experimentation and growth for the child. But the sad truth is that many children today are thought of more as burdens than as love objects. Their expenses, schedules, and needs are often in conflict with modern-day pressures on the busy parents, and there often just isn't enough time or energy on the parent's part to work, run the household, have some sort of life of his or her own, and pay attention to the children. Something has to give, and more often than not it is the care of the children. Though they may be dressed well, fed healthy food, and educated as best the parent can afford, they nonetheless can suffer from the worst kind of neglect—inattention. And the repercussions can follow them all their lives. A child who doesn't feel cared about doesn't learn how to care about anybody else—including himself. Though suicide among children five to fourteen is rare, the rate increased 150 percent between 1961 and 1975.[2]

There is no doubt that divorce also casts a pall, however temporarily, on the place of a child in the family. Begotten and born most often in love, children are living proof after divorce of love gone wrong, constant reminders of the broken promises of marriage. Too often, then, the children are either ignored or given short shrift by the parent who no longer has the motivation to invest heavily in their day-to-day lives. Child rearing requires enormous sacrifices and selflessness, and after divorce, both the support of the other partner and the eagerness to please are gone. The children can be left to fend for themselves, at least emotionally, until a new one-on-one relationship develops between parent and child—if it develops.

To be fair, the pressures on the single parent do not allow much time to concentrate on the personality development of a child. Instead of dinner hours with rambling table conversations in which the values and philosophies of the parents are transmitted to the child, single-parent families are apt to eat either separately or on the run. But the compensation can be dangerous. Aware of this lack of attention and guilty about it, many single parents instead put untoward emphasis on their children's achievements. If the child is on the honor roll or the dean's list, the child is said to be doing fine. But how does the child feel? Pressed. And often, throughout the interviews in this book, uncared for.

To counteract all the pressures on the single-parent family that allow for little meaningful parent-child interaction, it is essential to make time. The smallest gesture can make up for an enormous void of attention. A sit-down dinner at least once a week where the conversation gets beyond the "What did you do in school today" level can release all sorts of unspoken grievances. Tackling a chore together as simple as helping the child change the sheets on his bed (or him on your bed) can reignite a sense of intrafamily support. In single-parent families particularly, it is imporant to reassure the children time and again that the parent cares about them. And proof of it requires minimum effort on the part of the parent. "It's important that parents make it a point each day to do something for their children that the youngsters could do for themselves, such as making their breakfast," says author and psychologist Elkind. "That communicates to children that the parents really care."[3]

In the end, of course, much of the advice about the ways of handling divorce and children is pure common sense. But in the throes of divorce, common sense is not always operative. I know that in my case the divorce caused huge dislocations in my children's lives. Not only did they lose the day-to-day life with their father, but we moved from the city to the country, from an apartment to a house, to new schools, to new friends, to new everything. For the first time since they were babies, I didn't work full-time in an office but stayed home to work. Making up for lost time in mothering, I hovered over their characters like a vengeful angel, checking for lies, laziness, and sloth. For a while I played supermother, joining every car pool in sight and enrolling them in Brownies, Sunday School, and gymnastics lessons. Where once they had lived happily with the babysitter's fare of junk food, suddenly I became more nut-and-grain conscious than Ewell Gibbon. My son was away at boarding school, but for six months my daughters and I went everywhere together as if joined at the hip. I began to think I had six legs instead of two.

Then, in the erratic way of the recently divorced, I did an about-face and began to plunge into the greater world with the same vengeance with which I had hovered over the children. I traveled and took so many assignments that kept me away from home that they began to call the babysitter Mom. In short, I acted out the predictable patterns of many divorced parents.

Eventually, after two years of such confusion, I—and my children—settled down into a comfortable routine that persists to this day. We all grew very close, in the pattern of many single-parent families, and equally important, they continued to have a deep and consistent relationship with their father.

But I do wish that I had understood more about what I was doing, and why, and that I had known more about the effects of divorce on the children while we were all going through it. Such knowledge would certainly not have prevented the divorce. But it would have made it easier on me and them. I could have reassured my littlest daughter time and again that the divorce was not her fault, but was the result of differences between her father and me. I would not have spoken so freely about our money problems to my oldest daughter, who for a time squirreled away cookies in case we couldn't buy food. I would have been more sensitive to my son's reluctance to get too close to my subsequent male friends for fear of losing another father. And instead of expecting my children to act as little adults with too much responsibility for keeping their rooms tidy, getting to the school bus on time, and monitoring their own TV and homework time, I would have remembered just who was the adult here and who was the child.

Children have legitimate expectations of their parents, just as parents have certain expectations of their children. Children expect to be loved by their parents, to be sheltered, nurtured, protected, and guided. Parents expect their children to be loving, respectful, helpful, even grateful for parental sacrifices; and to be sources of pride. Too often the complications of divorce temporarily strain, even reverse these generational expectations. Predictably, the single-parent family flounders, caught short by the abrupt shift to the unexpected. Things just aren't the way they used to be. And no family member is quite sure how things are going to turn out.

This confusion of expectation hits the children of the eighties particularly hard, as they are growing up in a period of rapid social change. Between 1970 and 1980, the percentage of mothers with children under six who work outside the home rose from 29 percent to 43 percent. Over the same period, the proportion of children living with one parent rose just as dramatically, from 12 percent to 20 percent. There are now 8.5 million single-parent families, the vast majority headed by women. And the proportion is expected to rise, not only from divorce, but also from the increasing number of mothers who never marry at all; in the last thirty years, the number of out-of-wedlock births has tripled.

It is past time, then, not only to accept that the family has many new forms, but to deal with the resulting problems head-on. It does our society little good to pretend that this period of family flux is temporary and will simply go away. America has the highest divorce rate in the world, and there is no evidence to suggest that couples are suddenly going to decide that staying together unhappily is better than going it alone. Yet present social and legal policy still barely acknowledge, let alone address, the changing face of the American family.

Indeed, misplaced nostalgia governs the efforts of many among us who would turn the clock back to simpler and more rigid times. Though it is patently absurd to try to legislate family solidarity and a return to yesterday's norms, legislation has been introduced in Congress that would attempt to do just that. Amid the groundswell of the new conservatism, with its buzz phrases such as "secular humanism" and "the death of the American family," the Family Protection Act seeks to restore the saccharine values of fantasized family life by making it far more difficult for the family to come apart. Under the act, for example, legal services funds would be withheld from litigation in cases dealing with divorce. And federal support would be withdrawn from child and spouse-abuse programs. It is difficult to comprehend why a family that fights together is right together, or whether wife or child beating is a family tradition worth saving, but such is the stuff of the act.

The Family Protection Act also wants to see women go back home, not only as a cartoon of the past, but to do for free what the federal government helps pay for now. Tax advantages are proposed for women who stay home to take care of their elderly parents, for example, or, in an antiabortion ploy, to tend their unwed teenagers' children. Instead of proposing job training programs to lift women above poverty or near poverty levels, the bill would return women from public to private life. States would even be prohibited from using federal funds to promote material (including textbooks) that does not "reflect a balance between the status roles of men and women, does not reflect different ways in which women and men live, and does not contribute to the American way of life as it has been historically understood."

Children, too, are catapulted back in time by the act—not to Colonial times, when the sexes often toiled side by side, but to the more prurient Victorian era, when sex was deemed salaciously immoral. No child under eighteen would be allowed to have an abortion or even to receive contraceptives without notification of the parents, for example. Ridiculous in the extreme, even casual intermingling of the sexes in school sports or activities could be limited or prohibited outright by school systems and parents—as if coed trips to the local museum or the sight of a pair of gym bloomers might lead to a mass orgy.

To put it mildly, this is an absurd miscasting of the urgent debate on the shaky status of contemporary children. The proper debate should center on ways to stabilize the new forms of family life we already have. Much of the damage and distress that divorce inflicts on all family members develops from the confusion, dislocation, and loss of income that often follow. Children, especially, cannot successfully cope with too many changes. In a widely respected study, English psychiatrist Michael Rutter points out that children can absorb a single stress with no appreciable psychiatric risk. But as additional stresses occur, such as the typical postdivorce syndromes of moving, changing schools, mothers going out to work, and the resulting new child-care arrangements, the adverse effects multiply rather than just add up.[4]

The sorry, but remediable, truth about divorce is that much of the anxiety that follows is centered on money. The truth is that women are entering the job market in record numbers, less in a quest for self-fulfillment than for survival. In the great majority of single-parent families, mothers are the sole supporters. The figures on the nonpayment of child support and alimony fall on the far side of scandal in this era of cut-and-run parenting. And for all that some men (and increasingly women) continue to support their children faithfully and consistently, many more don't.

Consider the following from the 1980 Census Population Report: One-half of the 3.4 million mothers who were legally due child support received *none at all.* And the mothers who did received an average of $1,800 a year, or $150 a month—a sum representing 20 percent of their average annual total incomes of $9,000, for the greatest number of these women are those who gave up crucial earning years in the workplace in order to raise children. Furthermore, the situation is growing worse. In 1982, single mothers accounted for 15 percent of the population, but for 50 percent of all poor families. The outlook is even bleaker for their children: the bulk of the below poverty-level population in this country is children. One out of every five children in the United States is now classified by government standards as poor. Federal, state, and local governments now protect themselves by withholding tax rebates to child-support scofflaws. But these monies are routed to welfare agencies instead of directly to the single-parent families, who may be forced to live just above the poverty level because of nonpayment.

The paradox of it all is that while divorce tends to make women and children poor, it makes a far smaller dent in the wallets of men. Though there is much male chatter about the financial drains of divorce, much of it is hyperbole: courts rarely award more than one-third of a man's annual income to his family. The standard of living for the mother and children inevitably goes down, while the father's life-style, though he may move to smaller quarters, stays appreciably the same. The inequity between the two households becomes even greater when the father remarries. "Each person in the husband's new household—a new wife, a cohabitor, or a child—has three times as much disposable income as those living with his former wife," write the authors of *The Alimony Myth: Does No-Fault Divorce Make a Difference?* "When we realize that these 'other' members of his former wife's household are almost always *his* children, the discrepancy between the two standards of living seems especially unjust."[5]

Worrying about paying the rent or even putting food on the table makes any parent worry, and the children are quick to pick up on it—especially where the father appears to be living a high life while the mother and children aren't. In fact, many professionals in the field pinpoint loss of income as being a major factor in a child's psychological problems following divorce, as well as in his school and even health problems.

It is very expensive to get and maintain a divorce, but the

children, after all, should not bear the punishment for it. Costs should be shared proportionately between the parents, each sacrificing the same amount. Guidelines suggested by Stanford University sociologist Lenore Weitzman include setting the standard of living for the child in reference to the income of the wealthier parent, no matter who has custody. To ensure some sense of continuity, the family residence should not be considered part of the initial property settlement, but be maintained, if at all possible, for the custodial parent and minor children. Cost-of-living escalator clauses should be automatically included in every support agreement to protect the family's income against inflation. Where child-support payments are not forthcoming, courts could routinely order the garnisheeing of a scofflaw parent's salary, which they are now most reluctant to do. To expedite prompt and full payment of alimony and child-support awards, arrangements can be made, as they are now in Westchester County, New York, for automatic billing of a credit card account.[6] And to better the potential wage-earning power of the custodial mother, if she has been out of the labor market or sidelined her career to spend more time with her family, balloon payments for several years would enable her to get the training she needs to compete effectively.

Equality for women in the marketplace has also got to stop sounding like a practical slogan and instead become a reality. The number of female-headed households rose 51 percent between 1970 and 1980, making single-mother families the fastest growing family type in the country. Yet their median family incomes were *less than half* that of all other families. It is perfectly justifiable to point the finger at the ex-husbands who refuse to help support their families. But it is just as justifiable to wag the finger at business and industry, which continue to pay women 59¢ for every $1.00 earned by men, and at government, which is increasingly cutting back on the already stingy budget for job training for women, leaving them to scramble for whatever work they can get. The federal government's withholding of tax rebates is designed to protect *itself* against having to support single-parent families; but precious little has been done to train mothers to support their families themselves.

If a single mother is lucky enough to find work, she faces another Catch-22. What does she do with the children? The obvious answer, short of a live-in relative or babysitter, is a day-care center. But instead of providing more funds for day-care centers so single parents can support their families, the government in its wisdom has recently *cut* their funding by 25 percent. Crying "uncle" under their own financial burdens, states have also been excused from matching whatever federal funding there is for day-care programs, and have even cut the allowance for child-care costs for families already on welfare. This totally self-defeating, penny-wise, pound-foolish policy has forced many single parents who could work and get off the public dole to stay home with their young children at a much higher cost to the government.

Worse yet, current government policy actually breaks up some families and puts children at risk in others. Without anywhere to leave their children safely during the day, some single parents have to ship their children away to relatives so they can try to make a living. Other single parents are forced to leave their very young children by themselves or in the charge of their only slightly older siblings. One church on Long Island that sponsored a babysitting safety course for children twelve to fourteen was shocked when parents delivered children as young as six to learn how better to look after their younger sisters and brothers. Such precarious child-care arrangements take their toll on single parents, not only emotionally, but in terms of work performance as well. One mother was fired from three different jobs for absenteeism before finding a more flexible but lower-paying job. "Can you imagine leaving a house with a seven-year-old looking after a three-year-old with a temperature of a hundred and two?" she asks rhetorically. "I would cry the whole way to my job, immediately call home, which was forbidden because it was a personal call, then leave early because I was so terrified and guilty. And I kept getting fired."

Ever since the first mother walked out the door to go to work, child care has been a problem. But with divorce now isolating the nuclear family even more, and with over half of mothers with children under eighteen working, the problem has become critical. According to federal estimates, there are presently between 8 and 10 million children six and under in day-care programs, and many more waiting.[7] Even where mothers have enough money to hire private help, the pickings are slim. "I tried an employment agency and the Classifieds, and nothing," says one mother who finally worked out a child-care arrangement with a neighbor. "My six-year-old had more wits than the three people who applied."

Where child care is available, it is often less than optimal. Out of the some 100,000 family day-care homes in the United States, only 5 percent are licensed.[8] Operating mostly on faith, some mothers leave their children, especially infants, in what the government calls "family" care, a private home that can accept up to six children a day. When the number of children exceeds six, the label becomes "group home" but only some states require additional staff. The magic number of twelve turns a home or child-care facility into a day-care center, which though regulated by state law, often falls short of a parent's prayer. The chain of seven hundred Kinder-Care Learning Centers across the country, for example, has only one supervisor for every ten children, most of whom are under six. But for the working parent—and the child—the options are extremely limited. According to the Carnegie Corporation of New York, the average number of different day-care arrangements per family is *four a week*, which has to put a great strain on the bounced-around child.[9]

With its love of the private sector, the federal government

has passed the buck of providing child care to corporations, sweetening the proposition with incentive tax deductions. But though the idea of taking the children to the workplace is a good one, so far only about twenty-five U.S. corporations have installed on-site facilities. Other companies are taking advantage of the new corporate child-care tax deductions, either by contracting with a nearby child-care center for their employees' children or, like the Polaroid Corporation in Cambridge, Massachusetts, by issuing child-care vouchers to the centers of their employees' choice.[10] But all this is just a drop in the child-care bucket. According to the Children's Defense Fund in Washington, D.C., 5.2 million children thirteen and under are unsupervised a good part of the day.

It is both naive and dangerous to persist in thinking of the American family as a happy, autonomous unit headed by two parents when one out of every five children now lives in a single-parent home. Families, especially single-parent families, need help. Yet traditional mores persist in both public policy and social attitude, holding that the family is sacrosanct and can take care of its own. Meanwhile, no one is looking after the children. What single parents need is help from the government, from industry, from communities, from churches so they can get on with supporting their families. And the least society can do is provide a supervised haven for the children.

Though there is much that can be done in terms of public policy, the emotional work of the divorce has to be performed in the family itself. Just as it is impossible to legislate family togetherness, it is impossible to legislate away parental hostility or lack of concern for the children after divorce. Laws must be strengthened in the areas of child support, of inviting co-parenting through joint custody, of punishing childsnatchers. There are overdue reforms to be made in the school systems and in the courts to sensitize these formidable institutions to

291

the specific needs of modern-day children. But in the end, the one thing no institution on earth can legislate is love. And that, after all, is what all these children are after, be it in the form of a good-night hug, a special cookie in the lunch box, or college tuition paid on time.

We must learn how to divorce better, both for our own sakes and for the futures of our children. If divorce is handled well, the child may not only survive the aftermath gracefully, but even benefit from it in some ways. "If we can provide children with healthy divorce and healthy extended families, remarried families, stepfamilies, they can have lots of people in their lives, get ten times as much love and really do very well," says Nancy Weston, director of the Divorcing Family Clinic at the Center for Legal Psychiatry in Santa Monica, California. "There is no law that says they have to be in this one little nuclear family. They become enriched, they have more people that love them, they learn more what life is really about, and they're not nearly as protected. They learn to become more independent. There are a lot of positive things that can grow out of a well-handled divorce."

But too many parents are still too childlike themselves to put the children's interests ahead of their own. Like adolescents still locked in grudge matches, parents continue to taunt and fight each other, using the children as catalysts for their hatred. It's not divorce that handicaps kids. It's what comes after. Children from hostile, half-finished divorces grow up hostile and half-finished themselves. And their cynicism is, for the most part, well founded. "What I think is that there should be a fine for divorce just like there is for speeding," says nine-year-old Jeff, who hasn't heard from his father in two years. "There should be maybe ten thousand dollars for each kid, which for us would have cost him thirty thousand dollars. If he was thirty thousand dollars unhappy, then he would buy his way out. But now it's the kids who pay. Every day he's not here, we pay."

NOTES

CHAPTER 1

1. U.S. Bureau of the Census, *Marital Status and Living Arrangements,* March 1980, series P-20, no. 365.
2. E. Mavis Hetherington, "Children and Divorce," in *Parent-Child Interaction: Theory, Research and Prospects.* New York: Academic Press, 1981, p. 45.
3. *Ibid.,* p. 40.
4. *Ibid.,* p. 41.

CHAPTER 2

1. *New York Times* editorial, "Tess, Revisited," May 22, 1982, p. 26.
2. U.S. Bureau of the Census, *Child Support and Alimony: 1978.*
3. Graham B. Spanier and Paul C. Glick, "Marital Instability in the United States: Some Correlates and Recent Changes," *Family Relations,* July, 1981, pp. 329–38.
4. *Ibid.*
5. S. Houseknecht and G. B. Spanier, "Marital Disruption and Higher Education Among Women in the United States," *Sociologist Quarterly,* 21, 1980, pp. 375–89.

6. U.S. Bureau of the Census, *Marital Status and Living Arrangements,* March 1980.
7. The National Center on Women and Family Law.
8. Spanier and Glick, *ibid.*
9. *Ibid.*
10. Doris S. Jacobson, "The Impact of Marital Separation/ Divorce on Children: Parent-Child Separation and Child Adjustment," *Journal of Divorce,* Summer 1978, pp. 341–60.
11. Joan B. Kelly and Judith S. Wallerstein, "Part-Time Parent, Part-Time Child: Visiting After Divorce," *Journal of Clinical Child Psychology,* Summer 1977, pp. 51–54.
12. E. Mavis Hetherington, Martha Cox, and Roger Cox, "Divorce and Remarriage." Paper presented at the meeting of the Society for Research in Child Development, Boston, April 1981.
13. U.S. Bureau of the Census, *Marital Status, ibid.*
14. Paul Bohanan, "Marriage and Divorce," in *Comprehensive Textbook of Psychiatry, Volume III,* ed. Alfred M. Freedman, Harold I. Kaplan and Benjamin J. Sadock. Baltimore: Williams and Wilkins, 1980, p. 3264.
15. E. Mavis Hetherington, Martha Cox, and Roger Cox, "The Aftermath of Divorce," in *Mother/Child, Father/Child Relationships,* ed. Joseph H. Stephens, Jr., and Marilyn Mathews. Washington, D.C.: NAEYC, 1978, pp. 149–75.
16. Morton Hunt and Bernice Hunt, *The Divorce Experience.* New York: McGraw-Hill, 1977, pp. 43, 45.
17. Patricia B. Spivey and Avraham Scherman, "The Effects of Time Lapse on Personality Characteristics and Stress on Divorced Women," *Journal of Divorce,* Fall 1980, pp. 49–59.
18. Hetherington, Cox, and Cox, *ibid.*
19. Spivey and Scherman, *ibid.*
20. Hetherington, Cox, and Cox, "Divorce and Remarriage," *ibid.*, p. 5.
21. Hetherington, Cox, and Cox, "The Aftermath of Divorce," *ibid.*
22. *Ibid.*
23. *Ibid.*
24. E. Mavis Hetherington, "Children and Divorce," in *Parent-Child Interaction: Theory, Research and Prospects.* New York: Academic Press, 1981, pp. 33–58.
25. *Ibid.*
26. Hetherington, Cox, and Cox, *ibid.*
27. N. D. Coletta, "Divorced Mothers at Two Income Levels: Stress, Support and Child-rearing Practices." Unpublished thesis, Cornell University, 1978.

28. Hetherington, Cox, and Cox, *ibid.*
29. *Ibid.*
30. Spivey and Scherman, *ibid.*
31. Hetherington, "Children and Divorce," *ibid.*, p. 35.
32. Hunt and Hunt, *ibid.*, p. 10.
33. Hetherington, Cox, and Cox, *ibid.*
34. Hunt and Hunt, *ibid.*
35. Hetherington, Cox, and Cox, *ibid.*
36. *Ibid.*

CHAPTER 3

1. J. Louise Despert, *Children of Divorce*. Garden City, N.Y.: Dolphin Books, 1962, p. 171.
2. Linda Bird Francke, "The Children of Divorce," *Newsweek*, February 11, 1980, p. 59.
3. M. J. Power, P. M. Ash, E. Schoenberg, and E. C. Sorey, "Delinquency and the Family," *British Journal of Social Work*, 4 (1974), pp. 3–38.
4. Deborah Luepnitz, "Which Aspects of Divorce Affect Children?," *The Family Coordinator*, January 1979, pp. 79–85.

CHAPTER 4

1. Paul Henry Mussen, John Janeway Conger, and Jerome Kangan, *Child Development and Personality*. New York: Harper & Row, 1979, p. 176.
2. J. A. Martin, *A Longitudinal Study of the Consequences of Early Mother-Infant Interaction: A Microanalytic Approach*. Society for Research in Child Development, 1980.
3. E. Mavis Hetherington, "Children and Divorce," in *Parent-Child Interaction: Theory, Research and Prospects*. New York: Academic Press, 1981, p. 41.
4. Mussen *et al.*, *ibid.*, p. 91.
5. *Ibid.*
6. Benjamin Spock, *Baby and Child Care*. New York: Pocket Books, 1969, p. 216.
7. Maya Pines, "Baby, You're Incredible," *Psychology Today*, February 1982, pp. 48–53.
8. Alison Clarke-Stewart, *Child Care in the Family: A Review of Research and Some Propositions for Policy*. New York: Academic Press, 1977, p. 25.
9. Pines, *ibid.*

10. Clarke-Stewart, *ibid.*, p. 14
11. Mussen *et al.*, *ibid.*, p. 189.

CHAPTER 5

1. Albert Angrilli and Lucile Halfat, *Child Psychology*. New York: Barnes and Noble Books, 1981, pp. 92, 93.
2. Judith S. Wallerstein and Joan B. Kelly, "The Effects of Parental Divorce: Experiences of the Pre-School Child," *Journal of the American Academy of Child Psychiatry,* 14, 1975, pp. 600–616.
3. *Ibid.*
4. *Ibid.*
5. John F. McDermott, Jr., "Parental Divorce in Early Childhood," *American Journal of Psychiatry,* 124:10, April 1968, pp. 1427–32.
6. Wallerstein and Kelly, *ibid.*
7. McDermott, *ibid.*
8. *Ibid.*
9. Wallerstein and Kelly, *ibid.*
10. McDermott, *ibid.*
11. *Ibid.*
12. *Ibid.*
13. E. Mavis Hetherington, "Children and Divorce," in *Parent-Child Interaction: Theory, Research and Prospects.* New York: Academic Press, 1981, p. 43.
14. E. Mavis Hetherington, Martha Cox, and Roger Cox, "Play and Social Interaction in Children Following Divorce," *Journal of Social Issues,* No. 4, 35 (1979), p. 46.
15. Wallerstein and Kelly, *ibid.*, p. 605.
16. *Ibid.*, p. 610.
17. McDermott, *ibid.*
18. *Ibid.*
19. Hetherington, Cox, and Cox, *ibid.*, p. 40.
20. Hetherington, Cox, and Cox, "Family Interaction and the Social, Emotional and Cognitive Development of Children Following Divorce." Paper presented at the Symposium on the Family: Setting Priorities. Washington, D.C., 1978, p. 18.
21. E. Mavis Hetherington, "Effects of Father Absence on Personality Development in Adolescent Daughters," *Developmental Psychology,* no. 3, 7 (1972), pp. 313–26.
22. Hetherington, Cox, and Cox, *ibid.*

CHAPTER 6

1. Joan B. Kelly and Judith Wallerstein, "The Effects of Parental Di-

vorce: Experiences of the Child in Early Latency," *American Journal of Orthopsychiatry,* January 1976, pp. 20–32.

2. *Ibid.*
3. *Ibid.*
4. Judith S. Wallerstein and Joan B. Kelly, *Surviving the Breakup: How Parents and Children Cope with Divorce.* New York: Basic Books, 1980, p. 69.
5. Cynthia Longfellow, "Divorce in Context: Its Impact on Children," in *Divorce and Separation: Context, Causes and Consequences.* New York: Basic Books, 1979, p. 302.
6. Kelly and Wallerstein, *ibid.,* p. 22.
7. Joseph Goldstein, Anna Freud, and Albert Solnit, *Beyond the Best Interests of the Child.* New York: Free Press, 1979, p. 33.
8. *Ibid.,* p. 42.
9. Kelly and Wallerstein, *ibid.*
10. Goldstein, Freud, and Solnit, *ibid.,* p. 33.
11. Wallerstein and Kelly, *ibid.,* p. 71.
12. Kelly and Wallerstein, *ibid.,* p. 29.
13. *Ibid.*
14. *Ibid.*
15. *Ibid.,* p. 24.
16. John P. McDermott, Jr., "Parental Divorce in Early Childhood," *American Journal of Psychiatry,* 124:10, April 1968, pp. 1427–32.
17. J. Louise Despert, *Children of Divorce.* Garden City, N.Y.: Dolphin Books, 1962, p. 83.
18. Benjamin Spock, *Baby and Child Care.* New York: Pocket Books, 1969, p. 176.
19. Kelly and Wallerstein, *ibid.,* p. 24.
20. E. Mavis Hetherington, "Children and Divorce," in *Parent-Child Interaction: Theory, Research and Prospects.* New York: Academic Press, 1981, p. 37.
21. *Ibid.,* p. 45.
22. Wallerstein and Kelly, *ibid.,* p. 43.
23. Kelly and Wallerstein, *ibid.,* p. 25.
24. *Ibid.,* p. 26.
25. *Ibid.,* p. 25.
26. *Ibid.,* p. 25.
27. Wallerstein and Kelly, *ibid.,* p. 36.
28. *Ibid.,* p. 69.
29. Kelly and Wallerstein, *ibid.,* p. 27.
30. *Ibid.,* p. 28.
31. *Ibid.,* p. 27.

32. Hetherington, *ibid.*, p. 50.
33. Linda Bird Francke, "The Children of Divorce," *Newsweek,* February 11, 1980, p. 63.

CHAPTER 7

1. Judith S. Wallerstein and Joan B. Kelly, "The Effects of Parental Divorce: Experiences of the Child in Later Latency," *American Journal of Orthopsychiatry,* 46 (No. 2), April 1976, pp. 256–69.
2. Joan B. Kelly and Judith S. Wallerstein, "Part-Time Parent, Part-Time Child: Visiting After Divorce," *Journal of Clinical Psychology,* Summer 1977, pp. 51–54.
3. Wallerstein and Kelly, *ibid.*
4. Kelly and Wallerstein, *ibid.*
5. E. Mavis Hetherington, Martha Cox, and Roger Cox, "The Aftermath of Divorce," in *Mother/Child, Father/Child Relationships,* ed. Joseph H. Stevens, Jr., and Marilyn Mathews. Washington, D.C.: NAEYC, 1978, pp. 149–75.
6. Judith S. Wallerstein and Joan B. Kelly, *Surviving the Breakup: How Parents and Children Cope with Divorce.* New York: Basic Books, 1980, p. 78.
7. Wallerstein and Kelly, "The Effects of Parental Divorce," *ibid.*, p. 262.
8. E. Mavis Hetherington, "Children and Divorce," in *Parent-Child Interaction: Theory, Research and Prospects.* New York: Academic Press, 1981, p. 54.
9. *The Kids' Book of Divorce, By, For and About Kids,* ed. Eric Rofes. Lexington, Mass.: The Lewis Publishing Co., 1981, p. 62.
10. Wallerstein and Kelly, *ibid.*, p. 262.
11. "Our Neglected Kids," *U.S. News and World Report,* August 9, 1982, p. 55.
12. Hetherington, *ibid.*, p. 52.
13. E. Mavis Hetherington, Martha Cox, and Roger Cox, "Divorce and Remarriage." Paper presented at the meeting of the Society for Research in Child Development, Boston, April 1981.
14. Hetherington, *ibid.*
15. Wallerstein and Kelly, *Surviving the Breakup, ibid.*, p. 78.
16. *Ibid.*, p. 33.
17. Wallerstein and Kelly, "The Effects of Parental Divorce," *ibid.*
18. John W. Santrock, "Effects of Father-Absence on Sex-Typed Behaviors in Male Children: Reasons for the Absence and Age of Onset of the Absence," *The Journal of Genetic Psychology,* 130 (1977), pp. 3–10.
19. John W. Santrock and Richard A. Warshak,"Father Custody and So-

cial Development in Boys and Girls," *Journal of Social Issues,* no. 4, 35 (1979), pp. 112–25.

CHAPTER 8

1. Jack J. Sternlieb and Louis Munan, "A Survey of Health Problems, Practices and Needs of Youth," *Pediatrics,* 49:2 (February 1972), pp. 177–86.
2. Judith S. Wallerstein and Joan B. Kelly, *Surviving the Breakup: How Parents and Children Cope with Divorce.* New York: Basic Books, 1980, p. 83.
3. Arthur D. Sorosky, "The Psychological Effects of Divorce on Adolescents," *Adolescence,* Vol. XII, No. 45 (Spring 1977), pp. 123–36.
4. Wallerstein and Kelly, *ibid.,* p. 92.
5. *Ibid.,* p. 94.
6. E. Mavis Hetherington, "Children and Divorce," in *Parent-Child Interaction: Theory, Research and Prospects.* New York: Academic Press, 1981, p. 40.
7. Michael S. Jellinek and Louis S. Slovik, "Divorce: Impact on Children," *New England Journal of Medicine,* September 3, 1981, pp. 557–60.
8. Hetherington, *ibid.,* p. 40.
9. Jellinek and Slovik, *ibid.*
10. Wallerstein and Kelly, *ibid.,* p. 92.
11. *Ibid.,* p. 92.
12. *Ibid.,* p. 93.
13. Tom Demoretcky, "Father Sued for Tuition," *Newsday,* July 25, 1979, p. 9.
14. Jellinek and Slovik, *ibid.*
15. John W. Santrock, "Effects of Father-Absence on Sex-Typed Behaviors in Male Children: Reason for Absence and Age of Onset of the Absence," *The Journal of Genetic Psychology,* 130 (1977), pp. 3–10.
16. Jellinek and Slovik, *ibid.*
17. John W. Santrock and Richard A. Warshak, "Father Custody and Social Development in Boys and Girls," *Journal of Social Issues,* No. 4, 35 (1979), pp. 112–25.
18. Hetherington, *ibid.*
19. E. Mavis Hetherington, "Effects of Father Absence on Personality Development in Adolescent Daughters," *Developmental Psychology,* No. 3, 7 (1972), pp. 313–26.
20. Wallerstein and Kelly, *ibid.,* p. 93.
21. Jeri Hepworth, in *Marriage and Divorce Today,* March 29, 1982, p. 3.

22. Wallerstein and Kelly, *ibid.*, p. 83.
23. Hetherington, *ibid.*
24. Wallerstein and Kelly, *ibid.*, p. 86.

CHAPTER 9

1. Andrée Brooks, "For Stepfamilies, Sharing and Easing the Tensions," *New York Times,* January 10, 1983, p. 17.
2. E. Mavis Hetherington, Martha Cox, and Roger Cox, "Divorce and Remarriage." Paper presented at the meeting of the Society for Research in Child Development, Boston, April 1981, p. 8.
3. *Ibid.*, p. 10.
4. *Ibid.*
5. Ruth Roosevelt and Jeannette Lofas, *Living in Step: A Remarriage Journal for Parents and Children.* New York: McGraw-Hill Paperbacks, 1977, p. 122.
6. Hetherington, Cox, and Cox, *ibid.*, p. 7.
7. A. W. Simon, *Stepchild in the Family: A View of Children in Remarriage.* New York: Odyssey, 1964.
8. Hetherington, Cox, and Cox, *ibid.*, p. 6.
9. *Ibid.*, p. 7.
10. *Ibid.*, p. 9.
11. Frank F. Furstenberg, Jr., "Remarriage and Intergenerational Relations." Paper presented at the Assembly of Behavioral and Social Sciences, National Academy of Sciences, Annapolis, March 1979, p. 24.

CHAPTER 10

1. Sue Mittenthal, "When the School is the Second Parent," *New York Times,* May 3, 1979, p. C1.
2. "One-Parent Families and Their Children: The School's Most Significant Minority." Study cosponsored by the National Association of Elementary School Principals and the Charles F. Kettering Foundation, *Principal,* September 1980, pp. 31–37.
3. Sally Banks Zakariya, "Another Look at the Children of Divorce: Summary Report of the Study of School Needs of One-Parent Children," *Principal,* September 1982, pp. 34–37.
4. Judith S. Wallerstein and Joan B. Kelly, "The Effects of Parental Divorce: Experiences of the Pre-School Child," *Journal of the American Academy of Child Psychiatry,* 14 (1975), p. 609.
5. E. Mavis Hetherington, Martha Cox, and Roger Cox, "Play and Social Interaction in Children Following Divorce," *Journal of Social Issues,* no. 4, 35 (1979), p. 39.
6. Wallerstein and Kelly, *Surviving the Breakup: How Parents and*

Children Cope with Divorce. New York: Basic Books, 1980, pp. 271, 272.

7. *Ibid.*, p. 272.
8. "One-Parent Families," *ibid.*
9. Wallerstein and Kelly, "The Effects of Parental Divorce: Experiences of the Child in Later Latency," *American Journal of Orthopsychiatry*, no. 2, 46 (April 1976), p. 265.
10. "One-Parent Families," *ibid.*
11. *Ibid.*
12. Sue Mittenthal, *ibid.*
13. "Our Neglected Kids," *U.S. News and World Report*, August 9, 1982, pp. 54–58.

CHAPTER 11

1. *Ebert v. Ebert*, 38 N.Y. 2d 700, 704, 346 N.E. 2d 240, 243 (1976).
2. Andrée P. Derdeyn, "Child Custody Contests in Historical Perspective," *The American Journal of Psychiatry*, 133:12 (December 1976), p. 1370.
3. *State v. Richardson*, 40 NH 272 (NH 1860).
4. *Hall v. Green*, 32 Atl 796 (Me 1895).
5. Derdeyn, *ibid.*
6. *Carr v. Carr*, 22 Grat 168 (Va. 1872).
7. *Jenkins v. Jenkins*, 173 Wis. 592, 181 N.W. 826, 827 (1921).
8. *Tuter v. Tuter*, 120 S.W. 2d 203, 205 Mo. Ct. App. (1938).
9. *Meinherdt v. Meinherdt*, 111 N.W. 2d 782 (Minn. 1961).
10. Henry H. Foster and Doris Jonas Freed, "Life with Father: 1978," *Family Law Quarterly*, Winter 1978, p. 334.
11. *Chapsky v. Wood*, 26 Kan. 650 (1881).
12. H. Jay Folberg and Marva Graham, "Joint Custody of Children Following Divorce," *University of California, Davis Law Review*, Summer 1979, p. 534.
13. Minn. Stat. Ann 518.17 (West Cum. Supp. 1978).
14. *Garska v. McCoy*, May 26, 1981.
15. Susan Steinman, "The Experience of Children in a Joint-Custody Arrangement: A Report of a Study," *American Journal of Orthopsychiatry*, 51 (3), July 1981, p. 411.
16. Frederic W. Ilfeld, Jr., Holly Zingale Ilfeld, and John R. Alexander, "Does Joint Custody Work? A First Look at Outcome Data of Relitigation," *American Journal of Psychiatry*, 139:1 (January 1982), p. 64.
17. Georgia Dullea, "Helping Children Deal with Legal System," *New York Times*, January 4, 1982, p. B 14.

18. *Ibid.*
19. *Marriage and Divorce Today,* February 15, 1982.
20. *Ibid.,* September 28, 1981.
21. Joseph Goldstein, Anna Freud, and Albert J. Solnit, *Beyond the Best Interests of the Child.* New York: The Free Press, 1979, pp. 41–46.

CHAPTER 12

1. Anne Tyler, *Dinner at the Homesick Restaurant.* New York: Alfred A. Knopf, 1982.
2. "Our Neglected Kids," *U.S. News and World Report,* August 9, 1982, pp. 54–58.
3. *Ibid.*
4. M. Rutter, "Protective Factors in Children's Response to Stress and Disadvantage," in *Primary Prevention of Psychopathology,* Vol. 3: *Promoting Social Competence and Coping in Children,* ed. M. W. Kent and J. E. Rolf. Hanover, N. H.: University Press of New England, 1978.
5. Lenore J. Weitzman and Ruth B. Dixon, "The Alimony Myth: Does No Fault Divorce Make a Difference?" *Family Law Quarterly,* Fall 1980, p. 178.
6. "Westchester to Take Visa Payments for Support and Alimony," *New York Times,* March 21, 1982, p. 42.
7. "Our Neglected Kids," *ibid.,* p. 54.
8. *Ibid.*
9. Nancy Coons, "Child Care," *Vogue,* June 1982, p. 87.
10. *Ibid.*

ABOUT THE AUTHOR

Linda Bird Francke is a veteran journalist whose work has appeared in *The Washington Post, Esquire, The New York Times, Ms.,* and *McCall's,* among other publications. Formerly an editor at *Newsweek,* Ms. Francke is currently a contributing editor at *New York* magazine. She has three children and lives in Sagaponack, New York.